OFFICE
INFORMATION
TECHNOLOGY

OFFICE INFORMATION TECHNOLOGY

A DECISION-MAKER'S GUIDE TO SYSTEMS PLANNING AND IMPLEMENTATION

Randy J. Goldfield

QUORUM BOOKS

NEW YORK
WESTPORT, CONNECTICUT
LONDON

Library of Congress Cataloging-in-Publication Data

Goldfield, Randy J.
  Office information technology.

  Includes index.
  1. Office practice—Automation.   2. Business—
Data processing.   I. Title.
HF5547.5.G65   1986   651.8   86–614
ISBN 0–89930–108–8 (lib. bdg. : alk. paper)

Library of Congress Catalog Card Number: 86–614
ISBN: 0–89930–108–8

First published in 1986 by Quorum Books

Greenwood Press, Inc.
88 Post Road West, Westport, Connecticut 06881

Printed in the United States of America

The paper used in this book complies with the
Permanent Paper Standard issued by the National
Information Standards Organization (Z39.48–1984).

10 9 8 7 6 5 4 3 2 1

Copyright Acknowledgment

Exhibits are reprinted courtesy of The Omni Group, Ltd.

Contents

Exhibits

OFFICE
INFORMATION
TECHNOLOGY

1

An Introduction to Office Automation

1.1 THE OFFICE OF THE 1980S AND BEYOND

The office is an information clearinghouse that serves as the nerve center for today's business. Much more than a physical entity, the office houses and facilitates a set of business relationships centered on the generation and exchange of information. From it come lengthy and short reports, manuals and letters, documentation of orders, information on these invoices, and customers' records. In addition, the office has certain symbolic and human functions which, while not contributing directly to the bottom-line profit, are indispensable for the healthy business. First, it creates a sense of identity, a face to the outside world. The style of the organization is set in the office. Second, it serves as an organized space in which management can best direct all resources, human and otherwise. It is a headquarters from which the generals of business can best operate. Finally, the office environment can and should create the sense of community that nurtures an intangible but almost essential esprit de corps among the group of workers.

To underscore the central role played by the office in today's business, more and more Americans are finding employment in this environment. Whereas only 26 percent of the work force held white-collar jobs in 1960, by 1980 the percentage had almost doubled to 46 percent. By 1990, according to the Bureau of Labor Statistics, far more than half of the American work force will be occupied within the office.

1.2 THE INFORMATION REVOLUTION

Running parallel with the increased scope of the office itself has been a revolution in the tools used to perform its primary functions—the processing, collecting, and communicating of information. The new information technology of the 1980s can provide powerful and complex tools for the modern office. Top managers in all types of companies are realizing the potential of installing this new technology into the office environment. Unfortunately, the office automation boom of the recent past has not always been conducive to increased white-collar productivity. In fact, the flood of often incompatible machines and peripheral equipment that confronted the potential user has often been confusing and distracting. Technocrats often fell for technology for technology's sake, believing that a box or a button could magically improve the work flow. Merely increasing the capacity for the storage and retrieval of information itself is not the ultimate goal of office automation. Too many organizations have squandered resources on a massive system, only to find the full power of the system underutilized.

Consequently, the first step in effective office automation and in harnessing the revolution is the establishment of clear objectives based on the understanding that information is a resource not a commodity. Effective information resources management can only be accomplished by supporting general management goals. Management must insist not only on thorough planning but also on dependable ongoing management of newly installed systems.

The shorthand for this process is the formation of an office automation strategy. It is the aim of this book to provide the reader with a framework for developing and implementing such a plan.

1.3 A BRIEF HISTORY OF OFFICE AUTOMATION

To better understand the potential benefits of today's office automation technology, the informed reader should have a sense of its historical evolution over the past three decades. Office automation (OA) is inextricably linked with data processing (DP), although many data-processing professionals feel OA is merely an extension of DP.

However the cosmology is structured, it is clear that the information revolution began with the mainframe computer, whose size, complexity, and expense provided its own parameters for office organization and support. The mainframe era was characterized by a high degree of centralization, where access to computers was controlled by a few highly trained professionals in the data-processing departments. Most users, or management personnel, had little direct contact with these machines. It would be fair to characterize these two groups as speaking different languages—sometimes quite literally. While the business users talked of their business problems, the DP professionals, who work with COBOL, FORTRAN, BASIC, assembly and programming languages, operated too often within the realm of what the technology could do rather than what the business needs were. Understandably, this lack of communication created great gaps between the programs developed in the data center and the business information needs of the end users. The corporate manuals which spelled out computer procedures were usually rigid, formal, and highly standardized. They were often incomprehensible to any user outside the "DP brotherhood."

With the high cost of operation and the absence of off-the-shelf, "user friendly" systems software, most of the early applications had little to do with flexible day-to-day business, but were employed in basic number crunching operations such as payroll or accounts receivable. Developing new applications was a slow process, hampered by the inflexibility of the computer itself and of the institution which grew up to support it. One joke of the era had it that the DP professional was the best-balanced man in the company—he had a chip on each shoulder.

If there was a chip on the shoulder of the DP professional, it was no doubt a microchip. The introduction of the minicomputer into the office ushered in a second phase of the computer revolution. Its development was spawned in part by the functional inadequacies of mainframe technology. The upswing of demand created by these powerful machines outpaced the corporate data center's ability to expand. As the gap between supply and demand widened, users became frustrated. The minicomputer allowed the control of information processing to begin its shift away from the technical experts and into the arms of departmental managers and company planners. Because the minicomputer was more affordable both to own and run, individual business managers could justify their costs and perform "real-time" transactions without waiting for huge batches to run through the mainframe. Responsiveness improved. Applications could be input from remote terminals, thereby further decentralizing the processing activity and bringing even greater control to the user. By the time minicomputers were entrenched, a process usually referred to as "distributed processing," they had successfully drawn computer technology out of its air-conditioned tower and made it an integral component of the office.

Once the minicomputer put the first cracks in mainframe domination and DP hierarchy, it seemed only a matter of time before new technology would be able to make information processing accessible to not only the department but the individual user. The advent of the microcomputer opened the third and present phase of the computer age and brought with it a tremendous potential for restructuring the entire corporate organization. Computers at last moved down to the desktop and con-

fronted the business person. While this can be viewed as the next evolutionary step, in fact, it is a case of revolutionary change for the average
office worker.

With the trend toward distributed processing in full swing, the need
for data communication facilities has grown accordingly. As processing
became decentralized, a more flexible means to link distributed and
desktop computers became necessary. Direct cable links were augmented by voice lines with data capabilities, making electronic mail and
electronic messaging possible.

Although the mainframe has certainly not been rendered obsolete, its
power and storage capacity are now only part of the wide arsenal of
automation tools. The potential of both hardware and software systems
in the business environment affects everyone from senior management
to support staff and will inevitably redefine the activities of most white-
collar jobs.

1.4 THE IMPACT AND EVOLUTIONARY PHASES OF THE NEW WAVE OF OFFICE TECHNOLOGY

The streamlining of information processing can mean that tasks that
were previously processed manually, such as computation, editing,
scheduling and the like, become automated, and the transfer of such
information, once processed, becomes an instantaneous process with
the development of digital electronics. Electronic mail systems permit
the point-to-multipoint transfer of letters, orders, memos, or any type
of paper document. Progress in voice technology has accomplished the
same function for verbal messages. To top it off, the whole output process is considerably streamlined, as several workstations can share the
same printer, or output can be sent along telecommunications lines and
only printed in hard copy at the recipient's desk.

In addition, electronic storage and retrieval of information has altered
manual filing systems beyond recognition. Storage by computer saves
space and increases accessibility, as files can be immediately accessed
and transferred anywhere in the world. New computer programs for
the microcomputer actually give it the ability to retrieve information
from the corporate data base in a mainframe computer by key word or
content. This use of natural languages for mainframe-to-microcomputer
linkage opens up limitless possibilities for local information processing.

It is clear that manipulation of data, once reserved to central computer
operations, has now also been delivered into the hands of end users.
Database management programs are among the most powerful tools
that the new technology offers. Electronic files that contain information
on customers, products, or employees can be sorted, selected, and dis-

played on command. From his or her own terminal a manager can generate mailing lists, sales reports, and inventory locator reports. Electronic spreadsheets, one of the fastest-selling types of software programs, can create mathematical models for the purpose of budgeting and forecasting. They are especially valuable for hypothetical variable manipulation but, on a basic level, are meant to replace the calculator, the pad, and pencil. Word-processing programs, vastly popular, help expedite the writing process with text editing, formatting, and document printout capabilities.

Finally, the new technology facilitates human communication. Teleconferences among remote locations can be produced with simple speaker phones and inexpensive telephone equipment. Devices such as electronic blackboards, facsimile machines, and video scanners can add graphics capabilities to a teleconference. More simply, business people can engage in computer conferencing by transmitting terminal-to-terminal messages.

In addition to the streamlining of information processing which office automation promises, there is a significant cost factor pushing more businesses toward comprehensive automation schemes. As the work force continues to move from the blue-collar to the white-collar sector, the cost of benefits, salaries, and overheads is expanding as a proportion of overall office operating costs. Prior to 1980, the office consumed about 30 percent of total business costs, but by 1990 that figure will rise to 50 percent or more.

Meanwhile, information processing tools are becoming progressively cheaper and more powerful. As memory, logic, and storage components decline in price, vendors are able to build small computers with sufficient power to perform relatively large processing jobs. The flooded, competitive nature of the market adds its own incentive to the increasingly attractive pricing of equipment and software.

The process of implementing office systems throughout the organization can be divided into four main phases. In Phase One, office systems are installed to provide one or two isolated applications, such as spreadsheet routines or word processing, which are used by individuals rather than by groups of people working together. In Phase Two, further applications are added for individual use, possibly, but not necessarily, in the form of integrated office system packages such as Symphony or Framework. In Phase Three, specially designed office systems for group or departmental applications will be installed to perform specific functional activities, such as those associated with purchasing, sales aids, or an integrated departmental budget-monitoring system.

Finally, in Phase Four, companywide general-purpose office systems will be added to provide extra facilities for the large base of terminal users. These facilities will typically include a standard user interface to mainstream computer systems, store-and-forward electronic mail, and content-addressable electronic information retrieval facilities.

Although an orderly progression through each phase is an appealing concept, it is not necessarily the most appropriate route for all, or even most, large organizations. For example, several organizations have installed corporate electronic mail and electronic information retrieval facilities, which are Phase Four activities, without having made significant progress with Phase Two and Phase Three activities.

Indeed, since different groups of users will adopt office systems at different times, most progressive organizations are likely to have developments in all four phases taking place at any one time. Over the next five years, however, most large organizations are expected to move away from the current environment, which is predominantly Phase One or Phase Two, toward a much greater proportion of activities in Phases Two, Three, and Four.

1.5 AN OFFICE AUTOMATION STRATEGY: WHY, WHO, AND HOW?

Despite the compelling reasons to undertake major office automation efforts, progress has been checkered, and responses to the need for strategies to control progress have been mixed. Based on an extensive survey by The Omni Group, nearly 60 percent of the Fortune 1000 companies in America already have existing office automation strategies. There is hardly any difference in the commitment to office automation shown by the Fortune 500 industrial and the Fortune 500 service companies, either in the percentage that currently have strategies (59 percent versus 58 percent respectively) or the percentage that plan to formulate them (82 percent versus 86 percent respectively). Service companies, perhaps slightly more information dependent, project a somewhat higher incidence of OA strategies than do the industrials.

Among medium-sized firms (firms that are smaller than the Fortune 1000 but with more than 100 employees), 35 percent currently have formulated OA strategies, while 65 percent plan to develop OA strategies in the near future. For smaller firms (from 10 to 99 employees), 23 percent already have developed OA strategies, while 48 percent plan to develop them. While medium-sized and small companies have been less inclined to develop integrated policies, the trend even here is unmistakable. In only a few years OA has become ubiquitous to the point that virtually all large firms and more than half of the medium-sized firms have realized the need for an OA strategy. Clearly, such strategies have been recognized as necessary to each segment of American business.

Nevertheless, many companies have been reluctant to risk the necessary overhaul of the office and the creation of a strategy for a number of reasons. It is clear that there are problems in implementing OA, and these problems fall into three main categories. The first is technological. The gap between vendor promises and equipment performance seems to be a common complaint. Compatibility is another key question. Too frequently, hardware components, even from a single vendor, have proved incompatible. Maintenance and service support are not always reliable, and vendor training programs are often seriously deficient. Knowing whom to rely on and where to buy equipment requires a time and research investment that may seem prohibitive to the OA novice.

The second obstacle in the company may come from the centralized data processing and information services management (DP/MIS) departments. While users clamor for service, administration worries about costs, and DP/MIS operations have genuine concerns about the integrity and compatibility of new systems and often proceed according to more rigid, traditional methods of acquisition and implementation. This divided approach frequently creates a bottleneck or blocks departmental desires. Compounding the problem, most MIS departments are overloaded with applications development and maintenance tasks and have very little time to plan an office automation strategy. Finally, the process can reach a stalemate because many DP/MIS operations are reluctant to lose control of all computer systems planning and implementation. Yet administrators know little about the technology and are frequently intimidated by it.

Who, then, is in charge of OA policymaking? The responsibility for developing an OA policy has not yet been placed and varies considerably, in part, with the size of the company. Among the Fortune 500 companies, major OA policy development is the responsibility of an OA committee one-third of the time. About one-fifth to one-quarter of the time it is a single department's job. But in medium-sized and small companies the president is frequently involved. There are still no OA departments, and the confusion over who is responsible for OA has formed an obstacle to progress.

The third obstacle, perhaps even more fundamental, is the human one. Even when reliable equipment and MIS support are available, many employees remain wary of office computerization. Fears of a loss of status and control of technology per se, or simply of change itself, are fed by the hierarchy of the old computer environment and by the continuing obfuscation of "computerese." The manner in which new systems have been installed in the past does not ease the tension or the transition. Lack of attention by internal training staffs to how technology affects the lives of employees leaves them feeling intruded upon and computer illiterate. Successful office automation almost always entails the active involvement of the personnel department in helping office workers to accept and exploit the changes rather than to resist and be hindered by them.

Overcoming these technological, organizational, and human obstacles are preliminary steps to implementing any plan. Solutions to the problems do exist but take time, investment, and intelligent planning to unearth and implement. Dealing with technology and the vendors is still problematic, but data conversion technology and maturing product lines are resolving compatibility gaps, and competition is forcing increased attention to service and support. Also, the computer industry shakeout is narrowing the choice.

Meanwhile DP/MIS departments are realizing that their future lies in developing hybrid processing systems which can help corporations to meet all of their business information needs. Integrated systems would still rely on MIS's ability to provide a portfolio of hardware and software choices for end users, who would be responsible for defining their computer needs and designing their own solutions. Administrative and finance groups are becoming more sophisticated about the technology and its services and cost requirements.

Finally, the problems of human adaptation are being attacked from both technological and psychological angles. Using the science of ergonomics, or human factor engineering (see Chapter 8), vendors are producing hardware and software that is more comfortable and less threatening to use. In terms of training, companies are investing more time into diversifying and personalizing their methods of instruction (see Chapter 11). As an aid to this experimentation, hundreds of computer training products have come on the market in the past several years. Most important, corporations are realizing that the analysis of training needs and the selection of appropriate solutions are integral to the successful introduction of information technology into the office.

1.6 IMPLEMENTING AN OFFICE AUTOMATION STRATEGY

With the initial obstacles addressed or removed, the office automation process can be set in motion according to each company's overall strategic business guidelines. The establishment of a complementary, successful OA strategy depends on several things: a mandate from top management, an organizational structure to carry out new organizational policies, and an implementation mechanism. For a coordinated overhaul to be effective, top management must make it a global, organizational priority. Only in this way will sufficient human and financial resources be dedicated to the effort.

As just discussed, on the policy level, direct responsibility for the automation project is often delegated to an interdepartmental committee specially created to set strategy and review action plans. Representatives to this committee typically come from major operating units, as well as from corporate service departments, such as MIS, human resources, records management, administration, and facilities management. MIS is a strong member on committees, but to ensure effective participation, all committee members should have well-defined objectives actually written into their job descriptions and tied to their personal performance ratings. In fact, a critical success factor in OA policy setting and strategic planning (as well as the implementation) is the spreading of involvement down throughout the organization.

Later, as implementation progresses, even more specific operational responsibilities should be assigned to specialized departments. Thus, while corporate computer literacy training is often accomplished by the MIS department, it could be handled by personnel or training. Feasibility studies might be undertaken by an industrial engineering or adminis-trative services department. Cost justification can become the respon-sibility of the finance group, while relationships with vendors can be handled by purchasing, as well as by MIS.

To provide the link between strategic policy and actual implementation of OA plans, joint task forces composed of planners and departmental users should be formed. The undisputed need for this contact should be one of the enduring lessons inherited from the mainframe era. To avoid the ever present risk of gaps between needs and technology, user input is especially vital, not only in long-term policymaking but also when needs and objectives are assessed. As the purpose of these task forces is to reach the outer circles of end users, their concerns should be narrowly focused on a project-by-project basis.

Once the committees are in place, their success demands major amendments and additions to corporate policies in a number of key areas. To begin with, corporations are setting policies that link the OA process with business planning. The symbolic importance of this asso-ciation is that it recognizes the integrity of the office of the 1980s, with all its components. No longer are computers compartmentalized in data-processing departments. Now, the move to office automation requires a holistic strategy affecting all areas of operation. In a more practical sense, the link with the planning apparatus helps set funding levels, establish priorities, and provide objectives.

Other company policies must adapt accordingly. A policy which gov-erns information management, like information security and records retention, must face challenges and decisions which have never before existed. Policies for the purchase of technology are being honed to better evaluate and coordinate the machine network. Finally, policies directing human resources must confront the possibilities of substantial retraining and obsolete positions, as well as evaluate the existing pay scales and notions of career paths.

Once mechanisms for implementation are forged, the planning groups can create the OA strategy that will be implemented. The first priority is to ascertain what end users really want and need from the proposed system, that is, what they expect it to do. From a detailed examination of such goals, the planners' second priority is to identify a set of general objectives shared by most of the organization's users. These are likely to vary, depending on the company's market position, its operational methods, and its financial constraints. Some possibilities include increasing business volume, making information more accessible, developing new products, or speeding transactions.

With cost-effective objectives in hand, the third task of the OA planners is to establish company standards that are flexible enough to meet end users' needs and limited enough for the corporation to support. Not even the largest companies contain sufficient resources to maintain an infinite number of operating systems, programming languages, or database systems.

The last priority to engage the planners is the selection of vendors. Even with the trend toward systems communication and compatibility, most experts agree that unlimited vendor choice creates more headaches than benefits for purchasers. Many large companies, and an increasing number of smaller ones, are resorting to preferred vendor lists as a way to control proliferation and quality and increase their leverage as consumers.

Corporations that have followed well-defined courses of action have consistently been rewarded with automation success stories. Through eliciting involvement and commitment from everyone from top management to MIS to the user community, OA planners can build a successful relationship between state-of-the-art technology and business information needs. Maintaining and augmenting the independence of the end user within the structure of a controlled and standardized environment is the rock on which long-term strategies must stand. Given the potential for office automation to be completely integrated within its own technological components and its flexibility to adapt to the demands of the business community, it seems evident that information processing is entering a fourth era. Information resources management is coming of age and making major contributions to the achievement of business goals. Needless to say, it behoves today's manager to learn how to harness this powerful business tool before he or she is swept away in the wake of new developments.

QUESTIONS AND ANSWERS

Q. What is the impact of office automation (OA) on the modern work environment?

A. In the business world the effects of office automation are being felt universally. Not only is the manner in which business is carried out being changed, but the content of that work itself has been altered.

Corporations that have followed well-defined courses of action formulated with insight and understanding have consistently been rewarded with automation success stories. This is reflected in their service to customers, in their subsequent market position, and, ultimately, in their bottom-line results.

Q. *What questions should a manager ask when facing the subject of office automation?*

A. First, the manager should examine the state of the organization. Questions to be asked would be: What is the current level of involvement of my company in the office automation process? Is there an OA strategy and how has it come about? Is the strategy the most effective one and does it involve all the necessary departments and resources?

Second, a manager must determine his or her role in the organization with regard to office automation. Questions to ask would include: How am I affected by office automation? Will I help determine policy or simply follow the policy that has been laid down? Am I knowledgeable about office automation or must I educate myself?

Q. *Is office automation obligatory? What are other companies doing?*

A. The compelling reasons to undertake major office automation efforts are reflected in the number of firms that are addressing this issue seriously. A comprehensive survey made by The Omni Group (more than 800 companies were surveyed) indicates that over 60 percent of the Fortune 1000 companies have already formulated office automation strategies, and half of the remainder intend to establish them soon. Smaller firms are not far behind.

Q. *Who is responsible for office automation policy?*

A. A wide range of opinion exists as to where the responsibility for making an office automation policy should lie. When companies were asked who is in charge, it became clear that a broad consensus does not exist. The location of responsibility depends in part on the size of the company. Fortune 500 companies tend to place responsibility in the hands of one single department, or they set up interdepartmental committees for that purpose. In small and medium-sized companies, responsibility lies with the top levels of management.

Q. *What are some factors to consider when planning an implementation program?*

A. Early in the process one may divide implementation considerations into three central categories—technological, organizational, and human. Each category requires a varied blend of capacities and insights, but solutions do exist, and the evolution of technology, service, and a heightened awareness of the human factor all aid in the process. Additionally, any office automation process must fit within the overall strategic business plan of the organization. To ensure that this important requirement is fulfilled, the OA strategy should have a mandate from top management, a clear relationship to the firm's organizational structure, and a coherent, carefully staged implementation plan. All departments in the organization should have a voice in the development of the OA strategy.

2

Quantifying White-Collar Productivity

2.1 MEASURING WHITE-COLLAR PRODUCTIVITY

Although a coherent office automation plan is essential to the workings of the office of the 1980s, its implementation represents a substantial dollar investment. Therefore, the program must be carefully tied to concrete, measurable goals of productivity to ensure the success and justify the cost of the system.

The question of assessing white-collar productivity is a thorny issue, as certain tasks lend themselves more readily to quantification than others. The classical definition of productivity is units of output per unit of input, or, more simply, units of output per unit of cost. Improving productivity can thus be achieved by one of two methods—either by reducing the cost per unit of output or by increasing the volume of output while maintaining the cost. In the office environment, this approach has been translated into two methods: reducing staff or increasing the volume of work. Automation, such as word processing, is one of the more obvious means by which these goals have been achieved. If documents can be prepared more quickly with the use of a word processor, the secretaries can be more productive, enabling management to reduce staff or increase the work load.

2.2 GENERAL-PURPOSE OFFICE SYSTEMS

Studies to identify and quantify the theoretical benefits of general-purpose office systems have been carried out by Booz Allen & Hamilton and other consultancies. These studies were based on an analysis of work patterns for different types of office staff in a limited sample of companies. Assumptions were then made about the likely increases in productivity that would result from the application of office systems to each type of activity. From a knowledge of how office staff spend their time and an estimate of how office systems would increase the productivity of each activity, the likely productivity increase for different types of office staff was estimated.

To illustrate this type of calculation, suppose that a typical manager spends 12 percent of his time on the telephone. If this time can be reduced 20 percent by using electronic mail or voice-messaging facilities, then 2.4 percent of the typical manager's time will be saved by introducing these systems. It was found that the impact of office systems would save 15 percent of management time. Generally, the results of studies of this kind predict theoretical productivity improvements of between 10 and 20 percent for managers and professional staff, and improvements of between 20 and 30 percent for clerical and secretarial staff.

However, automation is only one of several tools and techniques that can be used to boost productivity in the office. Other methods include specialization, economies of scale, work simplification, training, and supervision. If workers are specialized in the sense that they are devoted to particular tasks, they can avoid the frustration and inefficiency of switching from task to task. If fractional productivity increases can be achieved across a large pool of workers, the resulting total increase can be translated into reduction of staff rather than extra time on the hands of single workers. Such marginal increases are said to result from economies of scale. If work processes are examined for redundancies and inefficiencies, these extra steps can be eliminated to streamline, to speed up, and to simplify the work process. If workers are properly trained in the use of their work tools, the nature of their work goals, and effective personal interaction of other workers, they will encounter greater success in executing their functions and discharging their responsibilities. Finally, in any work environment it is necessary to supervise workers— particularly in the lower echelons, but at all levels—to ensure that they are doing their jobs effectively.

These methods, developed to enhance industrial productivity since the pioneering work of Frederick Taylor, have been applied to the office environment with much success. However, these techniques cannot increase efficiency unless management devises a means to measure it. Without a methodology, reams of information can be compiled about professional activities without coming to terms with their relationship to the business objectives of the organization and, thus, without accurately assessing professional productivity.

To begin, one must be equipped with the proper tools for measuring occupational behavior, opinions, and activities. The tools include diaries or work logs, interviews, questionnaires, structured observations, and unstructured observations. The first three tools are relatively self-explanatory. Structured observations are conducted by an impartial observer or researcher who uses a form that breaks professional activities into components. Unstructured observation is essentially the same, but without the use of preconceived concepts or activities. The researcher is left to devise a framework into which professional and clerical activities fall. While placing greater responsibility upon the observer, this method has the virtue of enabling the observer to record the actual content, as opposed to the form, of these activities and to judge their appropriateness.

2.3 THREE METHODS OF ASSESSING PRODUCTIVITY

Tools for measuring occupational behavior can be integrated into essentially three methods of assessing office productivity: goal achievement analysis, time utilization, and work product analysis. Because the complexity of office work varies, no single method can be pursued exclusively. Rather, each method complements the others, allowing the researcher or planner to draw as detailed a picture as possible of what each staff member is trying to achieve, how he or she spends his or her time, and what he or she produces. The methods will first be briefly outlined, and the remainder of the chapter is devoted to an explanation of their use in evaluating both clerical and managerial functions.

The goal achievement method is at once the most valuable and the most difficult to implement. Managers, for example, are often unwilling or unable to communicate their objectives clearly to a researcher or a planner and may not feel they have the time to do so. Goal achievement analysis, however, is the cornerstone upon which all professional productivity measures rest. The goal achievement method attempts to evaluate qualitatively how well personnel are fulfilling the goals set for them by the organization as a whole. It makes little sense to measure quantitatively the time taken to perform a specific activity if that activity is not central to the achievement of a goal. For each person a goal priority list is developed along with a list of the typical activities performed by that person ordered by the amount of time spent on each. Given the purpose of each activity, it is possible to cross-reference the lists to determine whether the time spent to achieve certain goals matches the priority placed on those goals by the organization. Simply, goal achievement analysis attempts to relate the objectives of the organization to the activities of the individual in an organized and systematic fashion. For this reason it is particularly appropriate for measuring managerial productivity.

The time utilization method of measuring professional productivity is more useful for analyzing support staff effectiveness. Time measurement evaluates how professionals spend their time as they perform the tasks that compose their particular job function. As all activities are to some extent good and bad uses of time, the method provides an assessment of the worker's use of available time. The identification of poor use of time must lead, of course, to its reduction—for example, by delegating appropriate tasks to lower-paid staff and by redirecting the freed time to more productive activities.

The third method, work product analysis, focuses, in classical terms, on the output of the professional and is adapted from measures first applied on the factory floor. This analysis is particularly useful in assessing those aspects of professional work that have been formalized and turned into predictable routines. Each work product is broken down into the steps or tasks that compose it, and the time used to complete each activity is measured. Rating the efficiency of any activity answers only half the question, of course, as only an analysis of goals can determine whether the activity itself is valuable.

2.4 QUANTIFYING SECRETARIAL AND CLERICAL PRODUCTIVITY

In the quest to measure office productivity, it is appropriate to begin with secretarial and clerical tasks. Since these are the focus of the state of the art, they are more directly affected by current technology, and they are more easily quantifiable. In addition, with the rise in secretarial salaries over the past twenty years, a secretary's energies must be channeled more effectively than ever. Automation and procedural streamlining can be valuable tools to enhance clerical output, but these measures can only be implemented through a careful categorization of clerical functions. In contrast to managerial tasks, clerical work tends to be less elusive and less in need of definition. The relationship between measurement and productivity is thus easier to establish, but distinctions still dictate the use of different methods of analysis.

2.5 APPLYING THE METHODS TO SECRETARIAL AND CLERICAL PRODUCTIVITY

Clerical work can be divided into two basic areas of responsibility: document production and administrative support. As the former occupation generates tangible final products, such as typed reports, it is most open to an evaluation of productivity by work product analysis.

The key in using this method is to integrate both quantity and quality of output performance by using simple forms of record keeping.

Even with tangible products like reports, quantification can achieve varying levels of accuracy. When the number of documents or pages is used as a work-load estimate, the results can be very imprecise. Both documents and pages vary widely in terms of size, layout, or content.

Line counts are probably the most effective measure of volume, as they are neither too time-consuming nor too superficial. Although there is no standard line length, line comparison can easily produce a ballpark estimate of productivity and targets. Exceptions to this rule are found in the typing of heavy statistical or pharmaceutical formulas, which take so much longer to produce that line counts lose their validity.

For this type of work a precise keystroke count can be made, but unless the equipment can automatically tabulate strokes, this approach is ultimately impractical. Keystroke counts are justifiable only on documents that use complicated formatting, many Greek or other foreign symbols, and extensive statistics.

Once the unit of measure has been determined, automating the tabulation process is advisable. This can be accomplished relatively simply with either a minicomputer or a chip within a word-processing standalone. Each operator is responsible for dictating the amount of typing produced each day; the supervisor can then keep track of the sums in a log book. Document and page counts can be manually tracked, but the more precise measures of line and keystroke count require automation.

When first faced with this kind of record keeping, word-processing supervisors or managers will sometimes question its validity and resist its implementation. There is no question, however, that the contributions of this documentation far outweigh its inconvenience and cost. It is invaluable for charting the changing work flow and for determining the level of difficulty of each task. Furthermore, the data can be used as a planning tool as well as an evaluation mechanism. By noting trends in the work flow coming from different departments and comparing these with past measurements, the word-processing manager can predict ahead of time a need for additional staff or a reduction in work load. Advance budgeting is possible. In fact, when different departments are functionally related, a word-processing manager might be able to forecast a change in the work load of other departments before the managers of those departments can.

So that quality is not sacrificed for quantity in these line or stroke counts, revisions and error rates should be tabulated for the final assessment of each operator's performance. This calculation is essential for systems that use monetary incentives for increased productivity.

Systems that calculate both productivity and quality are fairly basic in design and implementation. They require some simple forms, the time to fill them in, and the effort to tabulate the data. A word-processing operation can thrive on the efficient use of this data, but amazingly enough some managers never take the extra step to utilize the information that they have collected.

For administrative support functions, which are neither easy to manage nor easy to quantify, the time measurement method of productivity measurement can be an effective tool in reducing the estimated 18 to 21 percent of the day that most secretaries spend waiting for work.

Administrative secretarial activities are varied in scope and function, from filing to answering telephones, from taking dictation to sorting mail. Although some tasks are department specific, most can be categorized and standardized. Again, quality of work must be figured in any measurement, as it is not only how many phone calls are answered, letters processed, or documents filed, but also how well messages are collected, mail prioritized, or files organized. Evaluation should aim toward establishing acceptable standards for the time required by administrative secretarial tasks. For example, a marketing secretary may need one minute to access a file, while a public relations clerk may need three minutes. Compilation of figures like these must precede the creation of departmental standards, which can then be used in much the same way that engineering standards have been successfully employed on the shop floor for many years. A problem with this type of evaluation, however, is that secretaries are unused to it and can be expected to offer considerable resistance.

Another time-oriented method for quantifying administrative secretarial activities is to make a comparative survey of how work time is being spent. Typically, this process is difficult to institute at first because secretaries and clerks feel threatened, intruded upon, and mistrusted. Less precise but perhaps less objectionable to office workers than the standardized time-per-task approach, this method is still accurate enough to expose major flaws in work distribution.

Whereas the control mechanism for document production will be a continuous process, the execution of time measurement surveys and audits on the administrative personnel should not be performed on a daily basis because they are too interruptive. Rather, they should be done only as required and performed by a project team authorized to review current procedures, refine techniques, survey the staff, analyze the data, and establish performance standards and procedural suggestions. In most cases, secretarial performance will be surprisingly constant. After a system has been broken in, periodic audits usually reveal very similar results. The experience of a Chicago petrochemical company is illustrative. The follow-up for an in-depth performance survey showed less than a 2 percent difference in secretarial activity.

2.6 ASSESSING PROFESSIONAL AND MANAGERIAL PRODUCTIVITY

Professional and managerial work has been radically restructured by the development of distributed decision support systems and the proliferation of microcomputers. Whereas end users were once isolated from the data processing and information services management (MIS) communities in American organizations, the need for these groups to talk with each other and better understand each other has grown in an unprecedented fashion. Managers now have immediate access to a wide range of computer applications, or tools, to aid them in nearly all of their business functions. As a result, MIS managers have begun to realize that there is an enormous potential to increase employee productivity within managerial ranks.

From an organizational perspective, however, the wealth of affordable computer power presents a range of difficulties to the office systems planner. Unlike the secretarial and clerical groups, managers perform functions that are not easily charted or quantified. Peter Drucker has pointed this out:

It is not enough that a manager perform his functions more quickly unless we judge the outcome of his actions. We cannot truly define, let alone measure, productivity for most knowledge work. One can define and measure it for the file clerk or the sales girl in the variety store. But productivity is already a murky term with respect to the field salesman of a manufacturing business. Is it total sales? Or is the profit contribution from sales, which might vary tremendously with the product mix individual salesmen might sell? Or is the sales (or profit contribution) related to the potential of a sales territory?[1]

The automation of managerial functions must begin with an assessment of business objectives and their relative value to the organization.

2.7 MANAGERIAL FUNCTIONS

What is it that managers do? The popular notion of the manager is that he or she is someone who makes decisions and develops business strategies. These decisions are essentially unstructured, insofar as it is still nearly impossible, even with the most sophisticated computer support, to predict the events which will impinge upon managerial decision-making.

Henry Mintzberg suggests that there are in fact three types of managerial roles, which are more or less common to all managerial positions, from the shop foreman to the chief executive officer. The first category is interpersonal functions, including his role as a liaison, leader, and figurehead of the organization. The second group is his informational roles as monitor, spokesman, and disseminator of business objectives and practices. The third group consists of decision-making tasks made as entrepreneur, negotiator, disturbance handler, and resource allocator.[2]

At the time that Mintzberg developed these categories, computers, while crucial to operational control of the organization, had little effect on any one of these three types of roles for the non-MIS manager. As recently as 1974, Peter Drucker wrote, "Every expert predicted a tremendous computer impact on business strategy, business policy, planning and top management—on none of which the computer has, however, had the slightest impact at all."[3] Today, thanks to the advent of microcomputer technology, computers directly affect the daily informational and decision-making roles of most managers, and their success in utilizing computers plays a large role in their interpersonal functions.

2.8 THE MANAGER'S INFORMATION REQUIREMENTS

What are the manager's information requirements? Managers are knowledge workers, whose work products are conversations, letters, analyses, and reports. Indeed, in the service sector, information is the work product of the entire organization. At different levels, managers have various information needs, according to their roles in the organization.

At the supervisory level, managers require tracking information to match employee performance against corporate objectives. Middle managers, such as plant managers, district sales managers, and bank branch managers, are suppliers of knowledge with diverse information requirements tied to the performance objectives of their enterprises. Professionals, such as lawyers, sales representatives, researchers, and systems analysts, have broad information needs tied to their specializations.

Finally, top managers require information in their roles as monitors, spokesmen, and disseminators. They have traditionally relied on a complex web of associates, peers, contacts, and subordinates for the most current information available. Furthermore, because of the time constraints imposed on managers in the past, most of this information has been verbally acquired and transmitted. As Mintzberg puts it, "Because he wants his information quickly, the manager seems willing to accept a high degree of uncertainty. In other words, gossip, speculation, and hearsay form a most important part of the manager's information diet."[4]

Today, electronic mail, computerized information services, local area networks, and micro-to-mainframe connections are some of the tools managers and professionals use to answer their information requirements. Yet while managers rush to acquire the latest in desktop hardware and software, the result is often a corporate headache for the DP/ MIS planner. Incompatible equipment, the lack of shared resources, and contending users of mainframe connections are formidable obstacles to professional productivity. And in the rush to "keep up with the Joneses" novice computer-using managers may unwittingly automate the wrong functions—with terrifying efficiency.

In summary, then, managers have enormous requirements for information collection and distribution. Yet their hectic work schedules and lack of technical expertise prevent them from planning adequately to harness their computer resources effectively. Simultaneously, the de facto evolution of distributed processing through microcomputer acquisition may pose an insurmountable obstacle to MIS staff, who see their corporate processing requirements growing by leaps and bounds.

Finally, the nature of managerial and professional work makes it virtually impossible to determine whether computerization actually results in increased personal productivity. Managers and MIS departments alike are likely to forego formal needs assessment on a corporate scale and simply figure that the new systems will just have to improve productivity whether they can demonstrate it or not. Unbelievers, on the other hand, are withholding financing in the absence of proven techniques for assessing professional productivity, leaving acquisitions to discretionary spending ceilings in a sporadic and unsystematic fashion.

2.9 APPLYING THE METHODS TO MANAGERIAL PRODUCTIVITY

In contrast to measures used for evaluating clerical work, the most effective measure of managerial productivity will be a goal achievement analysis. If a department's mission is clearly defined in terms of measurable goals that support the overall corporate mission, then the manager's contribution can be gauged in terms of how successful he or she is in reaching those goals. For example, if the department's goals are to increase revenue by 22 percent, reduce overhead by 15 percent, and introduce three new products, the manager's productivity can be clearly assessed in terms of those objectives, perhaps without focusing at all on the means he or she uses—that is, without applying time utilization or work product analysis.

To this end, the manager must list his or her objectives in order of priority. These should include those objectives tied to the long-term as well as the short-term performance of the organization. After consultation with the researcher or planner, the manager then recounts the activities which must be performed to achieve these objectives, again in order of priority. In this manner, the framework for assessing the effectiveness of the manager's work is established.

The manager's tools for analyzing goal achievement include a daily log in which he or she can correlate activities with goals and with time-tables for completion and contingency plans. Interviews conducted by an independent researcher in the Information Services Group are useful for clarifying the scope of managerial objectives and the likelihood of their achievement through current methods. Finally, a goal and task clarification form can be developed for identifying the interrelationships of goals and for establishing schedules for the completion of tasks.

The goal achievement method, while weighted toward the individual, should culminate in a roundtable discussion between the manager and his or her associates in which the outcome of the study can be voiced and the insights into managerial work can be shared. This is an especially useful forum for the product team, where duplication and redundancy can be identified and eliminated.

As a result of goal achievement analysis, the manager will have a matrix upon which he or she can assess the application of certain activities to the goals which they are meant to achieve. While the researcher can aid in the development of this matrix, it is finally the responsibility of the manager to weigh the relative benefits of one route for goal achievement against those of another. This approach should also help to identify the talents and orientation of professional staff, allowing top management to more effectively delegate resources and responsibilities among its employees.

Time measurement, while offering a less complete picture of managerial productivity, is useful in conjunction with other methods in making managers conscious of their own use of time.

The process may be conducted by the manager or by a researcher or both. In the first approach, the manager keeps a log of daily activities over a two- to five-week period, recording the following characteristics of each task: the type of task, its purpose, its location, the tools required to accomplish it, its content, the type of information exchanged, and its value. The manager may attempt to do this for every task or, randomly, at specific time intervals. For example, in one study conducted by Booz Allen & Hamilton, an automatic beeper would sound at fifteen-minute intervals, reminding the wearer to record in his log the activity he was performing.

In the second approach, an outside party uses a "structured observation" or "activity sampling" form. Activity sampling is discontinuous, while observations occur continuously at scheduled intervals. It provides therefore greater statistical reliability. The use of an outside party, while more efficient and less disruptive, unfortunately will not provide as much data on the activities recorded—for example, their value—as having the manager record his or her own activities.

The time measurement method provides a relative cost per activity in terms of professional time utilized. This method will allow the matching of costs to activities, thus providing an economic measure of the relative value of professional tasks. It will also help in determining whether environmental considerations—space, lighting, location—and support operations have been designed to maximize the potential for productivity, given the current pattern of professional time allocation.

Although the work product method is best suited to the assessment of clerical productivity, it can help the manager to focus on the appropriateness of existing products in terms of the business objectives and to judge the efficiency of their production. To do this, the manager must examine various means of collecting and distributing information. According to Drucker, "Every manager should ask himself, 'What information do I need to do my job, and where do I get it?' He should make sure that whoever has to provide that information understands the manager's needs—not only in terms of what is needed, but also how it is needed."[5]

This examination may unearth reports that are generated needlessly or that contain information which is unnecessary or duplicated elsewhere. As an example, a recent study of an insurance company's claims processing office determined that clerical staff spent nearly half of their time manually preparing inventory figures that were available on a computer-generated report of which management was completely unaware. It is often the case during the first year of implementation that the capacity of distributed information processing systems to produce automatic reporting and tracking figures is overlooked. Work product analysis can expose a redundant process or uncover a process of which no one was aware. In addition, work product analysis can contribute to the development of new automated systems by helping to define and communicate end user requirements to the DP/MIS staff, who can then design systems based on the availability of processing power.

2.10 DISTRIBUTED INFORMATION AND PRODUCTIVITY

The three methods as described and applied in this chapter can be highly valuable in assessing professional and clerical productivity and in performing feasibility and cost justification studies for the introduction of office automation into the managerial ranks. It should be stressed, however, that there remains a great deal of skepticism among the office automation and data-processing community on whether the quantification of productivity offers a realistic methodology for cost-justifying equipment expenditures.

Beyond the problems of quantification, the introduction of office automation will inevitably have far-reaching consequences in staff motivation, work patterns, and morale. This is the "soft side" of productivity, which cannot be quantified, yet most companies realize that these intangible human factors can have at least as much influence on productivity as overhead and equipment expenditures.

The availability of processing power and communications will restructure the organization of American business. And while some experts have predicted a Big Brother version of the future, in which top management uses the new technology to monitor the actions of staff and to consolidate their monopoly of information, it is just as likely that the future will see decentralization of functions and activities supported by sophisticated communications links that provide equal access to all users. A good example was the General Motors decision to disseminate financial information to its employees.

Bringing financial information down to the shop floor is a major step in bridging the gap between management and labor; more than any other single act, it makes the goals explicit and the nature of the partnership concrete. At the Bear (a huge old Chevrolet plant), managers tell workers the plant's direct labor costs, scrap costs, and profit (or loss)—and how these measure up against goals. Not even the foremen would have been privy to such information at GM in the past. The benefits, to GM's way of thinking, outweigh any harm that might come from revealing competitive information.[6]

The introduction of computers into business has brought about the decentralization of information control and the delegation of what were formerly professional tasks. Currently, well over half of managers in American corporations are having secretaries perform tasks the managers once did themselves. These tasks fall in the areas of accounting, spreadsheets, and database management, among others, giving these workers a more complete grasp of the operation and health of the business.

At the managerial level, not only information but the design of information systems will be greatly decentralized, thanks to such recent technological advances as the microcomputer, database management software, and the development of fourth generation programming languages.

Eventually, computers may become so flexible and easy to use that they will automatically adjust themselves to changes in user requirements, increased demands for processing power, and information handling behavior. Until that day, however, top management will have to plan for the coordination of increasingly decentralized computer resources if it wants to tap the full potential such systems contain for the enhancement of office productivity.

QUESTIONS AND ANSWERS

Q. Why look at white-collar productivity?

A. An increase in productivity, the ratio of output to input, is the goal of any office automation effort. A coherent office automation process requires a substantial investment of time and money to be successful. To justify the outlay of resources, to track the returns on investment, and to measure success in achieving established goals, some measure of white-collar productivity must be formulated.

Q. *How can productivity be increased?*

A. Several methods are available to increase office productivity: office automation, work specialization, economies of scale, enhanced training, staff supervision, and work simplification.

Q. *How can productivity be assessed?*

A. Utilizing various tools available to the observer, three methods of assessing office productivity can be delineated: goal achievement analysis, time utilization, and work product analysis.

Q. *Can the three methods be used throughout the organization?*

A. Yes, secretarial or clerical functions are easier to quantify or measure than professional or managerial functions. For this reason work product analysis or time utilization are better methods of measuring secretarial or clerical productivity. At the root of this difficulty in assessing managerial productivity lies the wide-ranging differences in managerial functions and activities. The popular notion of a manager as one who makes decisions and develops business strategies will in itself not provide a sufficient basis for evaluation. Goal achievement analysis is often the best of the three methods for evaluating managerial productivity.

Q. *What special needs or problems do managers present to productivity analysis?*

A. There are three aspects to the managerial function—interpersonal, informational and decision-making. Each of these functions requires informational needs. Furthermore, managerial responsibilities vary widely from level to level in the corporate hierarchy.

   Therefore, the accurate measurement of managerial productivity and the tracking of productivity improvements is fraught with complexity.

Q. *What special procedures are required to assess managerial productivity?*

A. Making a priority list of both short-term and long-term management goals establishes a yardstick or benchmark for the assessment of managerial productivity.

   In order of declining utility, goal achievement analysis, time measurement, and the work product method can be brought to bear. Each method will aid in the performance of feasibility studies and cost-justification analysis for the introduction of office automation into managerial ranks.

Q. What effects will be seen on organizations and their structure?

A. Office automation, along with the enhanced communications and increased processing power it provides, are contributing to the decentralization of authority in the American business organization. Tasks once limited to the upper and middle management levels, along with the information needed to carry them out, are being distributed to lower organizational levels.

NOTES

1. Peter F. Drucker, *Management: Tasks, Responsibilities, and Practices* (New York: Harper and Row, 1974), p. 177.
2. Henry Mintzberg, *The Nature of Managerial Work* (New York: Harper and Row, 1973), p.
3. Drucker, p. 332.
4. Mintzberg, p. 36.
5. Drucker, p. 415.
6. Thomas J. Peters and Robert H. Waterman, Jr., *In Search of Excellence: Lessons from America's Best Run Companies* (New York: Harper and Row, 1982), p. 267.

3

Information Processing

3.1 IMPACT OF NEW INFORMATION AND INTEGRATION NEEDS ON THE OFFICE

In the last decade a consensus has emerged that information is the lifeblood of the organization. It is recognized generally that new methods and technological means are necessary for dealing with information. The trend toward full office automation (OA) is the result of the application of new approaches to information processing. Computer-based information systems are transforming the values, the communication channels, and internal structures of entire organizations.

No level within an organization is exempt from the effects of the office automation revolution. For the full potential of the completely automated office to be realized, front-office systems for word processing and back-office systems for data processing must be integrated. The process of integration must be organized on a global, corporate level. An unplanned, bottom-up approach or a piecemeal, evolutionary development threatens the firm with technical and organizational chaos. If only local needs are addressed, global incompatibility, divisive competition for resources, or an interrupted information cycle may result.

Many companies today find themselves confronted with just such unintended results. To avoid organizational breakdown in the process of implementing new office automation systems, management must understand clearly the wide variety of tasks for which office machines can now be used. In order to integrate information processing, resources managers must be aware of the basic similarities and differences between front-office and back-office processing. The success of any global office automation strategy depends directly on the depth of management's understanding.

3.1.1 Why Integrate?

With large-scale data processing on mainframes, distributed processing on minicomputers, and desktop computing on personal computers, it is becoming increasingly difficult for companies to control the flow of information among all the information processing devices. In addition to the body of information generated internally, the flood of documents, reports, letters, studies, and invoices that come in from outside the organization imposes the need for an overall integrated information system.

The ultimate goal of integrated office automation is to increase productivity in the office. Although managers and decision-makers in all organizations commit vast resources and suffer temporary disruption to automate the office so they can achieve heightened productivity, very often an actual satisfactory return on investment is not obtained. The source of this less-than-expected return in many cases is a failure to integrate OA throughout the organization. Bringing together the front office and the back office is a key step in the integration process.

3.1.2 Basis of Integration

Most business tasks that address real business needs require a variety of thought processes, tools, and data sources to come up with a finished product. For example, a manager who is working on a proposal, which in this case could be either a proposal received from outside the organization for review or a proposal being generated internally for outside consideration, will consult several data bases for information. He or she will gather and manipulate the data for a variety of possible scenarios, express these results in graphs or tables, and incorporate these into a textual presentation. He or she will then circulate the document among a number of colleagues for comments, make revisions, prepare a final document, and present it for action.

This abbreviated description of a typical business occurrence shows how both back-office and front-office procedures are used in one task. Systems integration is required to create the final product. Both front- and back-office output is combined in a cohesive plan, scenario, or document. The better an information system can do this, the better it meets the needs of the users.

Historically, the development of modern office systems began in the 1870s with the introduction of the mechanical typewriter. Widespread use of typewriters generated an office productivity explosion. Later, advances in mechanical technology were employed to produce adding machines and mechanical calculators. Electricity was applied still later to office systems. Electric typewriters, adding machines, and calculators further increased office productivity. Nevertheless, the word-processing function in the office remained tied to the typewriter even into the 1970s.

The availability of magnetic storage and the development of solid-state electronics precipitated the wide use in a business environment of computer technology in the 1960s. With the mainframe computer, advances in data processing (DP) far outstripped those in word processing. Word processing (WP) began to catch up as the development of microprocessors brought computer technology into the front office.

Data and word processing today share many things in common. Both WP and DP are used by most personnel in the organization to send and receive information. Both are automated, use computer technology, and are software driven. With constant improvements and upgrades, DP and WP functions are changing rapidly, but until now keyboards have been the primary means of talking to the automated machinery. Both DP and WP are information processing functions, and they are critical to the business environment. As the earlier example illustrated, most businesses need both word and data processing to function effectively. The integration of DP and WP can make modern offices operate more efficiently and can also allow for the introduction and use of new information services such as electronic mail, message centers, and multifunction workstations.

The emergence of the personal computer has made a common bridge between DP and WP available for the first time. The personal computer (PC) has many functions. It can be dedicated solely to word processing, or it can be used to access a firm's data base, extract information or data, perform analysis of the data, and then incorporate this into the written report.

3.1.3 Obstacles to Integration

Although word processing and data processing are apparently converging, differences exist and must be faced. One fundamental distinction between the two is that data processing deals with numerical data whereas word processing deals with alphabetical or numerical characters in a textual format. There are also content differences. Data processing manipulates numbers, often on a regular cyclical basis. Once data is formatted, it is not often changed. Word processing, on the other hand, deals with person-to-person communication in a great variety of formats and often has a noncyclical use pattern. Additionally, applications for the two differ. The user of data processing output is primarily interested in the bottom line, the final result of the information manipulations. A word-processing user is interested in the entire file or, at the very least, some portion of the file.

In an organization, different functional areas are more apt to stress one type of processing over the other, although exclusivity is seldom the rule. For example, the accounting department would use numerical data manipulation and the back-office data-processing function, while the finance or marketing department has balanced needs for DP and WP. Customer service, on the other hand, may only use the WP function on a day-to-day basis.

Back-office data processing often operates in batch mode. Large quantities of data are input at one time; time-consuming, number-crunching operations are performed; and then large quantities of data are printed out as a result of such an operation. The process is sequential, and timeliness is a secondary consideration. Typically, such tasks must either be initiated days in advance of their scheduled completion or be part of a regularly scheduled protocol. Back-office tasks are usually performed by technical specialists with considerable experience and training in computer use. Frequently, these specialists have college educations and some background in science, mathematics, or engineering. Tasks and responsibilities are exacting and inflexible, and operating software is often designed in-house.

Word processing, on the other hand, is a very different beast. Because the central product of WP is the written document, batch operations are rarely used. Documents are produced interactively, typically with vendor-supplied software. Because specialized knowledge is not required, personnel on all levels of the company can use word-processing facilities. Word processing is much less repetitive than data processing, so procedures are not written in stone, and time constraints are more flexible.

As we have seen, data and word processing share many elements in common but have a number of conflicting differences. An effective functional integration must take advantage of the similarities and, at the same time, reconcile the differences.

The present-day organization finds itself with separate back-office and front-office processing departments. Both have different operating characteristics, controls, and functions, yet the two exist side by side. At the same time, developments in technology and equipment have created the personal computer, which is capable of merging the two. The unity of the information processing system, first broken by the divergence of data processing in the 1960s with the advent of the mainframe computer, can now be restored.

3.2 BACK-OFFICE PROCESSING: ARCHITECTURE OF THE PAST

In the early days of the technological revolution in the office, the data-processing (DP) manager obtained a firm foothold and insider advantage which today is still heavily entrenched in the back offices of many organizations which utilize mainframe computing power. Although recent developments are dictating a change in this status quo, familiarity with what took place is necessary to understand the shifts needed now. This section will therefore review the historical development and role of the back-office DP function and examine its new position in the organization that desires to implement integrated information processing.

3.2.1 Historical Back-Office Processing

When computers and their power to store and manipulate information were first applied to business needs, the early DP centers emerged. Over the period of the 1960s and early 1970s they gradually became recognized as a principal support function in many large organizations. The investment that companies made in mainframe computers was substantial, and DP departments grew quickly in size and importance.

Along with growth of budgets and personnel was a widespread feeling that DP was a specialized activity which required extensive technical expertise, special tools, and separate facilities. This was the time of the emergence of the white-coat-attired "priests" of computer and the DP function. The technology and equipment available required batch processing, which necessitated the compartmentalization of tasks by users in the front office. In addition to this division of tasks, the DP department imposed a schedule often of months or even quarters upon those to whom it provided services. The control of timeliness began to escape from those who needed the computing power and shift to those who operated the computers. Because the data-processing function was not understood by the layman, and this often included top management, DP departments acquired a tremendous degree of autonomy. Those in charge of DP departments found their influence spreading throughout entire organizations as reliance on this support function increased. The sanctity and mysteriousness of DP was also nurtured, often by the DP department itself. A shadow power structure gradually came into being, and in terms of the relationship between data processing and overall corporate activity, the tail began to wag the dog.

One of the principal faults of this situation was that users became alienated from the department designed to provide service to them. Disenchantment and outright fear of computers developed, and companies were divided into opposing camps for and against the new computing technology. Nevertheless, mainframes were too important to ignore and too widespread to avoid. Information processing integration was a foreign concept in many companies.

3.2.2 The Change in Data Processing

Advances in technology outside of the mainframe milieu which took place in the 1970s gradually challenged the autonomy of the DP department. The two developments with the greatest impact were the proliferation of more powerful and cheaper PCs and the development of "smart" word processors with computing and data access abilities. Improved software and interconnect facilities such as ports, modems, and office networks allowed these front-office tools to perform tasks and access information and data, which previously only the back office could.

As a result, the back office's monopoly over data processing was diluted. The very scope and nature of data itself broadened, and an increase in the role of the front office took place. The speed of data manipulation increased and the control over timeliness passed to the front office. The spread of microcomputers which could access a company's data base made the front office less dependent on back-office operations. Resources were gradually shifted to reflect this change, as OA expenditures showed.

Within the back office itself, DP/MIS departments are spending less time developing data-processing software and more time working on information management software. As always, the maintenance of a database and mainframe processing capability, which outside departments often utilize directly, remains its responsibility. With the spread of front-office technology, DP/MIS is also responsible for overseeing the development and implementation of a distributed information processing network throughout the organization.

The role of the back office in the modern office is changing drastically. New standards and procedures must be developed so that a company's back office may continue to make its vital contribution to the needs of a leading-edge business.

3.3 FRONT-OFFICE OPERATIONS: A CHANGING ENVIRONMENT

Someone returning today to the work force after a five-year absence would be surprised at the changes which have taken place in the modern front office. The terminology alone—VDTs, floppies, document search and replace, mail-merge—is daunting to the uninitiated. Following a typical document through its inception, revision, and final production would reveal much about a company's new internal organization.

At the heart of these changes in the work environment is the widespread use of advanced technology. Shared word-processing systems, personal computers and graphics devices, once considered exotic communication devices, are now common. In small and medium-sized businesses, such systems and devices are now selling rapidly. Of the major Fortune 1000 companies, more than 80 percent utilize some form of advanced OA equipment.

3.3.1 Merging Systems

Advances in telecommunications facilities have enhanced the versatility of many components in the automated office. New systems are now available to professionals, managers, and the support staff. Integrated tools with capabilities unheard of a few years ago are appearing in offices everywhere. Vendors of equipment are recognizing and promoting the synergy of these new systems. Office copiers now function as digital reading and printing devices and will soon perform facsimile transmission. Computer-based message systems (CBMSs) offer extensive features and function doubly as electronic mail systems. Private automated branch exchanges (PBXs) are software programmable, can store messages, and possess route forwarding ability within the company's telephone network. Database management systems (DBMSs) allow the front office, by means of minicomputers and PCs, to access information stored on mainframes in the back office. Word processors with greatly enhanced capability are becoming part of multifunction workstations and are performing tasks previously considered to be data processing. Shared word processing is transforming office procedures for document production.

All of these systems are changing the role of the front office and giving it more duties than it ever had before. More and more tasks once considered the domain of the back office are now performed in the front office. Packaged software allows front-office personnel to manage information with an expertise that reduces back-office dependence. With this development, response times are becoming shorter and shorter, and the pace of business everywhere is accelerating.

It is this difference in timeliness, from the weeks or months of the old back office, to the days or hours of the new front office, which distinguish the new era from the old. Dissatisfaction with the slowness of back-office processing provided the incentive for change up front. Lead times of months to incorporate a new program, and more if changes or debugging had to be performed, are no longer acceptable. The era of information processing has brought with it a new sense of urgency.

The new front-office environment has also brought about a need for greater standardization. For the efficient processing of information to take place on a large scale, a level of uniformity more commonly found in an industrial or manufacturing setting is becoming necessary. Document format, labeling, and storage must be increasingly standardized so that a new document entered into the information base can be accessed and updated later. Many companies are only beginning to recognize this as a key to the effective and efficient implementation of their new front-office technology.

3.4 THE INTEGRATION OF FRONT- AND BACK-OFFICE INFORMATION RESOURCES

Having reviewed the story behind the split between data processing and word processing, this section now looks at the developments that are pushing them back together.

Data processing and word processing are slowly becoming less and less distinct operations as technology advances. As the computing power of the desktop microcomputer approaches that of the dedicated mainframe, more and more users desire direct access to data bases which were previously under the strict control of the back office in order to integrate such information directly into their operations. Large-scale integration (LSI) has brought about size and price reductions which are nothing short of phenomenal. The integrated circuit and the development of the microprocessor chip have brought an amount of computing power to the PC which not all that long ago would have required rooms of equipment and all the accompanying costs of space, power, and personnel. Similarly, costs have dropped astoundingly. For example, in 1957 a Cadillac limousine cost $8,000 and a simple transistor $10. If the Cadillac had followed the cost reduction curve of the transistor, it would cost three cents today instead of $40,000.

What this has meant is that tremendous computing capacity available before only on mainframes is now widely available. A single small desktop PC is able to perform data-processing functions that were once widely thought to be far beyond its capacity. The PC also performs with ease and versatility word-processing tasks which once required dedicated machines. The gap between DP and WP functions is steadily shrinking with each new program and hardware product released.

3.4.1 Gains from Integration

The goal of the integration of data and word processing into one unified activity, which we have called information processing, is to help the members of an organization to achieve business goals in a more efficient (cost savings) and effective (value added) manner. The inherently integrative nature of business itself has already been discussed, but there are a number of specific benefits which follow from systems integration.

For one thing, costs can be reduced considerably both on hardware and personnel. Multiple function workstations integrate a number of tasks on to one machine. As the cost of office machinery continues to fall, companies that operate automated offices will realize considerable savings. Personnel costs can also be reduced. With integrated systems design, fewer people will be required to perform tasks which used to require many. In fact, the people-to-machine cost ratio has been climbing higher and higher recently. Control of personnel costs has now become a top priority item in many corporations.

Second, during the word-processing function, having direct access to stored data saves time and document production cost. Previously, with separate systems, integration of databank information with document production facilities required both the time and the effort of several people. Unless the desired information was included in regularly distributed reports, a special request was necessary to the database manager, and hard copy would be delivered from the DP department to the requesting user. If there was no delay and only one step was required, most users would have considered themselves fortunate. The disadvantages of such a system are obvious. With systems integration, workstation operators can request data directly from the computer files and display it immediately or store it for later use and revision. Additionally, the flow of information from the front office to a central data base is also possible.

Third, development of better hardware links ensures further advances in text manipulation and storage. Because remote terminals can be tied in to central data storage facilities, the front-office personnel will have a greater range of text processing functions at their disposal. On the other hand, advanced word-processing software has improved to the extent that microcomputers can perform a variety of functions that rival the word processors installed on mainframe computers.

3.4.2 Levels of Integration

The integration of computer and office systems, of back-office and front-office processes will enable various subsystems to be used cooperatively, allowing a user to apply a sequence of tools in a flexible order to a given document. Put simply, integration permits information to pass freely among users of different office machines. Higher levels of integration allow one to draw upon different subsystems without making special requests to send or receive data. Sophisticated integrated systems feature common data structures and the capability to automatically transfer data among subsystems and users.

In general, there are five stages or levels in the process of global systems integration. The most primitive is manual distribution, storage, and handling of data and text files on paper. When information is requested, it is delivered by hand to the desk of the user by clerical personnel. The second stage allows data to be transferred electronically from user to user over tie-ins to existing telephone lines employing interface processors. Data is sent or received only upon request from one place to another. The next stage permits the automatic transmission of data through its encapsulization. Data can be sent from one to many or received by one from many. Sender and receiver do not have to be operating terminals at the same time. Of course, this stage requires a network that supports full-time connections. The fourth stage employs common data bases with distributed processing capability. Any user can access any data set and design his or her own protocols for subsequent data manipulation and transfer. The fifth and highest stage of integration allows automatic and consistent interfaces across all operating tools. Complete integration provides a common, wide-open field which allows a user to move between various system components and operations without having to exit one system and enter another. A complex task, such as a marketing study which involves a number of discrete steps, can be approached and prepared in a continuous flow.

3.4.3 Integration and the Role of the Personal Computer

The system component that enables the integration of WP and DP in the modern office is the personal computer. The concept of the PC and its role as an information management device is different from the PC system most are familiar with to date—namely, a small desktop with peripheral devices and software on floppy disks.

Personal computers tied into a central data base make integration possible. The aggregate computing power of PCs in use today exceeds the computing power of all installed mainframes. In U.S. businesses the number of PCs per 100 employees has quadrupled in the last three years to an estimated 16 per 100 in 1985. Over 80 percent of the firms with more than 1,000 employees use PCs.

The integrated PC acts as a workstation within a large computerized corporate information system. It provides the user with personalized information support systems and word-processing capability. It is connected via telecommunications lines with a central facility. It offers the best of two worlds—access to a powerful central system from locations which are flexible and user oriented. It can be used in the office, on the road, or at home. For the PC to achieve this universal status, three requirements must be met. First, the information must be entered in machine-readable format and meet the requirements dictated by the software. Second, a suitable, optimal database management program must be installed on the PC. Third, a well-connected and secure linkage between the PC and the mainframe must be established.

Developments in office automation and office integration are clearly under way in a large number of America's companies, and the number is expected to rise very sharply over the next few years. Nearly 60 percent of Fortune 1000 firms consider integrated office communications to be essential in the planning of any new data transfer and access network. Interest has surged in linking the standalone PCs, which have become the workstation of choice for managers, professionals, and, increasingly, secretaries and support staff. Additional indicators that underline this clear trend are an expected doubling of modem use by 1986, a sharp increase in the use of digital PBX technology to interconnect office computers, and a surge in offerings of database management software programs for personal computers.

3.5 INTEGRATED INFORMATION PROCESSING: THE KEY TO LEADING-EDGE BUSINESSES

Integrated front-office and back-office systems which allow for total information processing will offer many advantages to leading-edge businesses. Information resources can be shared among all personnel in the company. Shared resources reduce the costs of duplication and eliminate the possibility of double-entry errors. Data bases may be designed and customized to reflect the needs of the organization as a whole. The records management function is simplified and improved since all information is located in one place. Global access to all information allows everyone to gather information quickly without imposing restrictions on the use of data by others. Individuals retain the right to design their own protocols and to change them at will. In short, data storage is centralized, but applications design is distributed to the users.

3.5.1 The Information Center

The integrating power of the personal microcomputer has allowed the multifunction workstation to become a reality. This workstation can be tied into a larger information center to allow users to become more self-sufficient and productive. The challenge to managers, especially in OA or MIS, is to make sure that these centers provide that increased productivity through the use of data, hardware, software, and applications to make users more efficient and effective.

Although the goal of full integration has not been achieved completely, the movement toward integration has gained momentum and affects all facets of business activity. For example, without integrated information systems, finance and accounting departments would quickly grind to a chaotic halt.

Every aspect of document production has changed. The compound, electronically generated document of tomorrow will have as major components text, data, image, graphic, and perhaps even voice elements. Creation of such documents is nearly impossible, and surely not affordable, without integrated information processing. Businesses that examine their needs and make plans for a sensible course of action will be on the leading edge of these developments and can hope to gain the benefits of a shared, global information processing capacity.

QUESTIONS AND ANSWERS

Q. What is integrated information processing?

A. Integrated information processing is the end result of a corporate strategy to bring all office automation equipment under common control. Full integration is achieved when every PC in the company can talk with every other PC, when a central data base is established that any end user in the company can gain access to, and when there are commonly agreed upon standards throughout the company for new equipment purchases.

Q. What distinguishes front-office operations from back-office processing?

A. First of all, the front office refers to that part of the business that is visible to the outsider; the back office is the part that is seen only by the company's employees. In the era of high-tech office automation, front-office operations include document creation and reproduction, information gathering, outside communications, and so on. Back-office processing includes central data storage, internal operations like payroll, and internal communications. Until the last decade, front-office operations consisted almost entirely of word-processing functions, and back-office processing involved the large-scale manipulation of data. This is no longer true. More and more, the front office is processing data without requesting back-office services, and the back office is taking on more of the repetitive front-office tasks. With integrated information processing, the front-office versus back-office distinction will dissolve completely.

Q. Why is integration necessary?

A. The very nature of business is changing. As more businesses move into service industries, information itself is becoming a resource and a valuable commodity. With so many workers involved in the "production of information," leading-edge businesses must be alert to cost-efficiency and value creation in order to remain competitive. Full integration of the firm's facilities for information management will open entire new vistas for cost savings and strategic product enhancement.

Q. Why is the personal computer so important to integration?

A. The personal computer is the centerpiece of the new office workstation. It incorporates a processing capability that can be used for document creation and data manipulation. The PC can be loaded with software that will incorporate it into a large data transmission network. Thus, the PC offers access to a large central information resource and at the same time permits the individual end user to employ custom-designed applications for specific tasks.

Q. What gains can a firm expect from integrated information processing?

A. First, a firm can reduce costs considerably on hardware and on personnel. Workstations built around the personal computer can perform a variety of functions that previously required several different machines. As the cost of personal computers keeps falling, firms will save a great deal by investing in them. Therefore, firms can realize cost savings on personnel. Second, the integration of word processing, data processing and retrieval, graphics capability, and printing into one workstation saves time in document production. Third, the flow of information among end users is faster and more convenient when everyone is tied in to one central data base.

Q. What challenge does full integration of information resources pose to the management information services (MIS) department?

A. The role of the MIS manager in all of this is of the broadest possible nature. MIS must coordinate the transition to full integration throughout the organization. MIS must design the central data base taking into consideration the various needs of all end users; MIS must choose the hardware that will best suit the data communications network; MIS must provide consultancy service to end users so that they can accomplish business tasks; and MIS must do all this with full attention to long-term business strategy.

4

Hardware Technology

4.1 THE DISTINCTION BETWEEN HARDWARE AND SOFTWARE

At the root of the revolution toward office automation lies the rapid pace of research into and development of new information technology. In today's world the term technology comprises both hardware and software. Without the hardware, software would not exist; without the software, office machines such as computers would be dead and functionless. Neither hardware nor software would be conceivable without its counterpart. Despite their mutual dependence, hardware and software can be separated into distinct categories. This chapter focuses on the recent developments and future trends in hardware technology. The next chapter reviews software technology.

Although it might be argued that the hardware-software distinction is somewhat artificial because the capability of the machine is determined by the characteristics of both simultaneously, it is convenient nevertheless to distinguish the two for the purposes of clarity. For our purposes, hardware will include the physical or material attributes of the office machine. Software will include everything that constitutes an instruction to the physical machine, that is, everything that makes the machine function. For illustrative purposes we will examine three tools or machines: a screwdriver, a clock, and a computer.

A screwdriver is a piece of hardware. Software is a concept completely foreign to the use of a screwdriver. In order to function, a screwdriver must be manually operated. It contains no logic of its own. The function of a screwdriver depends entirely on the knowledge of the person who uses it. An electric clock, on the other hand, is not dependent on its user. Once the clock is plugged in, electrical current operates it automatically. In this sense, the clock contains some logic. For every sixty cycles of AC input, the second hand on the clock advances one second. The electrical circuitry that translates an electrical current of 60 Hz into the motion of the second hand by one-sixtieth of a revolution around the clock face per second of time may be said to incorporate software. The important thing is that this software is "hard-wired." It cannot be changed without taking the clock apart and replacing certain physical parts. The software exists, but it is very primitive.

The computer, however, is a great advance in office automation because it can perform many different functions without the replacement of its physical parts. Like the electric clock it performs functions automatically, and it does contain some "hard-wired" logic. But a large portion of the instructions to the computer are provided from outside the machine itself, either by a person typing commands on a keyboard or by instructions stored on various media such as disks and tapes. Thus, the computer (or hardware) obeys its instructions (or software). If the software is changed, the hardware will perform different functions. Even with the computer, however, the distinction between hardware and software is not totally well-defined. Some software will not operate a given piece of hardware because it is not compatible. The logic that is wired into the computer places functional limitations on the machine that software alone cannot alter. In this realm the physical characteristics of the machine determine its functional capabilities. For our purposes we will consider as hardware all the physical elements of the machine, including the logic circuits that are built in. Hardware also includes all the peripheral devices that require a host computer in order to operate and that extend the capability of the computer, such as disk drives, video screens, printers, and so on. Software includes everything else.

In this chapter we will review the impact of advances in hardware technology on the office workstation and summarize advances in processing and information storage technology. We will also look at the development of printers and at the emerging field of voice technology.

4.2 OFFICE WORKSTATIONS AND THE PERSONAL COMPUTER

In the 1970s the standard office workstation was designed to perform the essential word-processing tasks. Late in that decade attempts were made to build more functional, albeit specialized, workstations for a variety of different tasks. This approach showed some promise of yielding productivity increases, but the introduction of the personal computer (PC) interrupted that progression and opened up an entirely new vista for development of office systems and, in particular, the workstation in the 1980s. The personal computer became the centerpiece of the new, professional office workstation and an essential component of the integrated office system.

There remains little doubt at this point that the personal computer must be the starting point for any comprehensive review of future trends in office workstations. The advent of the IBM PC and its widespread acceptance by users and other suppliers of compatible products created a de facto standard for the personal computer industry. Several features of this standard reveal potential long-term trends. For one thing, personal computer architecture is open. PCs are designed to be compatible with any number of different products. For most additional functional requirements it is therefore possible to design add-on products and adapter cards. For example, a larger screen with higher resolution could be added using a new adapter card with a faster microprocessor and a larger memory. Better keyboards, more powerful disk drives to support larger disks, printers, and data transmission devices may all be added as required merely by furnishing the proper adapter card. IBM anticipated the need for flexible personal computers by introducing a family of units with specialized functions. The PC 3270 provides superior terminal performance with switching between functions; the PC-XT contains a larger memory and greater disk storage capacity; and the PC-AT may be operated by more than one user.

The key word in personal computers is flexibility. The PC must be able to adapt to the need for new functional requirements. Thus, the trend toward workstations that are devoted to just one task was reversed overnight with the emergence of the PC. Now, the workstation is developing as a place for several different activities all aided by the personal computer.

4.2.1 Specialized Workstations

Nevertheless, despite the trend toward the multifunctional office workstation, there is still a need for specialized workstations dedicated to one particular type of task. One example is the engineering workstation, usually referred to as a computer-aided design (CAD) system. CAD systems have up to one megabyte of main memory, software to manage a display more sophisticated than the standard PC video type (usually larger than seventeen inches with much higher resolution), a 32-bit processor (the standard is 16-bit), and a detachable keyboard. Many of these systems provide features of large computer systems, such as virtual memory. With virtual memory the practical working memory available to the user can be much larger than the physical main memory, by shifting the data between disk storage and main memory as it is required. This process of shuffling data back and forth between disk and main memory is sometimes called checkpointing.

Along the same lines there are systems which provide a local area network (LAN) to allow all the units on the network to share resources. The LAN systems create a larger "virtual" system for all the users on the network. Each workstation enjoys greater processing power than it would have standing alone. Such a workstation network would cost more, but the benefits may justify the costs.

In an engineering workstation, the emphasis on processing power results from the need to produce complex graphics along with the associated engineering computations necessary to transform projections at high speed. Office systems do not require such a powerful processing capability, except for certain specialized document production applications, which include image processing for illustrations and graphics to be included in documents. Thus, specialized workstations such as adaptations of the engineering workstation may have some application in the office.

4.2.2 The Future Development of the Personal Computer

As the market for personal computers continues to expand, it can be reasonably expected that suppliers will seek ways to enhance the power of their machines. Several directions are suggested immediately by the needs of PC users and people who use the workstations. The areas slated for improvement include the provision for more local data storage, the need for additional main memory, enhancements to the terminal display, and the development of variants to the standard keyboard as the only mode of talking to the computer.

The most important PC developments will result from the quest to provide greater local data storage capability. The vast majority of currently installed PCs run from floppy disks, and many have only one floppy disk drive. Floppy disks have a relatively small storage capacity, so it is necessary to shuffle disks in and out of the computer as one changes the applications task. This leads to the proliferation of small floppy disks, each containing only one application and often with one application spread over several disks. With large collections of floppy disks comes the need for a filing system. By and large, users outside of secretarial or clerical groups do not manage floppy disk libraries effectively. Apart from choosing appropriate file names and managing the generation of files or the verions of files, floppy disks must be filed systematically. Furthermore, because the disks are fragile, they must be handled and stored correctly.

In the long term, these shortcomings will be corrected by the development of data storage on a hard disk within the PC or with small units that can be attached locally to the PC. Many personal computer suppliers have already developed PCs with fixed disks built permanently into the machine. These hard disks have a storage capacity equivalent to forty floppy disks. This allows a number of different applications to be installed in the PC simultaneously. The floppy disks are saved only to transmit data from one PC to another and to break up data stored on the hard disk. It becomes easier to maintain a library of floppy disks when disk circulation is no longer so heavy.

In the near future a work group file server will meet the needs of PC users who wish to remain on the forefront. The file server is a centrally located automated hard disk drive that can be linked to a local area network. In this scheme a number of PCs would be connected by a network, and all files and applications programs would be stored centrally. The file server would contain one or more disk drives and some processing capability to sort out the demand for files coming from a number of different nodes on the local area network at the same time. The central file server would be a shared resource and would obviate the need for a large central floppy disk library. In this sense the file server network mimics the minicomputer, which offers a central processing capability with slave terminals.

As the cost of hard disk storage continues to decrease, the workstation of the 1990s will probably incorporate some built-in disk storage, some remote, resource-sharing disk storage, and some removable disk storage such as the floppy disk.

Another need which suppliers will surely address is that for additional main memory. With the emergence of large integrated software applications, more sophisticated user interfaces, and telecommunications capabilities, the PC will require additional memory cards. The 512-Kbyte memory will be a standard attribute of the PC in the near future. Eventually, PCs may be endowed with a memory of one megabyte. To see just how remarkable this advance is, one might consider that in the early 1980s a minicomputer with a main memory of that size was considered top of the line.

Displays will also be improved, and a variety of add-on options will likely be available. As the PC becomes the standard for word processing, and as graphics output capabilities are developed and enhanced, the use of high-resolution display screens will become more commonplace. Again, costs will fall sufficiently to make high-resolution displays an attractive option.

At the moment color screens do not cost much more than monochrome screens, and they are used frequently in today's managerial and professional workstations. The future availability of reasonably priced, high-resolution displays will surely reduce the interest in color displays because shading and patterns can differentiate graphics effectively. Such shading can be reproduced readily on current hard-copy devices and office copiers. Until color reproduction and color printers become more widely used and affordable, the intrinsic value of color screens will remain limited. Only for applications where color representation is absolutely essential, such as the production of graphic art, will color display technology be developed further. In business applications, graphics are used primarily for communicating concepts, facts, and ideas, and, as such, color is not necessary, given high-resolution displays.

In addition to these other changes, the keyboard itself will probably be enhanced to include greater functional and command capability. The needs of different PC users vary tremendously. The full-time word-processing specialist needs a better-quality keyboard than that on the standard PC. Graphics applications need more direct methods of drawing onto the screen than the keyboard offers with its primitive directional controls.

Two prominent variants of the standard keyboard are likely to evolve. For visually oriented displays, the mouse has become a popular peripheral device. With icons or on-screen menus, decisions can be made without a keyboard, but instead by pointing at the option. For engineering workstations the data tablet has performed a similar function. A menu template is mounted on a digitizing board and commands are selected. The mouse will remain a standard feature in this regard, and it will probably supersede other options.

Another variant will result from recent attempts to incorporate voice functions into the workstation. Such incorporation in the form of a telephone link and a handset is an option that has been introduced by several suppliers recently. It seems unlikely that this will come into widespread use, except where the private branch exchange (PBX) is used as the preferred approach to local office communications. Advances in telecommunications technology will also create a demand for portable terminals with smaller keyboards. To keep size and weight down so that portables may travel, features will be limited to a subset of those available on the standard workstation. PCs will be developed to act as "hosts" for remote terminals. This will have the greatest impact on displays and on disk storage; in other respects, the compatibility of host to remote terminals should be almost total.

Specialized workstations for illustrations, image processing, and document production will be developed along slightly different lines, but they will likely be mere variants on engineering or architectural design workstations.

Exhibit 4.1
Evolution of the Office Workstation

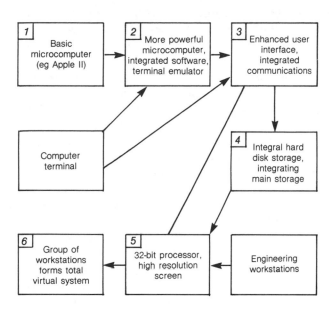

In general, the overall trend will be toward workstation integration. All the hardware changes itemized above follow from the clearly perceived trend to bring workstations into a shared local area network. Exhibit 4.1 illustrates the probable progression. The move toward integration can be considered as a reaction to the radical move toward distributed processing that followed the introduction of the PC. On the other hand, such integration is not the first step in an attempted move all the way back to the mainframe with central processing and dozens of "dumb" slave terminals that are incapable of independent processing.

4.2.3 Workstations in a Minicomputer System Environment

So far, the discussion of trends in the development of office workstations has assumed that the personal computer is the only possible starting point. This is not entirely true. Although the introduction of the PC brought into currency the idea of the office workstation, the workstation need not include a PC. As the previous section suggests, a local area network of PCs is very similar in character to a minicomputer-based system. Minicomputers can support PCs as peripheral devices, but more frequently they employ conventional computer terminals without independent processing capability which are enslaved by the central processor. In some cases the minicomputer can support a wide variety of different terminals, so that a number of different tasks may be performed efficiently. If both the PC-based local area network system and the minicomputer-based system can perform the same essential functions, on what basis does one choose between them?

In the short term, shared processing resources and direct connections between remote terminals are the primary advantages of the minicomputer system. Local area network developments have not proceeded far enough yet to offer the same high quality of support to a group of users that the minicomputer offers. In other respects, minicomputer systems do not support applications that are any better than those found on a PC, particularly in the areas of word processing and spreadsheet analysis.

The final long-term decision should be based primarily on cost trends. Such trends will likely go against the minicomputer system if it is required to support a full range of office systems facilities. Personal computer costs are falling rapidly and will soon approach the cost of a "dumb" computer terminal. Thus, the relatively high cost of the central minicomputer or network of minicomputers will soon make them uneconomical to use for functions that are now common on the PC. On the other hand, the minicomputer system already contains the necessary integrating links that would be supplied to the PC-based system by the local area network. In addition, minicomputers provide access to large data-processing systems, expensive peripheral devices such as high-speed printers, and a large data-storage capacity. Given these advantages, minicomputers will undoubtedly still be around in ten years. The degree to which they are used to serve as a host for large integrated office systems will depend on the success of the effort to develop local area networks and central access devices such as file servers.

4.2.4 Workstation Costs

As a general rule, the cost of a workstation falls the longer it is on the market. Prices are kept from falling to nothing by the continuous introduction of new technologies and better, more powerful features. The market remains stable because people are always anticipating the "next generation" of hardware. Thus, the costs of the state-of-the-art system follow a "saw-tooth" function illustrated in Exhibit 4.2.

When each advance in workstations is announced, the price of the new technology starts high relative to the broader market. As competitors launch similar products, the price begins to fall gradually. When

Exhibit 4.2
Costs of State-of-the-Art Personal Computers

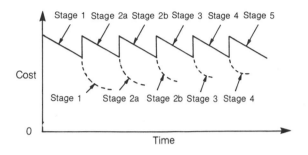

= cost of the "state-of-the-art" personal computer at that point in time.

the next generation is announced, two things happen: the costs of the state-of-the-art system jump back up, and the costs of the now-replaced product fall more rapidly than they had done previously. The prices of existing products drop at a faster rate so that the price differential will be sufficient to keep both on the market. Despite approaching obsolescence, the older products can still coexist on the market with the newer products. Thus, a cyclical scheme is established and is repeated each time a new stage is introduced.

The cheapest workstations, with a monochrome display, a terminal emulator, and a simple microprocessor will cost no more than $150 by the 1990s. Along with this fall in price of the simplest devices, office workstation capabilities will increase. By 1990, a unit that incorporates a 16-bit microprocessor, a range of communication protocols, a built-in hard disk, and a high-resolution display should not cost more than $1,000. Such a unit will run a variety of general-purpose software packages, and it will fit into a wide range of networks.

The cost of a state-of-the-art office workstation in the 1990s will be similar to today's leading-edge personal computer. Of course, it will include many of the advanced hardware and communications features that have been described above.

4.3 PROCESSING TECHNOLOGY

With the invention of the semiconductor in 1955, the revolution in information processing technology took off. Since the inception of the semiconductor, the technology has followed a nearly uniform seven-year cycle of leaps forward. Each of these developments has resulted in a quantum improvement in the processing power available from a single chip. Each has also expanded the information processing industry beyond its previous boundary.

The emergence of a new stage has two distinct consequences. First, it becomes economically feasible to computerize certain functions, the automation of which would not have previously been justified. Large-scale integration (LSI) made computerized word processing possible in an office setting. Similarly, with very-large-scale integration (VLSI) it is now possible for a computer to perform optical character recognition. Second, the falling cost and the reduced physical size of processors that accompany each new stage enable manufacturers to incorporate processing power into consumer goods, office machines, and system components. Automobiles and washing machines now contain small processors; pocket calculators and photocopiers contain more sophisticated processors. System components with built-in processors include intelligent terminals and printers and new disk controllers.

The falling cost of processors means that all systems will tend to become distributed, at least within the firm or local office. Mainframe computers have acted for a long time just like distributed processors in the sense that they are capable of running many different tasks simultaneously, either under a time-sharing or real-time priority system. Personal microcomputers will become more powerful with the penetration of VLSI technology, so that by 1991 2-million-instructions-per-second (2 mips) desktop PCs will be available at the price of today's PCs.

Developments in microelectronics continue at a greater rate than ever before. The technologies involved have not yet approached the fundamental limits of size and speed imposed by nature as we know it through the science of physics. In short, the book cannot be closed on the potential advances in processing technology.

4.4 STORAGE TECHNOLOGY

Along with the advances in solid-state physics that led to the development of the semiconductor came a number of engineering breakthroughs that created a variety of different storage media. All of these media are read from and written onto by electromagnetic fields. In this section we will describe five different types of storage technology: semiconductor memory, bubble memory, hard disks, floppy disks, and optical disks. We will also consider the progress that is being made in storing different forms of information such as digitized data, words and text, vocal utterances, and images.

4.4.1 Semiconductor Memories

Before 1970 most computer memories consisted of large arrays of ferrite cores. The cores were tiny rings of magnetic material only 1 millimeter in diameter, and they were strung on grids of conducting wires by the hundreds of thousands. With the advent of integrated circuits, semiconductors superseded ferrite cores as the basic element in computer memory.

In its simplest form the semiconductor memory cell consists of one transistor and one capacitor. The capacitor is extremely small, but its capacitance is large enough to hold an electric charge which indicates a binary value of one. The absence of an electric charge in the memory cell indicates a value of zero. Of course, at the elementary level a computer memory holds nothing more than binary values. Each element is called a "bit." The transistor enables reading the memory and writing to the memory. The transistor acts as a switch to connect the storage capacitor to the data line when the cell is selected for reading or writing.

The semiconductor memory cell loses its stored information each time it is read and also by leakage of the charge on the capacitor. Leakage can occur in only a few milliseconds. Thus, the cell must have its stored charge refreshed every 2 milliseconds, as well as after every access operation. For this reason this kind of memory is called "dynamic random-access memory" (RAM). Other designs, called "static RAMs," do not require refreshing, but they do require additional transistors. Static RAMs are larger since the transistors take up more area on the chip, and they cost more. Today single chip RAMs of 64K bits are common and chips with 256K bits are available.

Some computer applications require RAMs containing some permanently stored information such as control program instructions or constant data values. One common example is the control program for a pocket calculator; it is never changed. A read-only memory (ROM) is appropriate for this kind of information storage. In its simplest form, it is just like a RAM, but without the transistor. For a binary one, the capacitor is replaced by an open circuit; for a binary zero, it is grounded by a direct connection to earth. The desired data pattern is thus fabricated directly on the chip itself. Of course, this incurs a high initial production cost.

Despite these cost differentials, costs of producing all types of semiconductors have been falling rapidly. The falling cost of computer memory has been a driving force behind the reduced prices for computers and related technologies since the mid–1970s.

4.4.2 Bubble Memory

All the devices described in the section on semiconductor memories are randomly accessible. In other words, any piece of information in the memory may be read directly based on its location in the array of items without disturbing any other item. Magnetic bubble memory is totally different in the sense that it is a serial or sequential access device. This means that if one wants to read the sixth item on a bubble-memory device, one must read the five items in front of it first. Although this seems cumbersome, magnetic bubble memory is an important component of microcomputer systems.

Magnetic bubble memory exploits a physical phenomenon that was discovered only recently—namely, that certain magnetic materials such as garnet, when shaved to a thin film, will create local variations in otherwise uniform magnetic fields. Both the materials and the physical principles employed in bubble memory are quite different from those of transistor-based integrated circuits, which use semiconductors. Nevertheless, the bubble memory device may also be fabricated on chips of a sort, so it may be considered "microelectronic" in the broadest sense of the word.

The most attractive application of bubble memory is in replacing small disk or tape storage, two other media for serial access storage. With a storage capacity of 10 million bits per chip, bubble memory has great potential for use in microcomputer systems. When produced in quantity, it has a lower price than small disks with a comparable storage capacity. Bubble memory has similar performance characteristics, and it is also smaller and more reliable.

4.4.3 Hard Disks

A hard magnetic disk is a round metal plate, about the size of a long-playing phonograph record, coated with a thin layer of ferromagnetic material used for recording electronic information. A disk pack is formed when a number of disks are mounted on a common shaft. Disk packs may be permanently fixed inside an electronic reading and writing device called a disk drive, or they may be removable.

For example, the Winchester hard disk drive has one or more disks sealed hermetically in a nonremovable unit. Because the disks in the Winchester device are not subjected to the stress of insertion and removal, and because they are protected from environmental pollution, the read and write heads can be small, lighter, and closer to the recording surface. This provides for much higher recording densities. The time required to access information on a Winchester disk tends to be longer than the time required on more conventional, removable hard disk drives. Nevertheless, response times for Winchester disks are usually more than adequate for most business applications. Exhibit 4.3 shows the construction of the Winchester disk drive.

During the last fifteen years the improved performance and lower

Exhibit 4.3
The Winchester Hard Disk Drive

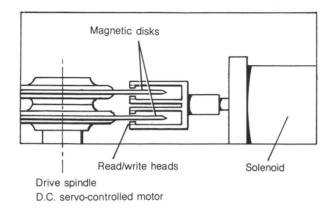

Magnetic disks

Read/write heads   Solenoid

Drive spindle
D.C. servo-controlled motor

price of disk products has been achieved by a continuing increase in the recording density. In turn, this has brought about the need for smaller read-write heads. Given the small scale that exists today, ferrite head technology is no longer adequate. Modern disk drives incorporate thin-film head technology, which uses VLSI chips. Thin-film head technology has a number of advantages over the older ferrite-head technology. Performance, storage capacity, and reliability of the device are improved, and it is easier to manufacture. Thin-film technology may also be used for the recording medium itself. The dominant electronic mass storage device today is the 14-inch diameter magnetic disk. It is considered the industry standard, and its familiarity can be attributed to its long history of ubiquitous use. Nevertheless, in the future, the 5 ¼-inch diameter disk will become the standard; the single-spindle 14-inch disk will be replaced by the multiple-spindle 5 ¼-inch disk. The well-known Winchester disk, now used in many personal computers, has a potential capacity of 300 megabytes and a diameter of 5 ¼ inches. The advantages of smaller disks are twofold. First, the units that drive smaller disks are smaller. More information can be stored without any increase in the space occupied. This consideration is relevant to large mainframe computer users and to small desktop microcomputer users. Second, the smaller disks require a lower torque to rotate them. Therefore, they expend less energy.

4.4.4 Floppy Disks

The floppy disk is a thin flexible disk about the size of the standard 7-inch single phonograph record. It stores information in an electronic form, and the technological principles involved are similar to those for hard disks. The floppy disk is undoubtedly the most familiar to the public of computer users as it is the standard storage medium available with the personal computer. It is used for word processors and micro-computers because its low weight and small size make it compatible with the small machines and easily transportable.

The volume of data that can be held on a single floppy disk has been increased substantially since its introduction in the 1970s. The improvement in access speed and transfer has been more modest, however. It appears that the continuing improvement of hard disks and bubble memory technology will displace floppy disks as the principal storage medium for business applications in the long run.

4.4.5 Optical Disks

The newest disk storage technology that has only recently broken into the market is the optical disk. Also known as video disks, optical disks have several attractive characteristics. They have a high storage capacity, are not costly for the amount of information they can hold, and employ a digital coding system. One weakness of optical disks is that previously recorded data cannot be amended. Data can be added, but not changed.

A single side of a 12-inch optical disk can store one gigabyte of information which is equivalent to about 400,000 pages of double-spaced typescript. The time it takes to access data is about 135 milliseconds, which is at least four times longer than the access time for hard magnetic disks. Optical disks are unsuitable, therefore, for any application that requires frequent disk access or extensive updating. They are excellent to use for most archival applications.

The optical disk gets its name from the method by which data is read from and written to the disk surface—namely, by means of an optical laser beam. Many mechanical or physical problems associated with magnetic disks are circumvented. The disk itself consists of a thin sheet of clear acrylic backed by a reflective surface. A laser burns small pits into the surface of the disk to record information. After the surface of the acrylic layer has been recorded, the disk is covered with a thin layer of a reflective aluminum material, and then the whole thing is sealed in a protective coating. To read information back from the disk, the device driver focuses a low-powered laser onto the pitted surface. The existence of or absence of a pit signifies the binary zero or one that constitutes

Exhibit 4.4
Optical Disk Storage

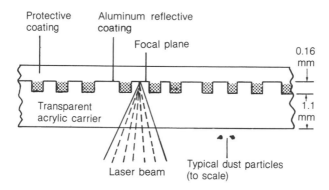

the elemental building block of all digitized information. Exhibit 4.4 illustrates the optical disk in schematic fashion.

Although the capacity of a single optical disk is much greater than that of a hard disk, the steadily increasing requirement for storing large amounts of information in a small space has led to the development of multidisk optical systems. These systems either stack several disks on a single spindle in a manner analogous to the disk pack or adopt the "jukebox" approach with a mechanical disk selector built into the system. This disk selection time increases the time required to access information, so most multiple disk systems employ magnetic disks to store an index and some sort of data storage buffer to improve the speed of operation.

For high-volume, archival storage of text, data, and especially images, optical disks are already more economical than traditional microfilm or microfiche systems. Responding to economic reality, more than a dozen companies have optical digital recording systems either currently available on the market or now under development for use with computer-based systems. Nevertheless, until the disadvantage of being noneras-able is overcome, optical disk technology will be confined largely to archival data storage, and it will not threaten the dominant market position of hard magnetic disks.

4.4.6 Multimedia Storage

With development underway on so many different aspects of data storage technology, the rising storage capacity and falling costs per unit

Exhibit 4.5
Storage Space Requirements of Various Modes of Communication

The table shows the space required to store one page of typescript
or equivalent information.

	Bytes
Data (say)	500
Text (250 words)	1,500
Facsimile image (with moderate data compression)	50,000
Facsimile image (without data compression)	500,000
Speech (at 100 words/min)	1,200,000

of information stored make it feasible for the first time to store images and speech digitally. Traditionally, images and speech have been stored in an analog fashion—that is, in photographs, on magnetic tape, or on phonograph records. The essential difference between analog and digital recording is captured by the difference between the gradual and the discrete. Digital data is discrete, binary, a zero or a one and nothing in between. Analog data is gradual, forms a continuum, like a spectrum of light generated by a glass prism. It is, for instance, the difference between a painting by a great master where color is blended gradually and by proportion, and an image on a color television which is composed of red, blue, and green dots that are either off or on. This difference lies at the heart of the current debate among musical aesthetes on whether digital recording, such as that on the new optical disks, or analog recording, such as that on the traditional LP, sounds better. Until very recently the idea of recording music or film digitally would have been inconceivable because of the vast quantity of discrete zeros and ones necessary to reproduce all the fine and subtle gradations that are easily reproducible with analog methods. Exhibit 4.5 gives some notion of the magnitudes involved. Continuous improvements in compressing techniques have made digital recording of images or speech feasible for routine business use. It is already possible to hold very large facsimile image files online for special purposes, and systems which enable the digital storage of speech have become available commercially in recent years.

Integration of data, image, and vocal storage poses more problems than that of cost-efficiency, however. Systems must be developed to handle the storage and retrieval of information of different types on the same medium. For instance, an integrated filing system must be able to handle records of any length from a few bytes to several hundred thousand bytes and to encode and decode in several different ways. Development of such a system falls primarily in the realm of software and not hardware, so it will not be treated at length here. It should be noted that development of the necessary software will be costly, and that without such software it would be difficult to maintain optimum efficiency.

By contrast, the integration of data and text storage is a relatively simple matter, and it has already been achieved in many office systems. For instance, any application designed to hold postal addresses has solved this problem. Increasingly, standard information management and retrieval systems have incorporated the capability to integrate data and text information.

In addition, the integration of text and facsimile images has been achieved in the more sophisticated office systems on the market. Text, data, and structured graphics have also been integrated in computer-aided design systems.

4.5 PRINTERS

Personal computer packages and word-processing systems provide the user with a document production capability that is well established. The user's view of word processing on the input side will not change a great deal over the next several years. In the overall document production process, the output side will likely improve in significant ways. The wide availability of lower-cost laser printers will raise further the quality of documents produced in the office, will lead to the integration of text and graphics, and will serve to make typesetting a more viable alternative for office documents, particularly for documents intended for customers and communications outside the firm.

Attempts have been made to establish a workable interface between data and text processing systems and typesetting systems for over fifteen years. The benefits of this idea accrue to the originator of the document and to the publisher or printer of the document. For standard published material such as reports, monographs, company brochures, and annual reports, typesetting has become standard. Now, the emergence of high-quality output technologies is giving the office system the ability to produce such output without employing the time-tested standard printing techniques.

4.5.1 Printer Technology

The well-known line printer still produces most of the printed matter generated by large computer systems. A revolving drum or chain or reciprocating train technology enables the line printer to generate a large volume of material.

The earliest electrical impact printer was the IBM Selectric golfball. Until 1972, when Diablo Systems invented the daisy wheel, the Selectric was the only letter-quality printer available. Users soon recognized the daisy wheel as more reliable, less noisy, and faster than the golfball; the daisy wheel could produce 55 characters per second as against 15 for the golfball.

Matrix printers are also single character printers, like the golfball and the daisy wheel. Unlike the others, the matrix printer forms each character from a dot matrix. Many of the smaller printers that can be run from a PC are matrix printers. Early matrix printing has been improved by electronic control and the addition of a second print-head. A print speed of up to 500 characters per second is now attainable with such improvements. The use of a single line of needles as opposed to a block matrix has reduced the cost of such printers. This "infinite matrix" principle enables the production of a more perfect letter image. The print-head makes a number of successive passes and distributes its imprint to give the letters a solid look. With this technical innovation, users can expect a large number of software products to make matrix printers into better quality tools that will enable line drawings and diagrams to be printed.

There are also a variety of nonimpact printing technologies; among them are ink-jet, reprographic, thermal, and electrostatic printers. One major drawback of nonimpact printers is that they are unable to produce multiple, simultaneous copies. In addition, thermal and electrostatic printers use special, costly paper.

Ink-jet printers squirt ink selectively from a print-head with many nozzles. (The ink is deflected by plates with an electric charge.) Exhibit 4.6 illustrates the principle by which ink-jet printers operate. Reprographic printers employ the same principles as office copiers. They can run up to 20,000 lines per minute and can overlay form headings as they print. Thermal printers exploit the reaction of a special paper to heat. Selected matrix probes heat the paper's surface as the print-head passes over. Thermal printers are small, light, reliable, and cheap, but the paper they use is expensive. Electrostatic printers apply a voltage to create an electrostatic image on sensitive paper. The image is then developed with a liquid toner. This printer is fast and silent. Its quality can be very high, and fonts may be changed. Electrostatic printers have no moving parts except for paper handling.

4.5.2 Laser Printers

The laser printer is a development that came out of photocopier technology. In practice, a laser is used only as a light source in some models,

Exhibit 4.6
Operating Principles of the Ink-Jet Printer

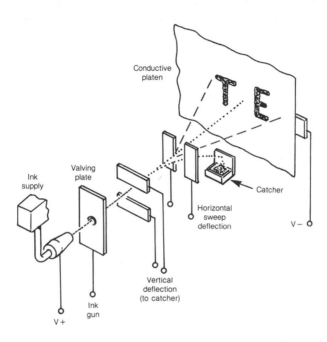

Conductive platen

Ink supply

Valving plate

Catcher

Horizontal sweep deflection

V −

Vertical deflection (to catcher)

Ink gun

V +

but the general term "laser printer" is employed anyway. Originally, laser printers were intended for use as high-volume line printers. Because they were capable of generating one hundred pages per minute, they were found in mainframe computer sites at companies with voluminous output requirements. A suitably equipped laser printer has one unique advantage in that it can reproduce graphics and approximate typeset printing. One early model featured high-volume output, printing on both sides of the paper, and text and graphics reproduction unified under software control. At the time, a printer with these features was very costly, had a complex protocol to step through in order to format the output, and had a dot density that was adequate for many uses, but which was not high enough to produce documents with a typeset, printed look.

More recently, some suppliers have introduced to the market low-cost laser printers suitable for office use. For under $5,000 a printer that can produce eight pages per minute can be purchased. Typically, the printer mechanism limits output to about 30,000 pages a month, however. One

can expect to see enhancements to these units over the next few years.
The volume of throughput will be higher (10 to 20 pages per minute),
and dot densities will be increased to enable output to appear typeset.
Laser printers will certainly displace standard line printers to some extent, but higher cost and the need for more frequent service to maintain
them will limit the extent of displacement.

From the user's viewpoint, developments to enhance the graphics
capability to include forms, illustrations, and exhibits will hold out far
greater promise. Potential applications of graphic laser printers include
the printing of technical service manuals, educational and training materials, customer proposals and quotations, and periodic financial
reports.

If color displays continue to become more prevalent, laser printers
may be used for color reproduction. Cost and technical issues that have
not yet been resolved suggest that some years will pass before color
laser printing will be a practical option. It is already feasible to produce
color output with color plotters and ink-jet printers. This may also dis-
courage the development of color laser printers.

4.5.3 Typesetting and Composition of Printed Matter

Choosing print fonts, handling letter and word spacing, laying out
pages and illustrations, and so on are complex activities; such tasks are
undertaken usually by professionals trained in graphics. For the typical
office that plans to typeset its documents or to engage in publishing
activity in-house, the lack of trained professionals can pose a problem.
If layouts are standardized, a predetermined batch stream may be set
up and run on a data-processing system and printed on a laser printer
with the requisite library of fonts. Thus, the burden of formulating complex code to insert in the text is lifted from the office worker. Still,
graphics and illustrations require special knowledge.

Certain units which enable the display of full-page layout can be operated by the office worker. Illustrations can be combined with text using
a scanner, but again knowledge of the application is essential. In the
future more and more functions will be built into a processor which
drives the printer itself. The processor will contain standard fonts, symbols, and line drawing capabilities. Specialized workstations to control
the printer processor will simplify the demands for special knowledge
on individuals operating nonspecialized workstations. High-resolution
screens will be required along with graphics applications to enable printing specialists to edit and check details.

Packaged systems will emerge over the next five years to allow
straightforward, word-processed text to be printed on laser printers.
Graphics applications will be included in such packages. The font library

will be limited; pagination, indexing, and layout will follow some simple rules. A series of standard options will be supplied to the user so that the need for graphics or layout expertise will be eliminated.

All of these developments, however, will not eliminate the need for special typesetting and printing services. The complexities inherent in all the tasks necessary to produce high-quality printed matter should not be underestimated. Extensive professional expertise will continue to be required.

4.6 VOICE TECHNOLOGY

Voice technology comprises all the technologies available to artificially generate human vocal utterances or to interpret and encode such utterances. Recently there have been rapid advances made in both computer-generated speech and speech recognition, which involves the analysis and interpretation of vocal input. Neither of these should be confused with voice messaging, which is the use of the computer to manage and control the recording, storage, and transmission of conventional audio recordings of voice messages.

4.6.1 Voice Output

Recent advances in voice output have been directed toward the aim of synthesis. Voice synthesis is the production of speech from text using phonemes (prototypical sounds) to construct words. The translation from text to utterance is governed by an elaborate set of rules. Again, this is not the same as drawing a limited set of messages from a tape recorder as required. The range of possible utterances that can be generated using voice synthesis is effectively infinite.

Voice output frees the eyes from looking at a screen, allowing the user to do something else. It allows telephone access to automated systems because the computer can quite literally talk on the phone. Instructions can be relayed to the system with a touch-tone phone. Voice synthesis chips are actually inexpensive, and a number of systems are available now to convert text into speech.

Systems which provide prerecorded or synthesized words or sounds directly under computer control are most frequently used for customer communications. Such systems cut down on the cost of staff devoted to answering the telephone, especially where the need for information, or the nature of customer transaction, is simple and straightforward. Typically, the customer keys in a simple inquiry using a touch-tone telephone and receives the voice synthesis response through the telephone handset. If the customer has only a dial phone, a touch-tone adaptor can be attached at nominal cost. Ideal applications for this technology are bank account status or financial inquiry systems, product price and availability quotes, and order processing. More complex applications may be provided when the customer is prompted for a response in much the same way that a cash machine at the bank operates, for instance. Up to now, banking, finance, and motor industries have employed this type of application to the greatest extent.

4.6.2 Speech Recognition

Automatic speech recognition is considered generally to be the most difficult and complex problem in the field of voice processing. The other areas such as voice synthesis, compression, analysis, encryption, and transmission are all much more narrowly defined, and all contribute to the solution of the voice recognition problem. Historically, the challenge has proved formidable. Some of the world's largest companies (AT&T, IBM, and ITT), the U.S. Department of Defense, and several universities have been developing speech recognition technology for years without the desired degree of success. Nevertheless, in spite of difficulties and setbacks, about a dozen companies have been founded to develop and market speech recognition products. Along with the major companies in the computing and telecommunications field, these firms preserve a dynamic market with open-ended growth potential.

Speech recognition draws on LSI and VLSI chip design, signal processing, acoustics, phonetics, natural language theory, linguistics, mathematics of stochastic processes, and computer science techniques. Because of the multidisciplinary nature of this field and because many competent people have studied this problem for years, a sudden breakthrough in speech recognition capability is unlikely. A number of hurdles must be surmounted, so a revolutionary leap into a new industry should not be expected.

Among the hurdles facing a workable speech recognition system is the tremendous variability of human speech. Since normal speech contains many words that are acoustically ambiguous, it is only through the context of words and a knowledge of linguistic constraints that speech recognition can be achieved. There is a great deal of difference between recognizing a few individual, isolated words (a problem of pattern recognition) and recognizing continuous speech using a large vocabulary of over 1,000 words (a problem of understanding). So conceived, the problem of recognizing a number of different dialects and accents has yet to be confronted.

Automatic speech recognition means a number of different things in different contexts. Speech recognition products capable of understanding isolated utterances have been on the market for fifteen years. "Isolated utterances" refer to words or short phrases spoken with pauses between them. "Continuous speech" refers to normal speech without pauses between individual words. Exhibit 4.7 illustrates schematically the way in which speech recognition can be expected to evolve.

Speech recognition systems differ greatly in technical sophistication, depending on the type of speech input expected. For isolated utterance input, a variety of signal-processing algorithms and classification schemes have been applied with success. In general, the more care and control exercised by the speaker on speech input, the greater the number of algorithms that work effectively. To reduce costs, some manufacturers of speech recognition devices specify that speech input is expected to be carefully enunciated, to consist of isolated utterances, to be spoken in a noise-free environment, and to be drawn from a limited vocabulary and a "known" speaker. (A known speaker is one whose voice characteristics have been previously analyzed and recorded.) Of the many techniques employed, few have achieved a useful trade-off between cost and the system's ability to cope with imperfect speech. Until this trade-off is found, as a result of both technological progress and better understanding of the speech process, recognition devices will be limited to special applications where speech is the only practical method of input. To be widely acceptable, speech recognition systems need to be able to understand word vocabularies of more than 1,000 words. Rapid continuous speech may not be a prerequisite since it is easier to train users to speak distinctly than to teach them to use a restricted vocabulary.

The technology and understanding of language required for the transcription of general conversational speech far exceeds our current capabilities. A number of suppliers are working toward the development of speech transcription devices, and, by the mid–1990s, cost-effective and useful products (such as automatic speech-input typewriters) will almost certainly be on the market. However, the social acceptability of humans talking to machines in an office environment might limit the market for these devices. In the meantime, the widespread use of speech recognition systems awaits both dramatic cost reductions and improved capabilities.

4.7 THE IMPORTANCE OF HARDWARE SELECTION

If an anthropologist were to undertake a comparative study of the office of the 1960s and the office of the 1980s, the first thing he or she would notice is the omnipresence of sophisticated machinery in the latter. The tasks performed by people staffing the two offices are not all that different, but the machinery used to accomplish those tasks has changed radically. On the one hand, it is not necessary for the office manager to understand in detail the internal working of modern office machinery to make decisions on which equipment to purchase. Expla-

Exhibit 4.7
Evolutionary Stages of Speech Recognition

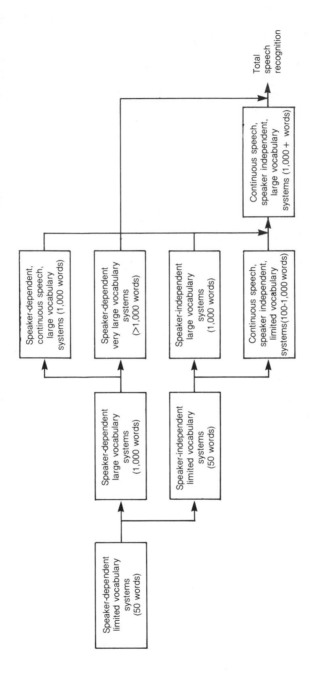

nations of the nuts-and-bolts aspects of modern, high-tech equipment are dry, long-winded, and tedious. On the other hand, the manager will have to make decisions based on vendor presentations which often employ technical comparisons between products in order to establish selling points. For this reason it behoves the manager to undertake some preliminary investigation of the technical, nuts-and-bolts characteristics of office machines that are under consideration for purchase.

In choosing office equipment it is also necessary to consider emerging trends in hardware development. The last thing a manager wants to do is to fill an office with equipment that will be rendered obsolete one year later by a new product. Maintaining the firm's competitive advantage depends on staying abreast of new trends in technological research and hardware development. The purpose of this chapter has not been to overwhelm the reader with technical minutiae on a wide range of automated products for the office. Rather, the aim has been to isolate the product areas where change is occurring most rapidly, to indicate the prevailing trend in each area, and to provide a brief technical introduction to the products under consideration. With this knowledge a manager should be able to make a case in management circles for an office equipment upgrade, to enter into discussions with a variety of vendors, and to select the appropriate product to satisfy the operational needs of the company.

QUESTIONS AND ANSWERS

Q. What is computer software and what does it do?

A. Computer software is the set of instructions which tells the computer what to do. At the most basic level, software instructs the computer where and how to store information. This type of information is contained in a computer's operating system (one type of software). Another type of software is applications software, such as word processing, electronic spreadsheet, and graphics. Most users rely almost exclusively on their applications software and only use their operating system occasionally for functions such as formatting diskettes and copying files.

Q. Why has the personal computer become such an important office automation tool?

A. The term personal computer is used today to refer to any one of a broad range of microcomputers manufactured by IBM, Apple Computer, and a variety of other manufacturers. IBM's personal computer has become particularly important in the office due to its relatively low price, its open architecture, and its flexibility. The IBM personal computer (as well as many competitive products) can accommodate a number of attachable devices, such as co-processors, special function cards and adapters, and monochrome and color monitors. Unlike the dedicated word processor that preceded it, the personal computer can run a wide range of applications software.

Q. What are the future trends in personal computer development?

A. Some of the future trends in personal computer development are greater random access memory, the provision for more local data storage, enhancements to the terminal display, and additional and improved input devices. Besides the ubiquitous keyboard, other input devices include the mouse, the graphics tablet, and speech recognition devices.

Q. What types of storage are used by computers?

A. Computers use both internal storage, or memory, and external storage, such as the floppy disk. Internal storage includes semiconductor and bubble memory. External storage includes magnetic media such as the floppy disk, the hard or Winchester disk, and, more recently, optical media. The optical disk is currently limited to read-only applications (such as large static databases), but will become an increasingly important form of computer storage.

Q. What types of printers are used in the office today?

A. The most common types of printers are the daisy wheel printer and the dot matrix printer. Non-impact printers include ink-jet, reprographic, thermal, and electrostatic printers. Laser printers offer very high quality printing for a variety of publishing and other applications and have recently dropped dramatically in price.

5

Choosing the Components of the Office of the 1980s: Software Technology Today and Tomorrow

5.1 SOFTWARE IN THE SPOTLIGHT: SOME PRELIMINARY ADVICE

As information technology gains prominence in the office environment, questions regarding systems technology selection and implementation multiply. While the last chapter focused primarily on hardware and product selection, some of the most difficult decisions you will have to make involve selecting the software that can best exploit the hardware. As office computers proliferate in businesses and multiply dramatically in the coming years, the product that unlocks the capabilities of these ubiquitous machines, the software, has assumed greater and greater significance.

While the appropriate software is an important key to higher productivity, greater profits, better decision-making, more successful ventures, and more efficient operation in today's technologically sophisticated business world, the selection isn't easy. Both large and small businesses look to a good software package as the solution to dozens of work problems. Frequently, when a large firm seeks to automate a process that is used widely within the organization, there is a deluge of requests from different departments and branch offices. Users are eager, but their needs are manifold and, to top it off, not always clearly perceived. Stories abound of users who make a software purchase with the understanding that the package will fulfill their need to a tee, only to discover that the new system does not do any of the things they had expected. Nevertheless, success stories are just as common, and when appropriate software is chosen, users often find the nature of their business changing in positive ways that had gone completely unanticipated.

To make even an informal proposal for the selection of the software, one must understand user needs as well as the range of software applications that address those needs. Making an assessment of secretarial and professional productivity should assist the software purchaser in defining user needs (see Chapter 2), but a broader overview is helpful in any case. There are essentially six categories into which all software applications for business fall: text processing (word processing, editing), data analysis (spreadsheets, models), data processing, communications (electronic mail), administrative management (scheduling, calendaring), and graphics.

In large companies, managers and professionals are involved far more often in data analysis and processing than in any other application. In mid-sized and small firms, managers are less prone to use computers, but when they do, they use a wider variety of applications.

Word processing (WP) is the application most frequently used by secretaries, followed by some sort of data processing (DP). Clearly, choosing the appropriate software for the support staff is essential to maximizing the productive potential of the office of the 1980s.

More than $15 billion is spent in the software market annually. Personal computer software accounts for at least a third of this market, and its share is growing at a rate of 50 percent every year. The Fortune 1000 companies are already spending over $1,000 per employee on software, and in smaller companies the figure is even higher. Unfortunately, the very nature of the software market does not make product selection easy. The software industry is volatile, growing rapidly, yet still in its infancy. Today's buyer often gets caught between sorting out the bewildering proliferation of packages and predicting future trends. The real mystery in the product selection process is how to choose the right program out of the more than 5,000 programs available from nearly 3,000 companies in a mushrooming market. Further complicating the choice is the fact that half the currently existing programs are expected to be rendered obsolete within a year. In addition, nearly 10 percent of the recent software offerings are what the industry calls "vaporware," products announced but not yet released. Under these circumstances, the safest bet is to pick an established brand although this may entail sacrificing top performance.

If the software market confounds the buyers, the sellers are equally confused. One of the difficulties is that the market does not stand still long enough for buyers and sellers to get a fix on it. Vendors complain that it is difficult to determine what users want. With the market carrying more and more sophisticated products, making a decision to develop a new product requires a willingness to accept some risk. Thousands of dollars can be spent on developing a new product that simply does not sell.

To top off the confusion, newly purchased software often seems to introduce more headaches for the user than there were in the first place. Although improved software can boost productivity, the end users should not entertain the visions of laborless ease or automated glory that seem inevitably to go hand in hand with an upgrade. The user's first priority must be to learn the program. A substantial investment of time and "grunt work" is required to set up a particular application program and to enter the facts and figures to manipulate it. As a further hindrance, program documentation is often spotty in its quality. One cannot expect to find all the necessary information in the manual; consequently, the software buyer is left to rely on either the corporate resource, the supplier, or even the developer's uneven technical support. For example, with or without a manual, the user can be entering figures on a spreadsheet after half an hour, but to manipulate columns or calculate projections is far more complicated and requires time and experience. Nevertheless, perseverance is amply rewarded. Once the program is mastered, it can generate budget projections or a new business plan within a drastically reduced time frame.

Information services management (MIS) is the group most influential in software selection. Frequently, control is handled through a list of vendors of choice, which precludes random purchasing of software packages. In the large companies these lists are already used extensively. Another tactic that is frequently employed to maintain control over the software selection process is to offer in-house training for approved software only.

This chapter aims to make the journey as smooth as possible. It will set out first to clarify a confusing and rapidly changing market and to give the potential user the information essential to evaluate the packages available today. Some attempt will be made to assess specific products: their ease of use, their functional limitations, and the gap between reality and expectation. Some guidelines for final selection will be provided. Finally, the chapter looks ahead and gives a glimpse of the future of emerging software technology.

5.2 GETTING STARTED

There are three basic ways to select the software best tailored for your needs: you can do it yourself, you can hire a consultant, or you can engage a "turnkey" (a supplier who will get the software running and train the operators to use it). No matter which approach you choose, you must do some homework. You must become acquainted with the software market, and you must have a clear idea of your need. The attractiveness of the last two options depends on the size of the firm, the computer expertise possessed by the staff, and the in-house labor that can be dedicated to the task. A large firm should have the internal resources to handle the process of purchasing and implementing new software. Many mid-sized firms will logically opt for relinquishing responsibility by letting outsiders shoulder the burden since they have no specialized staffs or expertise. For most small firms with limited means, the do-it-yourself method is the only feasible one. Whatever option you select, this chapter should help you determine all the questions, if not give you all the answers.

The assault on software selection must have two fronts: information gathering and needs assessment. As with hardware selection, the best place to gain information on products available is to read reviews in computer magazines like *Business Software, Byte, Infoworld, List, PC* and *PC World*, and *Personal Computing*. In addition, software guides are published frequently that give listings of programs available. These include *List* magazine's semi-annual Business Software Directory, *PC World*'s Annual Software Review for IBM PCs and their clones, and Data Source's quarterly software reference. These can be used to match a program's capabilities to the company's software needs. The product reviews can then be used to convey some ideas on how effective and user friendly a program really is. Even more complete information is available through user groups who can be more helpful and pragmatic than any other source. Unless it is very new, there is a good chance that somebody has already tried the software program you are assessing and can make recommendations based on hands-on experience.

Accompanying the gathering of information on available programs, however, must be the process of defining needs. It is essential that software requirements be specific and detailed. The best technique is to set out the user's requirements in the form of a proposal. The method of formulating a request for proposal (RFP) will be detailed in Chapter 9. To call for a payroll program, a spreadsheet program, a spreadsheet for forecasting, or a financial package for accounting will waste more time and money than it will save. The specification of software requirements will tell you whether to purchase generic, or horizontal, software (software designed to perform a general application in any business) or a vertical package, either customized to the needs of your company (and usually very costly) or industry-specific only (and far cheaper). Before specifications can be matched to software, it is important to fully understand these classifications.

5.3 SELECTING YOUR SOFTWARE

Horizontal software applications come in three forms: standalones, families, and integrated. Additionally, they are usually categorized by function: financial, which includes spreadsheets; file managers or processors, which includes data bases; integrated, which includes two or more applications; word processing; graphics; and communications. Horizontal software—WordStar, Lotus 1–2–3, dBASE III, Multimate, Symphony, Knowledge Man, Nutshell, and others—has a high advertising profile, as they are designed for a wide market. These word-processing, integrated, spreadsheet, accounting, and other business programs are, in a sense, generic. Given that the operating system and computer hardware requirements are fulfilled, they will do the basic job for just about anybody, but they generally cannot be tailored to specific requirements.

Vertical programs are created either for a specific industry or for a segment within an industry, but they are also broken into applications categories. Custom software designed for purchasing agents, attorneys, engineers, or research and development staff are nontransferable packages. Unlike horizontal software, vertical software cannot be widely used by personnel throughout the company or shifted among professions or applications. Thus, advertising in the market for vertical software is usually restricted to individual trade journals or an occasional feature about a particular type of vertical application in a computer magazine. Much of the marketing is by direct mail, word of mouth, or consultation.

Unique industries with particular sets of requirements are the ideal candidates for a vertical software package. Vertical packages tend to vary widely in quality, however, and range from being outstanding to useless. Traditionally, user friendliness has presented a problem with these applications, but giant strides have been made along these lines in the past two years. Software houses are now more sensitive than ever before to the problem of learning a custom-designed system. Recently, software companies or their representatives have begun to offer training, but the price of this service tends to be high—from $600 to over $5,000 for one training session. Depending on the needs of the firm, software consultants may be able to train the users more cheaply. For smaller problems one can inquire directly to the software dealership that specializes in the application in question. Of course, the great appeal of vertical software is that it can be used "as is" for a specific application or in a particular type of business. For an example of true specialization, train repair shops have a program, CATS–1, that diagnoses repairs needed for locomotives. It runs on a personal computer only.

Custom programs are the "Rolls Royce choice." If money is no object, a custom-designed program can always be written that does precisely what is needed in the easiest and most efficient way. Of course, the cost is often prohibitive, and most software programmers are not even familiar with how the particular industry or business operates. Nevertheless, if the business demands an automated procedure that is highly specialized and central to its operation, a custom-made software package may be cost-justified.

If no appropriate vertical software program is available and custom writing is too expensive, the company could buy the best available vertical package which fits the budget and then adapt the company's procedures to it. Similarly, the company can select a program close to the company's needs and adapt it to the company's procedures. Provided the application is not too complicated and the company has someone qualified to make the alteration, this may be the most cost-effective alternative.

5.4 SOFTWARE APPLICATIONS

With so many thousands of software products on the market and with the market itself changing so rapidly, any attempt to analyze the advantages and drawbacks of each product would be doomed to futility and ultimate failure. Instead, we will examine the market by dividing it into its basic functional groups and acquaint the reader with the most commonly used software packages in each group.

5.4.1 Financial

Financial software is often the first contact with PCs which many companies experience, and this software claims the largest groups of users in managerial and professional ranks. The tried and true approach has been to computerize the manual financial activities of the office using horizontal software packages. Effective manual systems must first be created or already be in place, otherwise the firm risks automating the wrong things. The three major types of financial applications are general ledger and accounting, accounts receivable and accounts payable, and spreadsheets. The biggest area in terms of sales, at $1.6 billion, and programs sold, 5 million units, is general ledger and accounting. Of course, most large companies run general ledger applications on mainframes, so mid-sized and small firms account for a major portion of the total purchases. On the other hand, spreadsheets, at 2 million units sold, have the greatest dollar volume annually at $600 million, much of it to large corporations.

A spreadsheet can act as the automated equivalent of the accounting pad or ledger sheet. It is a blank electronic blackboard divided into rows and columns that organize the data into cells and larger functional groups. It can manipulate data by row or by column, determine relationships (sales to inventory, for instance), and solve number problems according to formulae given by the user. It can produce profit-and-loss statements, budgets, and forecasts. The ability to produce quick answers to "what if" questions has endeared spreadsheet software to the business community. Once the format is established and the data is fed in, answers to "what if" questions can be produced in minutes instead of the days required in the past.

While spreadsheet programs have progressed by leaps and bounds, many OA decision makers still complain about limited spreadsheet functionality. Some users believe that spreadsheet applications process data too slowly.

A typical spreadsheet program includes a set of commands like Enter, Copy, Move, Format, Append and a list of functions that perform routine computations such as adding a set of numbers, producing an average, or coming up with the largest or smallest number within a range. More sophisticated programs have a host of special functions to calculate standard deviations, net present value, internal rate of return, and mortgage payments. Time effects can be factored into various calculations; adjustments for currency transfers and fluctuations can be added; and data cell size can be altered in existing files. The pioneer in spreadsheet analysis is VisiCalc, which came out in 1978. Although it has been updated to VisiCalc IV, newer programs like MultiPlan, Lotus 1–2–3 and SuperCalc 3 have established a solid niche in the market.

5.4.2 File Managers

Programs that handle files—that is, create and manage files, records, and data bases—have become more popular recently as computer usage has increased and spawned data management problems. Such software usually falls into two major categories: file management programs and relational database programs, with the latter currently in greater demand.

File management applications can work with only one file at a time. (A file in this sense is an entire data base of individual records, comparable to the contents of a file cabinet.) A file contains all the retrievable information of a certain type which has been processed. The advantage of data base programs is that they let you keep multiple files open at the same time. Some, however, only allow simultaneous access to two files. Others have no limits, and information can be fed in or corrected in any number of files at the same time.

Both types of programs, however, organize data in much the same way: first by files, then by record, then by field. Thus, files can contain a large quantity of information about a fairly broad category. For instance, a file might contain a warehouse inventory. In this case, each separate item in the inventory is represented by a record, which in turn contains fields of specific information about each item such as quantity, price, and order number. Although relational data bases view data much like the file management program does, they go one step further. By setting up what is called a "redundant" or "key" data field, relationships between data bases can be described.

As an illustration, think of a relational data base as having two discrete, but connected, records. The first holds the customer name, address information, and a customer number. The second file contains the customer history. The program enables the user to relate customer history to customer addresses by adding the customer number to the history field. This customer number becomes a unique field common to both records, a key field, which can tie them together whenever necessary.

To compare, when using a relational data base to procure a list of all of the customers' addresses from the first record and their total outstanding balance from the second record, only one step is necessary. Not using a relational data base, a file management program would have to sort the data at least twice, and perhaps more, depending on how the files are organized. In order to extract the desired information, one might have to sort initially for customers and orders and then for outstanding balances. More precisely, if you want to change a name or address, you have to call up the entire database file of records. In a relational system, you can change data held in a specific record without calling up the rest of the file. This speeds up access and cuts the chances of the user inadvertently changing information not intended to be altered.

The virtue of relational data bases is that they allow the user to classify information in whatever manner is most convenient. The user may put in and take out data at any time and in any order. This versatility and ease of entry has made relational data bases popular. Because of this capability, Ashton-Tate's dBASE II became the first of the powerful user-friendly relational database programs and sports a sales record which proves it.

Nevertheless, there are some difficulties with relational data bases. Frequently the link between files is artificially created by adding an extraneous field or, in some cases, three or four. For example, consider a business that requires files to be kept on a parts inventory, customer history, names and addresses, and salesmen. To retrieve data from all those files at once, artificial fields are created containing salesman numbers and customer numbers which can be related to sales, salesmen, inventory, and customer information. These fields are then added to the records in the relational file. Thus, relational files are larger, and records are more cumbersome. In a file management system these fields would not be necessary, so the files and records are more compact. On the other hand, relational information about which salesmen are responsible for what customers and what inventory would not be accessible.

Most relational data bases can be operated on two levels. The first is the simple command level. Such commands as Create, Append, Edit, and Sort allow the operator to create data bases of records and manipulate them rather simply. Although some file managers can do this, it is an awkward and slow process.

On the second level, the relationals have programming languages that allow manipulations of the data bases, report generation, graphics, and even interfaces to text editing programs. This programming language may be a relatively low-level one, like the relational algebra found in dBASE II, or a high-level relational calculus found in IBM's SQL (Structured Query Language) or MicroRIM's R:BASE. These powerful languages are time-consuming to learn and require expertise to use. Although the end user, a manager, professional, or secretary, may have neither the time nor the inclination to develop such skill, if the user's data structure is relatively complex, an effort to learn such applications will pay off in the long run.

The time involved to get a database management system running is much longer than the few minutes that it takes to figure out simple entry commands. The programming language takes weeks and months to really master. Frequently, the software seller or some other private concern offers training courses in using these languages, but these courses can cost significantly more than the software, not counting the trainees' time, and the courses are often inconsistent in quality.

In every case, the effort to learn the programming language will pay off. Without pushing the software to the limit of its capability, the user will not maximize the benefits to be derived from its purchase.

5.4.3 Word Processing

Word processing is perhaps the personal computer's most popular and enduring application for both business and home use. This year an estimated 3 million programs, more than in any other category, will be sold. Expected revenue from word-processing applications will rival spreadsheet revenue by bringing in approximately $525 million. In a market with great diversity in product offerings, users have few complaints with regard to functionality. For any specific type of word-processing application, there seems to be an appropriate software package available.

On the whole, word-processing programs have emulated dedicated word processing successfully. The applications are powerful, easy to use, and have advanced features. Multimate and Display Write are two such exemplary programs. They mimic Wang and IBM's Display Writer almost command for command, menus included, making them popular with users. Other programs have had less success, being bogged down with complicated command structures that make them much harder to use.

Approaches to word processing fall into either the format-oriented or screen-oriented schools. The consensus favors screen-oriented programs like WordStar, which shows page breaks, line length, capitalization, and spacing. This is the "What you see is what you get" school of thought. Very simply, what's on the screen prints out exactly as you see it.

Format-oriented programs operate differently. Perfect Writer, a format-oriented program, has "windows" that allow transfer of words between several different files. You can see what the text looks like, including paragraphing and capitalization, but line length, spacing, page breaks, page headings, and flush margins are not shown and must be set with special commands. You don't know what the copy is going to look like until you see it printed out.

Still, this simple dichotomy does not totally capture the variety of available word-processing packages. New entrants in the market, such as Samna and Leading Edge, have joined Multimate in the class of hybrid word processors that offer features from both the screen-oriented and the format-oriented approaches.

No matter which type you choose, your word processor should possess such features as automatic wraparound, choice of format for spacing and margins, automatic deletion and insertion of text, text-scanning functions such as find, search and replace, virtual memory (temporary storage capacity limited not by buffer memory but by disk capacity), automatic page numbering, and footnoting. Desirable, but usually sold separately, are spelling checkers, indexing and table of contents packages, and the so-called mail-merge features for generating form letters.

5.5 INTEGRATED SOFTWARE

The dominant software programs in today's software market are integrated. These programs combine the functions of word processing, spreadsheets, graphics, communications, and even accounting packages, often by using windows to promote ease of use and entry from one function to another. Today's integrated software takes four different approaches: tightly integrated, all-in-one packages; integrated series; systems integrators; and the background utility.

5.5.1 Tightly Integrated Programs

Tightly integrated software includes Lotus Development Corporation's Lotus 1–2–3 and Symphony, Ashton-Tate's Framework, Business Solution's Jack2, Xerox Microsystems's Encore!, The Software Group's Enable, Software Products International's Open Access, and many others. The applications are variations or extensions of one dominant program and are so tightly linked that they cannot be separated. The dominant function varies, depending on the package. For example, Symphony centers on a spreadsheet, Open Access on database management, and Jack2 on word processing. The trade-off is usually between the central function, which is the equal of any on the market, and the subordinate applications, which often fall short of more sophisticated packages. Lotus 1–2–3, for example, is based on a spreadsheet. It includes simple business graphics (bar and pie charts with line graphs) and a word-processing program. The graphics are good and the word processing adequate, but neither is quite as good as a first-rank standalone package. The advantage, of course, is that the tight links allow quick and easy data transfer between the different functions. Thus, when you update the data in one application, it is updated in all, something an integrated series of programs cannot perform.

5.5.2 Integrated Series

The integrated series approach works on a different premise. A series of separate programs contains a common command structure and provides a means of moving data from one program to another. Among the products in this category are Innovative Software's Smart Software, Software Publishing's pfs: family, Prentice-Hall's Profit Center Series, Chang Labs's Plan family, Thorn EMI's Perfect family, IBM Systems Product Division's Assistant Series, and VisiCorp's VisiSeries. The advantage of these packages is that each of the programs in the series has all the attributes of the most sophisticated programs on the market. The command structures of each program are the same, barring a few specific commands, thus cutting time and frustration in retraining. If a certain key produces the prompt on the screen, "Name of File to Open?" in the word processor, it will also produce the same prompt in the database file, the ledger file, and the graphics program. "Count" will give you the number of words in a letter in the word processor and the number of records in the spreadsheet or the database file.

Whereas the all-in-ones can deal with three or more programs at a time, the hardware in the series approach deals with only one. As a result, series require about half the memory space of integrated units. For example, a good word-processing, spreadsheet, and graphics program in a series package might take 128K of memory apiece, but because one program is closed before the other is opened, it only takes 128K to run them all. Alternatively, an all-in-one integrated program based on a word processor with spreadsheet and graphics units might take as much as 384K of random access memory (RAM) to run.

Unfortunately, choices are never black and white, and the transfer of data between integrated series programs is not as quick and easy as with the tightly integrated programs. Nor will correcting or changing data in one program automatically update it in the others. Because the integrated series approach employs a number of discrete, unconnected programs, task integration is inferior to the all-in-one packages. On the other hand, because each program runs separately with full processor dedication, each may be functionally superior to its counterpart in an all-in-one package.

5.5.3 System Integrators

The third approach, considered by some to be the wave of the future, is the system integrator. These include Quarterdeck Office Systems's DesQ, Digital Research's Concurrent PC-DOS with windows, IBM Systems Products Division's TopView, and Microsoft's MS Windows. Macintosh's hardware/software combinations fall into this group. These packages are attempts to combine the advantages of integrated packages with the strengths of the series approach. System integrators provide an environment within which standalone packages of choice can reside in memory and operate simultaneously. In essence, this approach constitutes a type of overlay structured, multitasking operating system. Ideally, one could simply retain the company's existing single programs and coordinate them under one of the system integrators.

Despite this potential, the lack of a common language among all the programs constitutes a major shortcoming in an integrated system. In addition, the ability of system integrators to handle diverse programs is somewhat limited. To run a program under the system integrator, it must be what is termed "well behaved." That is, it must operate totally under the computer's operating system, so it cannot make any commands directly to the computer hardware. This indirect command structure slows down the program's execution.

So far, none of the system integrators has really had a major impact on the software market. Success has eluded these programs chiefly because the independent software vendors have not supported them and because existing programs don't work well with them. And, like the all-in-one systems, the integrators are big memory eaters, 256K RAM and up. Nevertheless, system integrators are probably the next step forward from integrated systems like Lotus 1–2–3 and others. Although they are not strictly competitive today, they are a likely target for vast improvements in the next few years.

5.5.4 Background Utility

The fourth type of integrated application is the background utility. Examples include Borland International's Sidekick, Software Arts's Spotlight, and Belsoft's Pop-Up. The essence of these programs is to "hide" in the computer memory while other programs are being run and to appear into the foreground when called.

Background applications provide auxiliary side software rather than direct system integration. In short, background applications are passive in the sense that they are always there, ready to be used, but they are not the primary focus of attention. In this sense, they are equivalent to the desktop Rolodex for phone numbers and addresses, note pads, calendars, calculators, and other such accessories. Their virtue lies in their overlay capacity, which allows them to be called up in the middle of another program.

Each of the four types of integrated software has marked advantages over standalone applications packages. Through the use of windows and extensive menus and choices, they are more expansive and user friendly. They also save time. The all-in-ones, systems integrators, and background utilities allow several programs to be open at once, thus permitting text, data, and graphics to be moved swiftly from one program to another. For further versatility, programs themselves can be interchanged at will. From the spreadsheet, for example, it is possible to move to the word processor to write a report or memo, to move data from the spreadsheet to graphics, and to have a chart made from the data and moved to the word processor and finally placed in the report or memo. Throughout the process, program windows and continuous screen presentation help the user to visualize the results and to see how the final product is going to look.

5.6 GRAPHICS USE

Every year industry vendors predict that graphics will find a home in the office. Until now, however, penetration figures have continued to lag behind predictions. In 1985, about 1 million programs were expected to be sold for an estimated $225 million, up about 30 percent from 1984.

Still, there are problems, and the development of graphics packages has been hampered by the lack of an economical color printout method that will work with most graphics packages. Another problem is that most computers require an add-on board to be able to handle graphics. Despite its prospects, at the present time a graphics package seems to be regarded as a nonessential but possible future purchase.

Strictly speaking, there are five kinds of graphics packages, but most commercial graphics packages are combinations of two or more of the five types. They are business; screen dumps; statistical/graphics; general purpose or standalones; and computer show. Although not strictly graphics packages, there are also graphics capabilities included in integrated packages.

Business graphics packages are both the most basic and the top sellers. These programs, such as Software Publishing's pfs: Graph and Mosaic Software's Super Chartman II, present data in its most commonly used forms (pie, bar, and line charts and graphs from data entered by the operator), but they cannot manipulate or process data after entry. They are also the type included with integrated programs like Lotus 1–2–3.

Statistical graphics packages are much more powerful than business graphics, since the raw data can be manipulated after entry to allow regression, trend analyses, exponential smoothing, and other statistical tricks. The results of programs like VisiTrend/Plot and Graph'N Calc can be stored and put on the monitor and printed.

Graphics dumps are actually programs and are frequently included with the business and other types of graphics packages. These programs, like Paper Graph, allow the printout of anything seen on the computer monitor.

With more sophistication, computer show graphics packages and programs such as Frame-Up and Executive Briefing System make the computer into a kind of slide projector for presentations. The graphics can be mixed with other packages and arranged in order for showing. Like the screen dump, it is frequently combined with business and statistical graphics packages.

The most complex of the business graphics available are the general purpose software programs. They are not really business programs but can be adapted because their ease of use has great appeal to the business users. These packages offer more than pies, bars, and lines. They can generate three-dimensional images at a rate of 1200 baud. If you are tapping an outside data base, the cost of transmitting at 1200 baud is double the 300 baud rate. An additional consideration is that the telephone companies charge extra if the line is to be used for transmissions in excess of 1200 baud, since this requires a special line.

Graphics applications with animation, like most advanced packages, will drive a plotter and take input from a keyboard, mouse, and joystick, as well as from an electronic drawing pad.

5.7 COMMUNICATIONS: PRESENT APPLICATIONS AND FUTURE TRENDS

The importance of research into communications applications cannot be overestimated. In a sense, communication is the lynchpin around which a successful automation strategy revolves (see Chapter 6). Although much effort has been expended, this crucial area is still struggling to fulfill its potential. Fewer than a million programs will be sold this year, for a total of only about $125 million. Less than a quarter of the personal microcomputers have a modem attached, let alone any micro-to-mainframe links. Virtually untapped is the potential of telecommunications for teleconferencing, electronic mail, accessing outside data bases, and linking micros, minis, and mainframe computers.

Most initial communications applications should be limited to a general-purpose smart terminal communications program which works off its own memory and processing boards to execute calls to other computers. Modem software is by far the most common communications package, with the Hayes modem serving as the industry standard and compatibility model. Depending on the package, modems allow data transfer rates of 300, 1200, and most recently 2400 baud. Bauds translate into bits per second but are not quite the same thing. For example, it takes 12 minutes to transmit a 20K file at 300 baud and 3 minutes at 1200 baud. Higher speed programs, however, are usually too expensive for small businesses. They can cost up to several thousand dollars and are usually part of office automation packages. Modem programs facilitate automatic dialing and answering, up-loading and down-loading of files, phone number storage, and some subroutines that trigger phone numbers with one or two strokes. Sophisticated programs allow modems to set up the computer as an electronic mail drop, or automatic answering machine, and to get bulletin board programs for internal and external office communications. Modem software becomes a powerful information tool in its capacity to tap the wealth of outside data transfer services like the Source, Delphi, or TymNet. For this purpose, such software is frequently combined with database management systems.

Modem software is particularly important because it supports the linkage of microcomputers to each other. Without this software, an electronic messaging or computer mail service could not be supported. More and more firms are noticing the benefits that can be derived from implementing electronic mail systems.

Modem programs like Crosstalk, Mite/TS, and Smartcom II are not the only types of communications software. There are other communications packages that handle digital PBXs (private branch exchanges). In addition, applications exist to handle networks that connect various types of computers: microcomputers, minicomputers, and mainframes. Such applications are designed to resolve compatibility problems.

5.7.1 Voice Synthesis

In addition to addressing the problems of machine interface, communications research focuses on improving the effectiveness of the man-machine interface. Some of the most interesting experiments in expanding user friendliness are the attempts to fabricate voice for the computer. The option has existed for PCs since the late 1970s. Costs are falling and vocabularies are rising, but its appeal must compete with the cheap, quick, and memory-efficient entry and access device that is already familiar to the current generation of users—the keyboard. Voice systems are memory intensive and still fairly expensive. They run from $295, but cost more for anything with more than a few hundred words of vocabulary. Currently voice recognition devices have found their greatest market in security and emergency systems. These voice recognition systems should not be confused with the voice writers. The realization of the long-sought voice writer to replace the typewriter will probably not come until after the advent of artificial intelligence-assisted programs for personal computers.

5.7.2 Artificial Intelligence Programs

By far the most intriguing ideas for expanding PC software are, like the voice writer, in the area of artificial intelligence-assisted programs. In these new and still somewhat gray areas, concepts are just beginning to be translated into marketed programs. As yet they are so few and diverse that they are sometimes lumped under the title of human factors programs because they provide decision-making aids covering judgmental areas, or they attempt to duplicate some phase of human activity. Such software exists in various forms of sophistication, with borrowed techniques and programming concepts from artificial intelligence (AI) research. Some of these programs include Psycomp's Coping with Stress (or Depressed Feelings, Sexual Problems, Relationship Problems), Thoughtware's Managing for Success, Concourse Corporation's Participative Management Skills on how to deal with employees, and Compusophics System's KAMAS (Knowledge and Mind Amplification System), to name a few. Additionally, there are educational programs to teach anything from accounting to writing (although "teach" is a questionable word here).

Additional research is preparing mainframe programs for personal computer use, as in the area of expert systems in diagnostics and project management. These programs—like MYCIN, used to diagnose meningitis, or CATS–1, mentioned earlier and employed to spot locomotive malfunctioning—are true AI-based systems. Although most now run on mainframes or minicomputers, they are being reprogrammed to fit on personal computers, particularly as memory sizes increase.

Another domain of AI activity expected to affect PC programs is that of natural languages. Two programs, Savvy, which uses natural language-type commands to manipulate a data base, and Clout, which attempts to produce a general, natural language bridge between different data bases, are recent introductions. But most experts feel that true natural language programs will follow expert systems in market introduction and acceptance. Their biggest drawback is an excessive use of memory, which leaves little space for the program itself.

5.7.3 Networking and Multi-Tasking

Although the research into new communications applications is encouraging, one of the most nagging challenges in software development is to enable the linkage of several computers or, failing that, to get the computer to work on more than one program at a time. Following the PC boom of recent years, many small businesses are finding that standalone micros are not able to provide adequate "horsepower" for their sophisticated needs.

The path to multi-user systems which are capable of inventory management, full-scale accounting, and complex business procedures is not clearly charted. Networking microcomputers is one solution to connecting discrete units, but the technology is not available for all hardware and can be quite expensive. Alternatives to networked computers are multi-user microcomputers designed from the ground up that can support from 3 to 32 users. They range anywhere from just under $5,000 to the super micros that cost $30,000. These machines are usually furnished with various forms of multi-tasking software, which can increase both processing power and linkage capacity.

Multi-user microcomputer networks can be designed either by changing both hardware and software or by changing the software only. In the former case, memory and processor boards are added to each terminal in the network to produce "smart" terminals. The central computer handles only the interterminal traffic and the shared logic. This adjustment would cost over $1,000 per workstation. In the latter case, software is added to the central computer, and the terminals in the network are "slaves" to the central computer. Although this alternative is cheaper per terminal, system software will not run as quickly as in the former case.

Multi-tasking software systems can be valuable in increasing the sophistication of the workstation. Basically, they allow a PC to work on two or more programs at once. The functions and the potential of these types of programs are related to those of the system integrators—another, cheaper variation on the multi-tasking concept. But multi-tasking software goes one step further. Where integrators facilitate transfer of data between programs and allow the user to switch programs by issuing appropriate commands, multi-tasking gives the computer the capacity to simultaneously perform two functions. For example, while the user is manipulating an electronic spreadsheet in the foreground, the computer could be processing electronic mail in the background. As usual, increased performance is linked to higher cost, and multi-tasking software systems cost at least $600. Normally, unless the user wants to establish a link between two or more computers, a system integrator package is a more cost-effective solution.

5.8 SELECTING EASY-TO-USE SOFTWARE

In selecting software of any sort, one other crucial factor should be mentioned and considered, namely, user friendliness. The nature of its importance should not be underestimated. The aura of user friendliness about a particular program or computer will get people to use software and computers they otherwise would not. Users surveyed about software concerns cite ease of use and ease of learning as the two most important. Recently, there have been many improvements in user friendliness, but even the best program takes time to learn. To use today's state-of-the-art software, the user must still make some adjustments in his or her habits of thinking and working with the computer.

Currently, "windowing" is one of the prominent sales points in the latest software, touted for its user friendliness. This function allows the user to pause while working on one file and open a window, as it were, into a second or third file without closing the first. The user may now see what data or graphics he or she wishes to transfer into the first file from the others. The window might also show the menu of operations currently available without stopping work on the file. In the never-ending quest to make software easier to use, one of the major accomplishments is the electronic display of information through windows.

Other tools and methods have also been developed to enhance user friendliness. The roll-about mouse, which can position the cursor at any point on the screen and allow the operator to choose among the many options offered within windows and menus, is another noteworthy achievement in this field. But like any mechanical device, it takes practice to manipulate with efficiency and speed. (It is called a mouse because of its shape, the "tail" of connecting wire, and its gray or black color.)

Touching the screen with a finger, as with the Hewlett Packard 150, sounds great and is certainly easy, but a computer science major was observed struggling for half an hour trying to open a program without success. Even this type of user friendliness has its limits.

Light pens today are combined with an electronic drawing board or pad, like the popular Koala board, and are the visual equivalent to pointing fingers or mice. Currently, they are used more for graphics than as pointing devices.

Following the overall trend, these features form parts of integrated packages where word processing is combined with data bases, spreadsheets, and graphics, so that tabular data and graphics can be transferred directly into text instead of being generated separately and inserted.

Whether you select the software yourself or farm out that task to consultants or suppliers, it is imperative to have a workable set of objectives and a clear idea of needs (see Chapter 2), the appropriate hardware (see Chapter 4), an understanding of the telecommunications requirements (see Chapter 6), and an understanding of the software available, as laid out in this chapter. Above all, the purchase of software should not be based on an isolated decision but should be integrated into an overall strategy of automation.

QUESTIONS AND ANSWERS

Q. What are the most important business applications for today's software products?

A. A study by The Omni Group revealed that most software applications available today fall into six key groups. They are:

- Text processing (word processing and text editing)
- Data analysis (spreadsheets and financial models)
- Data processing
- Communications (electronic mail, video text)
- Administrative management (scheduling and ordering)
- Graphics

Q. How much is being spent on software by businesses?

A. A study by The Omni Group at the end of 1984 showed that it was already well over $1,000 per employee in the Fortune 1000 and almost twice that amount in smaller companies. Clearly, this constitutes a considerable sum on a national basis.

Q. How would the software market be characterized?

A. On both the side of suppliers and the side of users, the market is highly complex and dynamic. More than 5,000 programs are available from almost 3,000 suppliers with software volume totaling $15 billion. Approximately one-third of this market is aimed at personal computers, and it has been growing at a rate of 50 percent annually.

Q. Who is in charge of software selection?

A. Based on the results of 304 interviews with large corporations, MIS is the most influential department in the selection process. Control over software selection can be maintained by using approved vendor lists and by placing restrictions on in-house training and support.

Q. What are the selection options for a beginner?

A. Three basic modes of selection are available. They are self-selection, use of a consultant, and purchase of a "turnkey" operation. The beginner should keep in mind that the software selection process must have two prongs: information gathering and needs assessment. These are especially relevant distinctions to the user who manages the selection process alone.

Q. Is there a terminology a beginner must master?

A. A certain amount of jargon must be assimilated. For example, vertical, horizontal, and custom programs are distinct types of programs and have widely differing costs and usage limitations.

Systems integration and the four different types of integrated software have introduced another area of specialized knowledge with a specialized terminology.

Q. Are there additional factors a newcomer should keep in mind?

A. Yes, user friendliness should be kept in mind. It affects usage rates and the attitudes with which new users approach office systems. In fact, users state that ease of use and ease of learning are the two greatest concerns.

6

Telecommunications

6.1 TELECOMMUNICATIONS: THE CRUCIAL LINK

Telecommunications is the backbone of an integrated office system. In simple terms, it enables data to be transferred from one point to another within an information network. Through the incorporation of computer technology, the tools of telecommunications have the potential to connect every type of information processing equipment, whether it handles voice, data, text, graphics, or photographs. In the future, the industry may be able to create a global communications network, providing instant transfer of information in any form to any remote terminal in the world.

In the business world, telecommunications is not simply a futuristic vision. The information that travels along the telecommunications highways is the lifeblood of business operations. Timely access to information gives firms in any industry the competitive edge which they need to survive. The effective use of telecommunications tools allows businesses to react promptly to oscillating market conditions, to break time and transport barriers, and to make more informed decisions in periods of crises.

The growth of the telecommunications industry demonstrates that firms are treating its products as valuable assets. At present, however, the far-ranging potential of the field is largely unrealized. The reliable delivery of timely information to the desks, telephones, and terminals of the end user is an unsolved management issue. Telecommunications is one of the most rapidly changing facets of office automation. It is highly technical and requires considerable expertise and capital investment to use its tools effectively. In addition, it is the aspect of office automation that most clearly demands a holistic approach and a long-term corporate strategy. This chapter will help you get started, by reviewing the basic elements of telecommunications technology and by introducing some of the state-of-the-art office applications.

6.2 OPERATING IN THE DEREGULATED ENVIRONMENT

Before any firm can employ telecommunications tools effectively, its management must be aware of developments in the industry at large. The current national telecommunications infrastructure was constructed by AT&T and affiliated independent telephone companies. Before AT&T's divestiture, it coordinated the operations of all local branches through granting licenses, setting standards, and providing certain services.

Public criticism over the last ten years, which pointed to, among other things, the lack of technological advances in customer-provided equipment, led to AT&T's divestiture of the local operating companies in 1984.

The deregulation of the U.S. telecommunications industry radically altered the nature of the market. A wealth of competitors have parceled off shares of the market, while the competitive environment has produced a variety of new services and products. Interconnect companies have established their niche; bypass technologies have created return service offerings; and computer and office automation manufacturers have begun turning out communications products. Communications giants like AT&T and Western Union began offering voice, data, and electronic mail services. The merger of computer and telecommunications technologies pushed the industry into a new and more dynamic phase.

The impact of deregulation on the user community is tremendous. Whereas telecommunications was once tied to a stable structure, it now operates more like the volatile computer industry. Evaluating the myriad of products offered by dozens of vendors is an enormous task. Further, deregulation has complicated the user's efforts to maximize the two most important equipment selection criteria—support and compatibility. Users find they need support for equipment and services from a variety of vendors. Compatibility has been endangered by the proliferation of private networks and transmission facilities.

A firm's ability to survive and succeed in this environment requires thoughtful planning and a clear notion of present options and future potential. In this rapidly expanding field, it is absolutely imperative to avoid decisions based only on short-term considerations. The effects of deregulation have made it more essential than ever to build a long-term, integrated office automation strategy.

6.3 RECENT ADVANCES IN TELECOMMUNICATIONS: TRANSMISSION MEDIA

Communication and computer technologies have evolved along separate if parallel paths over the last hundred years. While recent telecommunications applications utilize computer technology, it is not only computers that have made the communications industry as dynamic as it is. None of the current merging of technologies would be possible without the cumulative improvements in the way voice, television signals, and data are transmitted over both long and short distances.

From the 1950s the standard transmission media have been radio and co-axial cable. Cable can transmit its signals without interference and with no limits to the number of cables which cross over each other. Radio, or wireless systems, operate within a limited spectrum of frequencies. As such they must be rationed and carefully regulated. Developments in both media over the last 20 years have led to the use of higher frequencies and more powerful transmitters. Their expanding capacity has opened the way for more sophisticated and integrated networks.

6.3.1 Radio

Developments in radio technology are less significant for our purposes. Even with the high-frequency radio transmission of today, the problem of signal attenuation caused by rain and atmospheric abnormalities is unsolved. It is still possible for a heavy storm to completely cut off radio communication. Radio transmission has the advantage of not needing heavy cables, but its powerful transmitters can be just as costly. Small microwave radio systems are used for receiving satellite transmissions, but it is not clear that they are more economical than cable links.

6.3.2 Coaxial Cable

After World War II, the coaxial cable replaced the common carrier cable by being able to transmit at higher frequencies and to carry more signals simultaneously. The coaxial cable consists of a hollow cylinder, made of copper or some other conductor, which encircles an internal, single-wire conductor. The first cables carried only several dozen calls at a time. The most sophisticated coaxial cables in current use are those built by the telephone companies on their well-traveled routes. They can carry up to 100,000 calls at one time.

The capacity of coaxial cables was surpassed with the development of millimeter waveguide pipes for long-distance transmission. These pipes are about two inches in diameter and constructed to allow the transmission of very-high-frequency radio waves. A single pipe can carry over twice the number of calls as the highest capacity coaxial cable. For this reason, it can transmit signals at the lowest cost per circuit of any medium. Waveguide pipes are, however, costly to install and, as yet, not economical except on a very large scale.

6.3.3 Fiber Optics

The most recently developed transmission medium is the optical fiber. Rather than converting signals to electrical impulses, the glass fibers convert them into light pulses, which have a higher transmission frequency. The potential for this medium is tremendous, as light is a much more efficient transmitter than electricity. Light pulses neither generate nor are affected by electromagnetic interference. They are thus more reliable and impossible to intercept or tamper with. Furthermore, the fibers are lightweight and have an extremely high capacity per square inch when compared with the bulkier co-axial tubes. Fiber optics applications, however, are still in the experimental stages of development. It will probably be a few years before the practical problems of deployment can be worked out, but many people consider optical fibers to be the transmission medium of the future.

6.3.4 Communications Satellites

Satellites have always been powerful communication tools, but they have only recently acquired the potential for widespread use. The capacity of satellites to transmit large quantities of undisturbed signals to any receiver on the globe has been improved by various transmission and reception techniques. The construction of larger and more powerful satellites has resulted in ever cheaper earth stations. New microwave devices make it economical for individual homes with rooftop antennas to receive satellite signals. As with fiber optics, however, satellite potential is presently unrealized. Part of the problem lies in the highly regulated nature of the industry; to put a satellite in orbit, it is necessary to fire a rocket. Most of the limits, though, are financial and technical. Although the cost of transmission per circuit continues to drop, satellites are still only economical when transmitting large volumes of data.

6.4 COMPUTERS AND TELECOMMUNICATIONS

The dynamic nature of the telecommunications field is due in part to improvements in transmission quality and capacity. More crucial, however, is the integration of computers and computer logic with traditional telecommunications technology. Several developments in the computer industry laid the groundwork for this merger.

Innovations in electronic circuitry have improved long distance communication, at first for computer data but eventually for other information media as well. The electromagnetic transistors which filled huge rooms have been replaced by tiny silicon chips. The computer circuitry is etched onto these chips in a process called LSI, or large-scale integration. Integrated circuits not only allow computer power to be concentrated in ever smaller containers, but they can be inexpensively mass produced once the first "mold" has been made. Newer chips, called VLSI (very-large-scale integration), incorporate more complicated logical patterns and command structures.

The impact of low-cost, concentrated computer power on electronic communication has been great. "Smart" remote terminals are now capable of standalone operation and of communicating with mainframe central terminals. In other words, electronic circuits allow more computers to talk to each other.

The storage capacity of chips allows them to carry out sophisticated command structures. Now software programs bring this potential to telecommunications. For example, telephone lines have traditionally been constructed to transmit analog or continuous frequency signals. Computers, on the other hand, process digital or discretely variable signals. Without the modems for converting analog data to a digital form, computers could not use telephone wires to communicate. With the new fiber optic cables, however, digital data may be transmitted through telephone lines by converting digital electronic signals into light pulses for transmission. New electronic switching systems, based on microchip technology, have been developed to translate analog into digital electronic signals.

As computer circuitry is applied to telephone systems, electromechanical switches are being replaced by computerized exchanges. Switches have always been a crucial component of a telephone network, as they route calls between millions of users. Computerized switches also link telecommunications facilities, without the need for huge central switching offices. The old private branch exchanges (PBXs) were clumsy and inflexible. The computerized PBXs use the capacity of LSI circuits to move signals at high speeds with no moving parts. Furthermore, they can store program information so that every decentralized switch takes on the characteristics of a smart computer terminal. For example, they can route calls by the cheapest route, set up conference calls, redial numbers, or send electronic mail.

6.5 COMPUTER NETWORKS

Electronic switching systems, designed with microcircuitry, are the central component of the new computerized networks which are becoming crucial to business operations. The goal of these networks is to interconnect all the office technologies, from data processing and word processing to micrographics and optical disk technology. The purpose of such a network is to allow users to share information stored in many different places and in a wide variety of different forms. Networks place the power of many separate office machines at the fingertips of each workstation operator along the network.

The implications of networking systems for business operations are vast. Users will have access to extensive pools of shared resources, which could be stored in a central data base thousands of miles away. Any type of information could be sent instantaneously along telephone lines or between satellites to remote locations on the globe. And finally, the information which is accessed, stored, and sent could be controlled and manipulated by any number of sophisticated software programs.

6.5.1 Local Area Networks

Local area networks (LANs) are private systems linking a number of computers within a limited radius, usually up to 50 miles. A LAN allows any computer on the network to operate independently or to access any of its linked companions. Local area networks fill a recognized need for in-house communication capabilities, since a great deal of terminal-to-host communicating takes place within a single building or group of buildings. LAN applications can also provide host-to-host linkage, desk-to-desk communication, and shared access to data bases or expensive specialized machines such as printers and duplicators.

The power of a local area network lies in its potential to subordinate all other operations to its own organization. The network does not simply provide lines of communication, but the means to coordinate them as well. It can be an essential tool, for example, for a data-processing department trying to retain control of decentralized processing capabilities. It can also allocate user access to central resources in the manner of a switching system. Or it could act as a tool for creating and enforcing a uniform filing format for the firm's records.

Local area networks receive a lot of media and advertising attention, but they have not yet established themselves in the corporate world. It is not easy to achieve an effective LAN system. First, the installation of a local area network often involves costly structural changes to accommodate cabling and building code restrictions. Further, a host of competing technologies and incompatible products often confuses buyers. Users cannot simply purchase a network, but must consider network media (that is, voice or data transmission), protocols, the LAN's basic configuration, and optimum transmission speed. Basically, there are as yet no accepted standards and procedures for transmitting information.

The setting of standards will be crucial if networks are to be extended to global proportions. The long-term goal of computer networking is to establish a worldwide integrated network which links all of the existing data, voice, message, and image networks. The fully integrated network is still only an emerging concept. Before the end of the century, however, most computers will be able to exchange information with any other terminal in the world.

6.5.2 Data Transmission Services

If a private local area network is unfeasible, firms can always utilize a carrier service. There are four types of carriers, each of which offers a variety of both regulated and unregulated data transmission services. The most familiar of these are the common carriers like the post office and telephone companies, which transport goods for public use according to a set tariff of averaged rates. These entities now offer telex, electronic mail, voice messaging, and facsimile services, in addition to the basic telephone and mail services.

Since the 1960s specialized carriers have provided limited service, usually among high-traffic metropolitan districts. Understandably, common carriers resented the incursion of subscriber services like MCI's microwave radio links. These services were able to build selective networks in lucrative high-traffic areas without having to cover the less profitable routes. Despite objections, the specialized carriers won their legal battles to provide interstate communication. They offer conventional voice as well as data transmission services to subscribers through the use of switched access, leased line, private switched network, satellite channel, or packet messaging.

Value added carriers also offer specialized services, but they act in tandem with conventional carriers. Thus, these carriers probably lease facilities from common carriers and provide the computers which can store data, correct errors, send electronic mail, or convert incompatible computer code. For firms unable to justify the overhead and operating cost of building their own network, the value added networks, like Tymnet, Graphnet, Autonet, or FaxPak, can offer a viable alternative. It is important, however, to keep track of the carriers that are employed and the technologies they use. Some of the value added services are subject to regulation and others, such as electronic or voice mail, are not.

The last type of carriers are international. Some carry only voice and data messages, while others include image services like facsimile or electronic blackboard. With the deregulation of the industry, there are now various alternatives for setting up international communication networks. Some international carriers provide only long-haul service, while others offer domestic linkage as well. The new carriers have tailored services to the needs of end users, but the result is a rather confusing array of options. Developing international communications capability involves coordinating domestic carriers with international connections, international records carriers (IRC), and the foreign telecommunications companies (PTT).

6.6 TELECOMMUNICATIONS AND DATA TRANSFER

Computerized networks, whether public or private, are the information highways for today's businesses. The ways for firms to use voice, data, image, or message networks are infinite. Here we will discuss a few of the more promising applications that are already widely used.

6.6.1 Image Networks

Two of the most useful image applications are facsimile and the electronic blackboard. Both technologies allow photographic or graphic representations to be transmitted over telephone lines. The ability to instantaneously send exact replicas of documents, including signatures, sets facsimile apart from data transfer devices. Depending on whether the facsimile equipment is analog or digital, a normal business letter can be transmitted, in either hard copy or on a video screen, within a few minutes. Electronic blackboards allow graphics presentations which are drawn in one location to appear on the video screens of any number of remote terminals. Although they have difficulties as an interactive device, they can significantly enhance the effectiveness of one-way presentations. Facsimile and especially electronic blackboards are often used in conjunction with other equipment for conducting teleconferences.

6.6.2 Message Networks

Businesses have taken advantage of the digitization of telephone signals by using telephone lines to mail messages. Both electronic and voice mail have decreased the communication lag time which results from using public mail routes and redialing busy numbers. Electronic mail can be transmitted directly from computer to computer without the intervening costs of typing, delivering, and distributing. Voice mail differs from electronic mail in that the voice itself is recorded and stored for audio as opposed to visual reception. Users have voice mailboxes which store these messages in digital form. To retrieve them, they can simply call the mailbox from any telephone. A response can also be fed intc the mailbox for transmission back to the sender. Voice store and forward (VSF) devices are computerized message storage systems usually connected to a PABX switching system.

6.6.3 Teleconferencing

Many of these transfer technologies are used for holding teleconferences. Teleconferencing is one of the most well-publicized telecommunications applications for business use. The staging of electronic conferences over long or short distances can save significant sums in travel expenses and travel time. Through the use of electronic blackboards, computer terminals, facsimile, satellite communication, and video facilities, firms can design the teleconferencing system which best meets their needs.

The most expensive and sophisticated system is the full motion, two-way videoconference. This system operates much like a closed circuit TV, by recording and transmitting all activity, both audio and visual. A video conference room would be equipped with a video camera, a speaker, video screens, microphones for each of the participants, and a control panel. The cost of full-motion video conferencing is steep because it requires a tremendous transmission capacity. With the growing accessibility of satellite transmission, these costs should drop significantly in the next few years.

In the meantime, by far the most common type of teleconferencing is audio. The band width requirements are much narrower and thus cheaper than for video transmission. Besides, audio conferencing can be made available to anyone who has access to a telephone, without the expense of constructing a video conference room. The simplest audio conference connects a number of users by a computerized bridging device through their telephone receivers. For greater ease, headphones or speaker phones can be used to free hands for taking notes. More complex setups involve audio conference rooms equipped with a number of microphones around a table and a speaker to amplify responses. These facilities are usually enhanced by graphics visual aids, like facsimile or electronic blackboards.

Despite the obvious advantages and cost savings of teleconferencing, many businesses are still hesitant to incorporate the technology into their everyday operations. As communication costs continue to fall, and as travel costs and headaches increase, teleconferencing will certainly become an accepted business practice and an important communication tool.

6.7 ESTABLISHING AN INTEGRATED TELECOMMUNICATIONS STRATEGY

Telecommunications technology is complicated and costly. While its tools can increase business productivity, they provide no instant panaceas. Telecommunications, more than any other area of office automation, requires careful and systematic planning. Unless it is coordinated centrally, a telecommunications network will not achieve its goal of integrating all users. Unless every link in the chain is compatible with every other, the chain will be broken. Only a corporate plan can ensure that the parts are integrated.

A telecommunications plan is a work strategy that coordinates telecommunications equipment and services with the long-range goals of the firm, the departments, the divisions, and each work group. A plan must begin with a blueprint showing where the components of the corporate communications network are located, how they interact with each other, and what roles they perform. The blueprint is not meant to serve as a still photograph of the firm's telecommunications network, but as a guide to its progress over a five- or ten-year period. The plan should allocate resources and define future projects, while leaving room for flexible reassessment. In addition, the plan must consider the legal and regulatory restrictions that govern the telecommunications industry, as well as the competitive forecasts which affect a firm's future.

Management must not see telecommunications planning as simply the allocation of technological resources. It is above all an organizational tool which can better position the company for future growth. Thus, top management should treat telecommunications as a valuable corporate asset and design the framework and feedback mechanisms for managing the asset in accordance with its importance.

QUESTIONS AND ANSWERS

Q. What role does telecommunications have in the world of information technology?

A. Telecommunications plays a crucial role in an integrated office system and can be considered its backbone. Simply put, it enables data to be transferred from one point to another in an information network. It presents real problems, affects every user of the system, and is growing in importance and influence.

Q. What must one be aware of when considering telecommunications and office automation?

A. A manager or other interested party must realize that this is a complex and far-reaching area which must be approached holistically and with a long-term orientation. The shock waves of divestiture and deregulation are still spreading, affecting households and all businesses.

Q. What developments in telecommunications will affect the user?

A. Developments are myriad. Fiber optics, satellites, the miniaturization of integrated circuits, and the linking of computers and transmission systems are among them. Quality has improved and costs have declined.

New players have emerged in offering linkups on local, national, and international bases. New services such as teleconferencing, electronic mail, and electronic blackboards are available. All of these can, and in the future probably will, affect American businesses and their personnel.

Records Management

7.1 THE CASE FOR CORPORATE RECORDS MANAGEMENT

Automation advertisements often promote a seductive vision of the "paperless" office of the future. In this new office, the flow of information moves along electronic highways from one desktop to another. The automated office, according to this scenario, need not generate paper records, since the computer will meet all business information requirements. As a logical consequence, the traditional records management function, with its filing cabinets and storage boxes, would be a phenomenon of the past.

Unfortunately, the existing office environment seems far removed from this paperless paradise. An Omni Group study on image technologies, completed in 1985, clearly illustrates that paper consumption in the office is on the rise (see Exhibit 7.1). Over half of the Fortune 1000 respondents indicate that paper generation in their firms had increased greatly while only 5 percent saw a significant decrease. These findings are supported by an American Paper Institute projection that the use of business forms and writing paper will rise steadily throughout the century.

Ironically, office automation is one of the leading causes of this glut (see Exhibit 7.2). While it is true that computers have propelled us into

Exhibit 7.1
Directions in Paper Consumption: 1983–1987

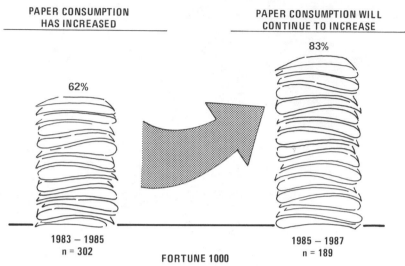

PAPER CONSUMPTION
HAS INCREASED

PAPER CONSUMPTION WILL
CONTINUE TO INCREASE

83%

62%

1983 – 1985
n = 302

FORTUNE 1000

1985 – 1987
n = 189

the information age, their potential to generate data has created as many problems as it has solved. Paper production has been increased by new copiers and printers which can generate documents faster and cheaper than ever before. But automation's impact on paper production is even more complicated. Much has been said already about the advantages and disadvantages of desktop computing. One of the major disadvantages, of course, is the proliferation of incompatible systems. Most companies today have not gained control over their purchasing policies, with the result that corporations are still installing PCs and other products which cannot communicate or share files or resources with each other.

As a result, firms continue to maintain a variety of information systems in order to meet their needs for timely and efficient informational exchange. The keynote for records management is the hybrid system, which integrates the strengths and avoids the weaknesses of various paper, microform, and computer-based systems. Thus, although documents are now created on a variety of electronic media, paper has not yet been rendered obsolete. Since paper is the common denominator among all these electronic and manual systems, it remains the universal medium through which businesses communicate.

While document production soars, document management has not always kept pace. A significant portion of America's largest companies

Exhibit 7.2
Impact of Office Automation on Paper Explosion

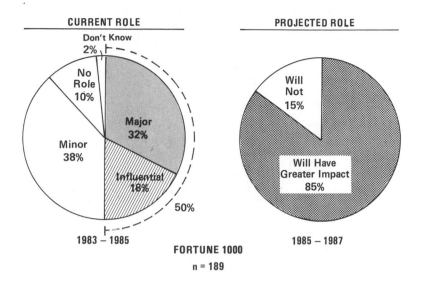

CURRENT ROLE

Don't Know
2%
No Role 10%
Minor 38%
Major 32%
Influential 18%
50%
1983 – 1985

PROJECTED ROLE

Will Not 15%
Will Have Greater Impact 85%
1985 – 1987

FORTUNE 1000
n = 189

lack confidence in their own ability to gain control of the paper explosion (see Exhibit 7.3). Because timely access to documents can create an important competitive advantage, more firms are treating records management as a vital business function. An effective records management program can transform mountains of inaccessible data into timely business information. This chapter will discuss basic concepts in records management and how the records management function can be expanded to meet the document needs of the automated office.

7.2 WHO SHOULD MANAGE RECORDS?

With new pressures and responsibilities being added to the records management function, it is not clear who is most qualified to manage the corporate records. In today's business environment, no one group has a monopoly on records decision-making (see Exhibit 7.4). While control of office automation purchasing has fallen to the MIS department, records management decisions remain dispersed. In over two-thirds of the Fortune 1000 firms, there is no centralized authority responsible for the handling of document management systems. In the one-third of the companies that have a centralized records management function, no one department dominates. The field is evenly divided

Exhibit 7.3

Dissatisfaction Index: Document Handling

TYPE OF DOCUMENT	PARAMETER			RESPONDENT GROUP
	RETRIEVAL TIME	FILE INTEGRITY	SECURITY	
Corporate/Vital	16%	32%	15%	Records Managers
	34%	33%	21%	MIS/DP
Active	22%	36%	23%	Records Managers
	35%	41%	36%	MIS/DP
Personal	24%	35%	22%	Records Managers
	36%	37%	40%	MIS/DP

FORTUNE 1000
n = 302

Exhibit 7.4
Decision-Making in the Fortune 1000: Office Systems

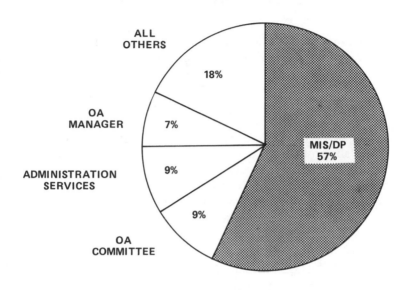

ALL OTHERS 18%

OA MANAGER 7%

ADMINISTRATION SERVICES 9%

OA COMMITTEE 9%

MIS/DP 57%

MOST INFLUENTIAL GROUP

among records management, DP/MIS, and administrative services departments.

Part of the problem seems to be in how records management responsibilities are defined. Traditionally, records management has been grouped under administrative services. But because of the impact of automation on the field, some argue that records management should be placed under the supervision of DP/MIS. This argument stresses the centrality of automated storage and retrieval systems in the records management program of the future. Only MIS, then, could provide the technical expertise needed to make purchasing decisions.

Therefore, the records management function is currently in a state of flux. The same challenges that face other office decision-makers—to master new technology, to keep up with user needs, to integrate the old and the new—also face records managers. Records management is neither a purely technological issue nor a strictly administrative one. Whether DP/MIS managers or records managers eventually get the upper hand in the decision-making process, they will have to incorporate new skills. Records management is likely to remain a mixture of automated, semi-automated, and manual systems, and whoever wrests control of the function must be adept at managing all of them.

7.3 THE BASICS: WHAT ARE RECORDS AND HOW ARE THEY USED?

Records can be any official document that contains information of value to the operation of a firm. They can document any facet of business activity, from security procedures to correspondence. The value of each record depends on the information it provides, but any record can fulfill a variety of legal, administrative, fiscal, or archival requirements.

Records are also categorized according to their function, or how they are used in the organization. Records move through a four-phase life cycle, consisting of generation, active status, inactive status, and destruction (Exhibit 7.5). A record's position in the life cycle determines the policies which will govern its existence.

Records generation is the period in which records, in the form of letters, reports, forms or statistics, are produced. They can be created on a variety of media, either electronic, paper, voice/video, or microform, and then distributed to the workers who will use them for reference. The major problem in this phase is to control the generation of useless documents, such as outdated forms and superfluous reports.

The second phase of the record life cycle covers the period of active use. When the document has been produced, it must be classified and filed for easy reference. In this period, rapid, cost-effective retrieval is of primary importance. Thus, active records must be conveniently located and organized for immediate and accurate retrieval.

When the information provided by a document is no longer relevant for everyday reference, the record becomes inactive. Records retain this inactive status for varying amounts of time, depending on the need for occasional retrieval or the fulfillment of legal regulations. As large volumes of inactive records are accumulated, the chief concern is to store them as cheaply as possible in a minimum amount of space.

The final phase of the record life cycle is document destruction. At the end of the life cycle as at the beginning, the primary task is to limit the number of unnecessary records which are stored. To this end, it is imperative to set strict retention schedules. These schedules can be one of the most effective ways of controlling a firm's paper explosion.

7.4 STORAGE AND RETRIEVAL SYSTEMS AND EQUIPMENT

Several factors determine what type of storage and retrieval systems are appropriate for each firm. However, a complete records program for most businesses will probably include a mixture of paper, micrographic,

Exhibit 7.5
Records Life Cycle

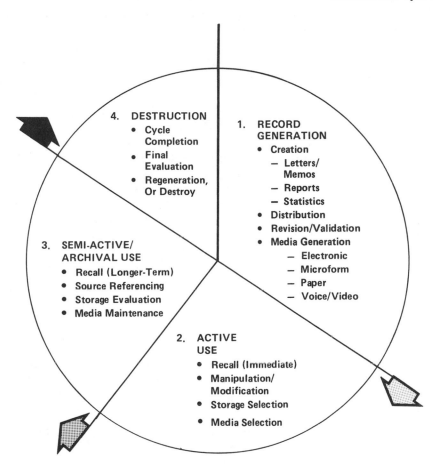

and computer-based storage and retrieval systems. Each system has its advantages and disadvantages. The ideal combination would seek to minimize the limitations while reaping the benefits that paper, micrographics, and computer-based systems have to offer.

One of the important factors to consider in choosing storage media and equipment is the cost and availability of office space. The amount of space available for records storage will become more limited as office rent continues to climb. Space concerns, of course, become more prominent as the volume of records increases.

An equally important consideration is that of retrieval time. The more often records are referenced, the more important the turnaround time is. A related issue for active records is whether they need to be updated. Some storage media are more easily altered than others.

And finally, the degree of security which a record requires determines how and where it must be stored. With the growth in decentralized information systems, more people can access vital company documents. Because of this potential, many managers remain unconvinced of the security of electronically stored data.

7.4.1 Paper Storage and Retrieval Systems

Some of the technical reasons for the survival of paper business records have been discussed, but paper has the additional psychological advantage of being familiar and accepted. Also, the equipment which supports and maintains a paper storage system is less expensive to purchase than equipment for the other media. On the other hand, it takes up more space and is therefore more costly on an operational basis. The two basic aspects of a manual filing system considered here are the classification scheme and the equipment.

For documents to be retrieved from filing cabinets and boxes, files must be given an internal organization. Obviously, different classification schemes are appropriate for various types of documents. Each file series, or group of related files, can be ordered alphabetically, numerically, or by subject. Alphabetization is appropriate for client or personnel files; numerical filing, usually according to the date, can be used for purchase orders or checks. Filing by subject is a way to enhance an alphabetical scheme by providing more information about the content of the file. Thus, files can be cross-referenced under subject headings or key words.

Paper filing equipment is the least expensive to purchase, but it is often the most costly in terms of the space it utilizes. Therefore, it is important to choose manual equipment which makes the best use of available space without sacrificing convenience and accessibility. Other factors to consider are security and fire protection, the potential to expand, mobility requirements, and the size of the documents.

Filing cabinets are still the most basic and widely used manual filing equipment. Traditional vertical filing cabinets are still installed in small offices, but recently they have been superceded by other, more space-efficient cabinets. Lateral file cabinets, which file documents from left to right rather than front to back, are narrower and take up less aisle room. Another, even more space-efficient alternative is open shelf filing. Open files are quickly accessed, have no drawers to block aisles, and can cover the entire wall. On the other hand, they cannot be monitored for security purposes and are fairly vulnerable to dirt and fire.

For large offices with great volumes of paper records, individual cabinets are probably not the most efficient option. Compactible files consist of a series of open shelves packed together and loaded on sliding tracks. Rather than having permanent aisles, access space is created by pushing apart the appropriate unit. This process can either be done automatically or manually, but in either case retrieval is a rather slow process. If turnaround time is more important, automated files, which are the state of the art in paper systems, can be installed. Files are stored in a large metal box equipped with an electronic sorting device. An operator pressing a button can call up any file, and it will be automatically located and retrieved within seconds.

7.4.2 Micrographic Storage

Micrographics is the process of reducing documents by recording them on film. Depending on the film, reduction ratios can range anywhere from 18 to 1 to 90 to 1 for certain types of ultrafiche. Although businesses have been utilizing microform storage for over 50 years, it has become an increasingly popular practice in recent years. The deluge of information has made many managers receptive to microfilm's potential contribution to the records control aspect of office automation (see Exhibit 7.6). Microform users cite improved space utilization, cost savings, and greater retrieval speed and file integrity as the major benefits of image media storage (see Exhibit 7.7).

In addition to microfilm's inherent attractions, it has the advantage of being easily integrated into computer-based storage and retrieval systems. Rather than making microfilm obsolete, micrographics is augmenting its tremendous capacity for cheap and efficient storage by tapping into the computer's ability to sort and retrieve information.

Despite its powerful advantages, microfilm is limited by the expensive and specialized equipment which is required to film, develop, and display microfilmed documents. In addition, the conversion of paper documents to microforms is costly and time-consuming. Finally, some microforms are difficult to update because it is hard to locate specific frames. However, some of the storage and retrieval systems that combine computer power and image technologies have provided viable solutions to these problems.

There are several types of microforms, each with its own potential and limitations. The oldest microform is roll film, now available either on open reels, in cartridges, or in double reel cassettes. Roll film is the most economical method of filming and preparing sequentially ordered inactive documents which do not need to be updated. However, there are many disadvantages. First, it tends to be inconvenient for calling up specific images since many images are stored on one continuous roll.

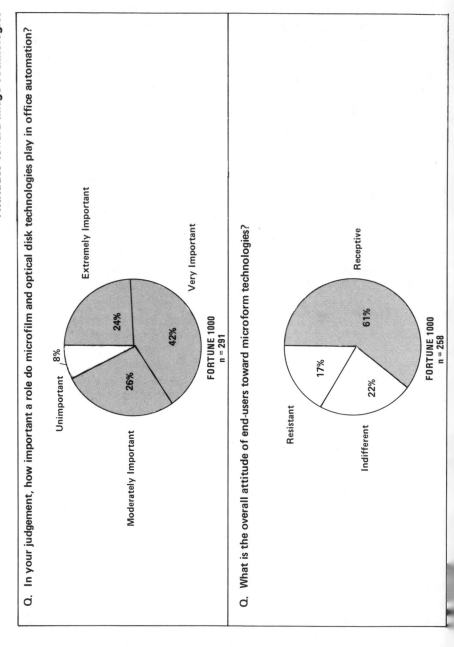

Exhibit 7.6
Attitudes toward Image Technologies

Q. In your judgement, how important a role do microfilm and optical disk technologies play in office automation?

Unimportant 8%

Extremely Important

24%

Moderately Important 26%

42%

Very Important

FORTUNE 1000
n = 291

Q. What is the overall attitude of end-users toward microform technologies?

Resistant 17%

Receptive

61%

Indifferent 22%

FORTUNE 1000
n = 258

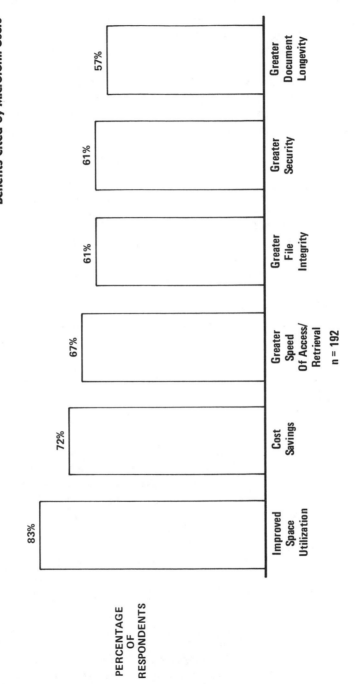

Exhibit 7.7
Benefits Cited by Microform Users

PERCENTAGE OF RESPONDENTS

Improved Space Utilization — 83%
Cost Savings — 72%
Greater Speed Of Access/ Retrieval — 67%
Greater File Integrity — 61%
Greater Security — 61%
Greater Document Longevity — 57%

n = 192

Although cartridges and cassettes can be indexed for manual or electronic retrieval of specific frames, microfilm readers that use indexes are considerably more expensive to purchase than open reel projectors. Even with the special readers, retrieval time is slowed by the need to find the appropriate roll and load it in the reader. A final disadvantage is the bulky size of rolls, which are somewhat inconvenient to store.

Thus, despite the advances in reel film retrieval, reels are still more likely to be used for inactive record storage. For active filing, unitized microforms like microfiche, aperture cards, and jackets are more commonly used. In fact, microfiche is one of the most preferred storage media used by businesses today. The unitized microforms have the advantage of dividing information into discrete frames. Information is thus easier to locate and display. On the other hand, the frames are more expensive to produce, as each document must be individually filmed.

The convenience of unitized microforms is enhanced by combining them in various ways with other forms. Thus, microfilm cards and jackets include space both for strips of microfilm and for written or key-punched information. The added information makes them easily located, either by the human eye or by an electronic reader. The versatility of unitized forms has also been enhanced by the innovations in fiche that can be updated. Such fiche can be refilmed until all the unused space is filled. Some film can even be erased to allow for the deletion of outdated information.

Microfilm's impressive potential for space reduction and speedy retrieval is limited by the expense of related micrographics equipment. In order to convert paper documents to microfilm, special cameras must be purchased. Variations in the size and condition of the documents to be filmed might even necessitate the purchase of more than one type of camera. Rotary cameras can only handle normal-sized, single sheet documents which are in good condition. Planetary cameras can be used for oversized or fragile documents. Finally, step-and-repeat cameras are used specifically to create microfiche. Many firms will find it more economical to hire microfilm service bureaus to transfer records to microfilm, especially for a one-time conversion.

While firms can rent cameras, microfilm readers and reader-printers are purchases which cannot be avoided. Without these machines, the information stored on the film will not be available to the reader. Readers can be categorized by their size and by the microforms they are capable of reading. The cost of these readers varies tremendously, from the simplest reel spindle viewer to the most sophisticated image retrieval systems, such as Kodak's KIMS or Image System's ISI 4000. It is therefore essential that the cost of readers and printers be kept in mind when the feasibility of microfilm conversion is being evaluated.

7.4.3 Computer-Based Storage and Retrieval Systems

The great power of the computer has rested in its capacity to manipulate and control large amounts of information. For records management, this power had limited applications. Electronic file storage was and is expensive and has not yet posed a viable alternative to film or paper storage. But, as in other areas of office automation, computer technology has blended with other technologies to produce hybrid systems. Thus, these systems combine the data-processing capabilities of the computer with the inexpensive storage of microfilm. The hybrid storage and retrieval systems consist of a device for creating microfilm, a unit for storing it, and a device to display it in a usable form.

Microfilm can be created by cameras, or, alternatively, it can be produced directly off a computer terminal by a COM (computer output microfilm) recorder. COM recorders have the attraction of avoiding paper production entirely. In essence, the recorder replaces the normal computer printer. Since a few frames of microfilm can hold as much information as a sheet of paper, direct microfilm generation is inexpensive and rapid. In addition, the COM recorders can be easily integrated into an electronic store and retrieval system. The COM recorder (as well as some of the more sophisticated microfilm cameras) can record a computer-readable index, such as a blip or a notch, as it generates the film from computer data or source documents.

The computer-managed index is the key to the most sophisticated marriage between computers and micrographics. CAR (computer-assisted retrieval) systems vary in their degree of sophistication, but all of them use a computer-generated index to locate and retrieve microfilm images. CAR can solve some of the chronic problems of manual filing and retrieval systems which are error-ridden and time consuming to use. CAR systems can stand alone, or they can access an index stored in a host mainframe or stored off-line on microfilm. When a request for a particular document is made, the computer can scan the index in seconds and pinpoint the location of the desired image.

After the document search has been completed, the document must be retrieved from its storage area. If the computer is only used to generate the index, the microfilm can be manually retrieved from a filing cabinet or cartridge rack. Then the operator must load the film in the reader for viewing. But by establishing a link between the computer and the retrieval unit, this step can be automated as well. The computer can direct the search, and an automated arm can bring out the appropriate roll or fiche. Finally, the highest level of integration can be achieved by a CAR system which can scan the desired image, translate it into digital form, and move it into a data buffer display on a terminal. This function operates much like a facsimile device, which transports visual images over telephone wires by digitizing them. The advantage of the highly integrated systems is that the documents can be searched, retrieved, edited, and displayed in seconds. In the process, the microfilm need not be removed from its storage unit nor loaded into expensive readers.

Another variation on the hybrid storage and retrieval systems involves the use of optical disks for data storage. The disks, no larger than a record album, can store up to 200,000 pages of text in digital form. The disks are made by a laser scanner which burns ridges onto their surface. At this time, optical disks are too expensive to produce and too difficult to update to be widely used in records management applications. However, when combined with a CAR system which can index, retrieve, and display its recorded information, the optical disk may in the future offer a powerful alternative to microfilm storage.

Not all firms can justify the expense of computer-based storage and retrieval components. As in all facets of office automation, there are trade-offs between speed and efficiency and the cost of installing and maintaining new technology. However, in today's office environment many complex factors must be considered in justifying the cost of records systems. The timely access to business information is a valuable commodity which is difficult to quantify. CAR systems and COM recorders which are expensive to install might be easily justified by the speed with which they can generate and locate information. In addition, with the falling price of hardware and the greater concentration of computing power, CAR systems, once reserved only for the largest file collections, have become more practical for smaller firms.

7.5 ESTABLISHING A RECORDS MANAGEMENT PROGRAM

As office technology establishes more links between previously unconnected functions, the need for central coordination increases. Records management is no longer an isolated administrative service but a function which must take into account technological developments, business objectives, and organizational imperatives. Records management has become part of the overall OA strategy of building an information network in the office. As such, top management should not underestimate the importance of giving records managers the mandate they need to establish an effective records program.

The process of creating a records program, or of overhauling an existing one, should be carried out according to a standard set of procedures. Once top management has given a mandate to proceed, the records or DP/MIS manager must design a plan for creating and implementing an image management program which best suits the firm's needs. The work plan should allocate resources for collecting data on records management needs, for analyzing the data, and for using the results to design and implement a program. If no one in the firm has the expertise to complete this task, a consultant can be brought in to oversee any or all of the steps.

7.5.1 Conducting an Inventory

A working knowledge of records management concepts and equipment is useless unless it can be applied to meeting specific requirements. Before the records analyst can decide what procedures and equipment best meet the firm's information needs, it is imperative to define the scope of the document collection which needs to be managed. Therefore, conducting an inventory is the first step in the data collection process.

An inventory should serve several purposes. The inventory should reveal how many documents exist, where they are kept, what they are used for, and what phase in the records' life cycle they are in. In other words, the inventory will be a tool to gain control over the life of each record series, and hence over the physical flow of information within the firm.

An inventory process has four phases. First, the current records policies must be reviewed. Second, a methodology must be developed to catalog records which are stored on a variety of media: electronic, micrographic, paper, voice, or video. Third, the inventory itself must be conducted through the use of interviews, survey sheets, and floor plans of storage areas. Finally, the results must be analyzed and summarized for presentation to top management.

7.5.2 Establishing Records Control

After the data collection process has been completed, the records manager can use the information gathered to design a complete records control program. The overall goal of the program should be to provide, within the budget constraints, the most accurate and timely information to whoever requires it. To this end, the first object of the program should be to establish policies which regulate every phase of the records life cycle. Second, it should set standardized guidelines for purchasing records management equipment. Third, it should design and implement new storage and retrieval systems. Fourth, it should establish policies for auditing and improving the system in the future. Fifth, it should define and delegate records management responsibilities, both for users and for records management personnel.

The policies which control each phase of the records life cycle should be designed to minimize the creation and storage of useless documents and to maximize the accessibility of those which are valuable. Records generation can be monitored by strict procedures for the creation and distribution of forms and reports. Record retrieval can be facilitated by implementing a coherent and uniform filing system. Files can be either centrally located or decentralized throughout the departments, but most firms will choose a combination of the two approaches. Wherever files are located, they should all be subject to the same classification scheme, so that files can be accessed by anyone in the organization.

Regulating records storage is one of the most important parts of the program. Records retention schedules should be set for all records series, and procedures for enforcing them must be implemented. Retention schedules are essentially contracts on record disposition and agreed to by those who produce records, those who use them, and those who monitor them. The schedule will indicate how long a record series remains in active status, when it is to be transferred to inactive status, and when it is to be destroyed.

The setting of retention schedules is a complex process and involves an evaluation of the legal, administrative, fiscal, and archival regulations that pertain to each records series. Restrictions can be set by outside organizations, such as federal or state regulatory agencies or the IRS, or by internal requirements. Retention schedules for various types of records can be purchased off-the-shelf, but each company will have slightly different retention requirements. It is best, therefore, to invest time and effort into customizing the firm's retention schedules.

Defining systems requirements and putting together the most appropriate combination of technology requires a working knowledge of the records management applications presented in this chapter. The process of researching and selecting individual office automation vendors and products is discussed in chapters 9 and 10. For more specific information on image management technology, several organizations and publications provide a good starting point. The Association of Records Managers of America (ARMA) and the Association of Image and Information Management (AIIM) provide information in the form of conferences, product comparisons, publications, and seminars. Other good sources are the Auerbach and Datapro subscription services, which offer product-by-product comparison and vendor background information. Finally, records management trade journals, such as *The Journal of Information and Image Management* and *Information and Records Management*, can be consulted for reports on new trends in records management.

Finally, the whole records program should be supervised by a procedures manual which includes all of the records policies, guidelines, and standards. The purpose of the manual is to provide a standard reference for both users and records management personnel. In addition, it should include job descriptions for records management personnel and a flowchart outlining the distribution of records management re-

sponsibilities. Whether records are centralized or decentralized, the procedures manual can be invaluable in tying the whole records
management program together. For this reason, the manual must be
clear, readable, and appropriately illustrated.

With the completion of a new or updated manual, the records control
program should be set in motion. If it is successful, it will contribute as
much to a firm's competitive advantage as will an efficient local area
network (see Chapter 6). Although records management has not received as much attention in trade journals as the highly volatile field of
telecommunications, its role in disseminating valuable information is
equally important. Records management must be considered carefully
in the development of any global office automation strategy. Office automation does not do away with the need for an efficient records management program. Rather, technological advances have made records
management more complex and more vital than ever before.

QUESTIONS AND ANSWERS

Q. What role does a manual filing system play in the modern office?

A. Although advanced paperless records management systems are making substantial inroads into today's offices, most systems still consist of
a mixture of computer retention and paper-based manual files.

Q. What classification schemes are commonly used in manual systems?

A. Most frequently, alphabetic or numerical classifications are used in
conjunction with a system of file series which can consist of anything
from correspondence to invoice notices to pension records.

*Q. Why examine manual filing in a book which covers the automation of records
management?*

A. For two reasons, the first being that unless one's manual system is
up-to-date and well organized, it is not possible to effectively automate
a company's record program; and second, a company's current system,
while it may be capable of improvement, gives clues as to the particular
needs of that company.

Q. What are the elements of a filing system?

A. File classification has a number of aspects. Primarily, it provides a
means of document identification and document location, as well as a
means to assemble individual documents into categories which become
files or file series, the building blocks of any file system.

Q. What are archival or inactive vital records?

A. Archival records are those which a company would need to start its business from the bottom up if all others were destroyed. Such papers would include incorporation documents, patents, property rights or leases, tax and pension records, and the like. In most cases these documents compose less than 2 percent of a firm's document inventory and are consulted only rarely.

Q. What are some of the major types of manual filing equipment available?

A. Major equipment categories include vertical and lateral file cabinets as well as open shelf, compactible, and automated files.

8

Office Ergonomics

New machines and tasks require new types of workspaces and furniture design. Although the need to adapt to new technologies has always been recognized, the microcomputer revolution has introduced so many changes to the office environment so quickly that the relationship between machines and human beings in the office has become a central focus of research and concern. As David Elowitz, space utilization consultant and president of Michael Laurie & Partners in New York, asserts, "Before the microcomputer, people could simply go on as they always had, and ignore the computers locked away in DP. But now they've really been jolted, and everyone's working to establish a new equilibrium." Following the tradition of scientific management and measurement, this concern has been incorporated into the discipline of ergonomics—the study of workers' interactions with their environment.

Stemming from the field of biotechnology, which uses engineering principles to measure the impact and adaptive responses of man to machine, ergonomics seeks to find the balance between worker satisfaction and efficiency in today's work spaces. Although books have been written outlining quantitative methods for evaluating factors from space division and chair height to muscle fatigue, none has been accepted uncritically. Indeed, many people question the validity of the science itself, insisting that no one has proved any measurable relationship between office design and human output.

"We read the books and have our own technical people working on the stuff," admits Stephanie Hendricks, architect and vice-president of St. Hendricks and Associates in New York, "but no one's really sure how to apply all the figures, or what they can tell us about how people work." Nevertheless, no one would argue that workers' physical, social, and psychological needs are unimportant components in a functioning office. Ergonomics, whether science or nonsense, does address issues that cannot be ignored. Corporations are recognizing the importance of this whole category of problems by incorporating facility management personnel into decision-making processes. "Office workers spend more time and direct more thoughts on their work than ever before. It's not just a way to make money, it's a home," explains Phil Muller, automation consultant. "Ergonomics can contribute to this feeling. When the environment is comfortable, people work harder. It's the key."

Design of office space in the past has always held to the general maxim that form follows function. But although this basic belief still stands, offices continue to be constructed as if their functions have remained unaltered from the precomputer era. Richard Weisenthal, architect at Skidmore, Owings & Merrill, agrees, "It's amazing how slowly people are willing to change their conceptions of how things should look—even in the face of obvious inconvenience and discomfort. A lot of the offices I see out there probably look exactly as they did fifty years ago."

The desk in the corner, surrounded by its wastebasket, filing cabinet, unimaginative chair, and ceiling light is a testament to the endurance of traditional notions about the nature of the office. Layouts often reflected management's ideas about status and comfort, and discussions focused on questions of period, style, and color. Secretaries were either pooled in drab, utilitarian typing quarters or given extravagant desks outside their bosses' offices. Although many companies are experimenting now with new spatial arrangements, most miss the larger implications—that the new office equipment networks have changed beyond recognition the way the office works.

"Most firms that want us to come in and redecorate have quite narrow ideas—give us a bigger desk here, a padded chair there. But no one wants to hear anything about restructuring," says architect Barry Bronfman, president of Bronfman and Associates in New York.

8.1 STRUCTURAL PROBLEMS

Restructuring cannot be avoided. When buildings or offices which were designed without computers in mind have to be "retrofitted," there is more involved than just redecoration. Computer technology affects the structural components of the building itself.

"The first three things we look at, before we even think about furniture, are air conditioning, power and cabling," says Robert Reich, president of Design Technologies in New York. Computers generate heat, and a powerful air-conditioning system is a must. On the other hand, computers can cut down on heating bills without draining much extra power. One firm that Reich has worked with is even experimenting with having no heating system at all.

Computers also make power distribution more complex. First, they need separate circuits in order to assure uninterrupted data transmission. And second, they need special cabling that distributes the power to each desk terminal and is flexible enough to accommodate change. As Phil Muller, automation consultant, notes, "What firms think they need when they start is constantly changing. Cabling thus becomes a major problem, with cables being dragged around through ceilings and floors. New computers are brought in all the time, and you can't get technicians in fast enough to rewire everything."

One solution to the cabling problem is to prewire buildings with floor cabling. However, this method is costly both to install and to change. A more flexible solution is flat electrical cabling, which does not require ceilings or floors to be knocked out. Or offices can run movable cable tubes which attach to walls and ceilings.

The solution that the firm chooses will depend on whether the building must be retrofitted or is already built to suit their needs. But whatever structural solutions are chosen, it is clear that business as usual is no longer an option. It is crucial for facilities management personnel to consider the most basic design problems when planning for the firm's future development. Without this foundation, ergonomics can have only a weak impact on the office of the future.

8.2 LANDSCAPING: OPEN OR CLOSED

A traditionally structured office consists of a number of private executive offices and corridors staffed with secretaries. Although open landscaping for the support staff has its advantages—the staff are more easily supervised, flexible, and accessible—it also has its distinct drawbacks—noise and a lack of privacy. In the last 15 years or so, partitioning has become a fashionable and cost-effective way to divide space into individual workstations. The panels normally employed for this purpose, however, do not ensure either auditory or visual privacy. There are options, like altering the height of such panels or equipping them with acoustical screens, but these improvements can be fairly expensive.

The pros and cons of various landscaping alternatives can be argued without much difficulty. The bottom-line distinctions are fairly clear; open landscaping is more expensive than closed to set up, but cheaper to change. Making value judgments, on the other hand, is not so easy, as there are no hard and fast rules associated with the division of space.

"I've worked on a lot of interiors, and the arguments for one over the other are always different," notes Andrew Vines, architect at Kohn, Pedersen and Fox. "A lot of it seems to come down to personal philosophy." Much depends on a company's own objectives, its philosophy, its growth pattern. Thus, a firm that expects to experience rapid expansion in the next few years should design a layout which can be altered with minimum cost and disruption. Other companies hold particular principles which indicate appropriate spatial design. M&M Mars, for example, is constructed without interior walls to symbolize and promote the concept of a tightly knit organization.

Whatever the general guidelines, when it comes to the specifics of noise and privacy, workstations should be individually evaluated where possible. Thus, workers engaged in creative or thinking tasks place a premium on minimum acoustical distraction. Data-entry people, on the other hand, can be grouped together without disrupting their work process. Meeting space is another consideration that affects mainly management personnel. Privacy requirements again depend on how business is conducted. Andrew Vines adds, "I always ask them how they do business, if they work in teams or alone, if everyone gets together once a year or weekly. At first, people don't always see the relevance, but once they work in the space designed for them, they become planning converts."

8.3 LIGHTING: GENERAL OR AMBIENT

As with spatial design, there are no clear directives to be given for lighting arrangements. Traditionally, offices have been lit by blanket ceiling fixtures which produce a general, fixed level of light. With rising energy costs, however, experiments have been made with ambient lighting or task spotlighting. Responses to these new systems have generally been favorable, and some researchers have drawn implications of improved productivity, but again no clear answers have been provided.

"In most cases," asserts Richard Weisenthal, "I think task lighting gives workers a better feeling, helps them focus on their job. Ceiling lights have a kind of dulling effect, making everyone and every space look the same."

Specific factors which are easier to evaluate are things like reflected and differential lighting patterns. Reflected light has only become a problem with the proliferation of video display terminals (VDTs). When screens are placed opposite windows, users consistently complain of eye strain.

Lighting level requirements have also been altered by the presence of VDTs, as recommended levels are lower in these workplaces than in traditional, nonelectronic offices. If terminal-generated light is taken into account, offices can significantly reduce their level of general lighting and save much of the extra power used by the computers. Bob Reich of Design Technologies tells of a project in which ceiling lights in the terminal room were fitted with 25 to 30 watt bulbs. If additional light was needed for desk tasks, programmers could simply switch on a small lamp next to their PCs. "Most people don't realize how little artificial light the automated office actually needs. Even we made the same mistake in our office," Reich admitted. "Sometimes we don't turn on the lights at all."

8.4 FURNITURE

As cost of space continues to rise and workspaces inevitably shrink, the shape and functional efficiency of office furniture will take on new meaning, even though smaller spaces will be somewhat compensated for by the reduction in storage space provided by computer record retention. Trying to accommodate worker comfort and contribute to job satisfaction and productivity while operating within more stringent spatial constraints is the challenge of the future for facilities management planners.

"More than ever," says Barbara Turner, vice-president of Michael Laurie & Partners, "facilities management personnel are being incorporated into central planning groups. Finally, we are seeing management accept that a happy balance is not just going to happen accidentally."

Furniture designers and office planners can benefit from the research undertaken by related applied sciences. Biomechanics, which measures stress on muscles, tendons, and joints, can contribute to reducing the fatigue caused by awkwardly shaped work surfaces and uncomfortable chairs. Anthropometry calculates body dimensions of general populations and is used to determine the shape, size, and contour of office furniture and individual workstations. Attempts at quantification in this field compile detailed estimates of arm span and reaching capacity, leg room, and chair height. Seat contours are calculated to provide maximum weight distribution without reducing the variety of people the chair's design can comfortably accommodate.

While it is helpful to know that these efforts go on behind the scenes, most buyers will be concerned with more general features. A chair is probably the purchase with the most far-reaching effects and the most individualized requirements. "With proper air conditioning, power distribution and a good chair," states Phil Muller, "everything else is secondary."

"And yet," comments David Elowitz, "the way chairs are generally picked reflects ideas about status and office hierarchy. To get a padded armchair is like having the corner office with a window. Meanwhile, the functional requirements are neglected."

Chair height is fundamental, although, surprisingly enough, adequately adjustable chairs are a sparse commodity on the market. If chairs cannot be lowered to accommodate the shortest office workers, then foot stools must be provided. Other considerations when choosing chairs, especially for word processors and secretaries who spend long hours at their desks, are seat contour and back support. Arm rests are also important, as they vary in order to meet both secretarial and executive needs. That is, executive armchairs require no special height ratios, but typists need a certain distance between elbows and keyboard.

After all is said and done about scientific design, however, it must be remembered that comfort is essentially personal. For this reason, worker input into the decision-making process should not be neglected. "We looked at 40 chairs before we made a decision, and everyone got to sit in each one," said Bob Reich. "Don't be afraid to get the vendor to bring over a sample—a good chair is a substantial investment. Besides, for programmers today, their chair and terminal are practically home."

Work surface and desk design is the second important category of office furnishings. Again, height is critical, as surfaces which are too high or low will defeat the purpose of adjustable chairs. Ideally offices should possess a variety of surfaces which can be adjusted by cranks, friction devices, or even motors. On the other hand, most workers would probably not go through the trouble to adjust the height of a work surface, and the money might be better spent on easily adjustable chairs and detachable keyboards. Desk size obviously depends on what it is used for, as does the ratio of surface space to storage space. New desks include 120-degree models for accessibility and roominess. "Mini-offices" are directed toward multi-task support staff and are meant to facilitate various operations within a reachable sphere.

8.5 SOUND DAMPENING

One of the facts of life in the electronic office is that the new machines are noisy. Although acceptable noise levels vary from place to place, from data-entry stations to telephone centers, some general attempts at noise reduction can be made. None of the office-generated noises has the capacity to damage hearing, but printers, telephones, and conversation contribute to work disruption and stress.

"Stress on the job is high enough as it is, and noise levels rank high up there on complaint tests. But the thing is, noise is one source of stress that can be dealt with more or less effectively—at least in an office—so why ignore the problem?" asks Stephanie Hendricks. If offices are partitioned, the dividing screens can be made more substantial, in size and width, with special attention paid to the conduction and absorption of sound. Acoustical devices of various sorts, like acoustical ceiling tiles, floors, and windows, help maintain acceptable noise levels, but a full-scale, sound reduction treatment can be rather expensive. Sound-absorbing drapes and carpeting can serve as noise dampeners while enhancing the attractiveness of the office environment. These items should be chosen for sturdiness, in colors that neither distract nor need frequent cleaning.

Finally, machines themselves can be fitted with noise dampeners—an option which should be seriously considered for the word-processing center.

8.6 LOCATION STRATEGY

Location of equipment and work-space arrangement is tied in some way to all of the previously mentioned factors. For noise control it is inadvisable to place word processors inside top management offices. Grouping depends on the general divisions of space within the office. Lighting arrangements vary with how people's work is physically structured. Finally, planners need to take into account the relationship between available space, furniture, and equipment and the tasks workers are expected to perform. "It's a bit like putting together a puzzle," explains Barbara Turner. "We figure out what shape all the pieces are and then sit down and try to make them fit together."

Beyond these correlations, a location strategy should attempt to minimize inefficient movement and the expense of wasted energy. Tools that are used in consecutive processes should be placed together, like large volume photocopiers and binders. Although this may seem an obvious point, consultants continue to find numerous infractions of this commonsense rule. For instance, at one New York office, word processors shared space with graphics functions, while printers and binders were both located on the floor below. This arrangement resulted in unnecessary travel time between word processor and printer and between graphics and the binding station. A simple shifting of equipment ended by saving the company considerable daily time and energy. Location signifies not only workstations but the paths between them. To avoid unnecessary stress and strain, aisles should be wide enough to negotiate without twisting or bumping into objects.

Warns Barry Bronfman, "Sometimes planners are so focused on each individual desk or machine that the larger picture gets lost entirely. So you have these beautifully tailored little workspaces separated by obstacle course nightmares."

Deciding where people will be located depends on privacy requirements, as mentioned previously, but also on technological imperatives. For example, VDTs must not be placed opposite windows or printers. The advantage of grouping data and word-processing equipment into an accessible entity suggests work-space sharing for these functions, but varying degrees of centralization are possible.

"Whether you're talking about space or about the processing itself, the key issue with these new machines seems to be whether to set up centralized or distributed networks. The potential can be great either way, but you have to decide what your objectives are," asserts Barbara Turner. If word processors are completely decentralized and placed in proximity to the principals whom they serve, problems in work balancing and distribution may arise. On the other hand, a totally centralized word-processing unit may, depending on the size of the firm, create too much physical distance between managers' information needs and the document production area. Medium-sized firms may find the most optimum solution in a series of minicenters which balance both accessibility and the efficiency of work-space sharing.

Another issue to be raised when considering location of workstations is cabling. With the advent of computer terminals, which are now ubiquitous in some companies, the need to cable these workstations together to share information within local area networks (LANs) has arisen. In some cases this is an important cost consideration as the types of cable required for some equipment are rather expensive, even when purchased in bulk.

The fivefold increase in terminal penetration that will very likely occur in the offices of large organizations over the next five years will lead to cabling and physical environment problems on an unprecedented scale. These cabling problems will lead to increasing demands for advanced forms of local networks. Toward the end of the 1980s, therefore, the long-predicted "take off" of local networks (probably based on a combination of LANs and data-switching PABXs) will begin.

The installation of these new networks is, however, likely to lag behind the increase in terminal penetration, since smaller office system installations will not usually require extensive communications facilities. But as organizations begin to build specially designed group applications and corporate general-purpose office system facilities, the demand for telecommunications and data communications facilities will increase dramatically.

The high penetration of terminals will also increase the demands made on office planners. Not only must office planners create the working environment in such a way as to conform with health guidelines regarding the use of visual displays, but they must also design the cabling network so that each desk may support a terminal that is interconnected with others. The physical consequences of high terminal penetration have been the focus of concern particularly in large organizations that already have more than one terminal to every five employees.

8.7 THE COST OF SPACE

As with the control of document production and the quantification of white-collar productivity, the bottom line in spatial design is cost-effectiveness. Clearly the escalating cost of space itself has given the field of ergonomics its power and interest.

"There's quite a simple correlation, actually, between cost and concern," David Elowitz says. "When secretarial salaries began climbing, suddenly managers wanted to be able to quantify clerical output. Now there is the same urgency about space, so a lot of energy is going into finding solutions."

With population and demand for space increasing steadily, and with rents expected to climb some 30 percent over the next five years, floor space has become yet another scarce resource to be preserved and carefully managed. As the investments in office space, automation equipment, and personnel continue to absorb increasing chunks of a firm's budget, managers cannot afford to ignore these facets of the modern business environment.

To be competitive, today's company is compelled to make substantial capital investments in high-tech office equipment that promises a high return. The money and time spent on facilities design and management are as crucial to keeping productivity ahead of cost as the resources funneled into electronic equipment. At the same time, however, the outcome of such design efforts is more difficult to ascertain and quantify. Although most people are convinced that ergonomics cannot be simply ignored or dismissed, no one is sure exactly how the relationship between workers and their environment should be taken into account. What can and has been offered, however, are guidelines for making decisions based on factors pertaining to office ergonomics. From this point, each firm must make its own analysis of spatial and human relationships within the office environment.

QUESTIONS AND ANSWERS

Q. What is ergonomics?

A. Ergonomics is the study of a worker's interaction with his or her environment. It seeks to find a balance between worker productivity and efficiency within the workplace. It relates form and function.

Q. What does ergonomics have to do with office automation?

A. In the process of office automation, new machines and new tasks will be introduced to the office. Along with this development, a re-orientation of the layout, furniture, and interaction of the work space takes place. Conscious control of this process and its intended result is preferred over chance.

Q. What are special requirements to keep in mind?

A. Computers and other electronic equipment have a number of characteristics which need to be considered during the office design process. Computers generate considerable heat and have more complex power distribution and interconnect needs, and their video screens have ambient lighting requirements.

Sound, both in terms of generation and control, is another factor which requires attention.

Q. Why should one pay attention to these matters?

A. There are a myriad of reasons for thoughtful design of the work environment. Among these are employee satisfaction and efficiency, organizational productivity and flexibility, operating costs, and, in the case of space requirements, fixed costs. At issue here is an important component of an organization's competitive position.

9

Getting the Most out of the Vendor: Developing a Strategy for Equipping Your Office

Over 150 vendors compete aggressively for computer users' business, and jumping into this chaotic and rarely stable market can be intimidating. This chapter is designed to help you construct a systematic program to assess vendors and to save your firm from the pitfalls of systems incompatibility and unnecessary purchases of equipment. The vendor-approval process, from the initial information survey to the final framing of the contract, constitutes the first step in implementing a strategy for bringing modern automated equipment into your office. Operating successfully in the new environment is the second step toward getting the optimum results from your office automation strategy. Several case studies will be included to illustrate options and pitfalls for different types of companies.

9.1 APPROVING THE VENDORS

In order to implement an office automation strategy that is consistent with the principles of integration stressed in Chapter 3, many large companies have resorted to the tactic of creating an approved-vendor list. Essentially, this list includes all the vendors that the company will turn to when it needs to purchase any piece of office automation equipment from mainframe computers to personal computers, from telecommunications networks to specific software applications. The purpose of such a list is to render the product selection process manageable given the huge and bewildering array of products currently on the market. By restricting purchases to several product lines, vendor support can be better assured, product compatibility can be guaranteed, and the purchasing process itself can be accelerated. Companies with approved-vendor lists increase their clout with their "vendors of choice" and gain some control over the multi-vendor environment.

The process of initially establishing the approved-vendor list requires some lead time. The company must undertake a systematic process of "playing the field." The company as a user and potential purchaser of office automation equipment lets its intentions be known to suppliers or vendors of that equipment. Vendors then court the user, attempting to get on—or stay on—the user's approved-vendor list.

The practice of establishing and working from a list of approved vendors has become widespread in the last few years. A majority of the Fortune 500 companies already have such lists, and a sizable portion of the smaller companies have begun to follow suit. Currently, three out of four large companies use lists for purchasing word-processing equipment and microcomputers. Among medium-sized companies (defined as those with over 100 employees but not in the Fortune 1000) 40 percent make their purchases from approved-vendor lists. Similarly, one-fourth of the small companies (those with at least ten employees and fewer than 100) employ approved-vendor lists.

Given the common use of the vendor list, the user or purchaser really has only three options: to use the list to mandate purchases, to use the list merely to recommend purchases, or not to use a list at all and simply ignore purchases. If a company chooses to create an approved-vendor list, some central functional group will have to bear the responsibility for establishing the list. An obvious candidate for this task is the MIS department. Relative to other departments in the company, the MIS department is likely to have a better technical knowledge of the products available and a broader knowledge of the needs of the company as a whole at least from an automated systems perspective.

Mandated purchases of personal computers provide all the benefits of centralized control and are on the upswing. Future integration is facilitated best by up-front compatibility screening. The mandate strategy assures compatibility, while the recommendation strategy advocates—but does not guarantee—compatibility. Given the accumulated evidence, a company will be pushing its luck to plan some form of integration and yet ignore the acquisition process. The process of establishing an approved-vendor list requires staff time and money, but companies initiate an approval process for a good reason. Vendor approval allows the user to achieve optimal satisfaction under all the various criteria for purchases that are established throughout the organization. In short, the vendor-approval process works hand in hand with the broader strategy to achieve integrated information processing (as discussed in Chapter 3).

9.2 THE PLAYERS IN THE APPROVAL PROCESS

There are really only three major groups involved in establishing the approval process: the users who must establish the approved-vendor list, the vendors who seek inclusion on the list, and the consultants who advise the users on how to select vendors and advise the vendors on how to be selected. With users taking the initiative in the vendor list trend, the vendors will undoubtedly be eager to join in the approval process. Vendors will have to reorganize their priorities so that, rather than generating immediate sales, getting onto the approved-vendor list should become a paramount marketing objective. Vendors who want to survive in today's marketplace have no real choice in the matter. There are four types of vendors under consideration: hardware manufacturers, software houses, service bureaus, and computer supply companies.

Hardware manufacturers are at the greatest risk. In the process of equipment design, all the major issues of product compatibility must be resolved. In addition to the manufacturers' selling directly to the user, this group includes original equipment manufacturers (OEMs) who sell other manufacturers' equipment. Original equipment manufacturers who sell directly to users, distributors, or dealers naturally play a direct role in courting users.

Software houses may not play a visible role for the user in the approval process. Nonetheless, they will certainly be working behind the scenes. Software houses design their products to be compatible with selected hardware. As the use of approved-vendor lists increases, the hardware vendors selected by software houses for compatibility are sure to correspond to the approved-vendor lists established by users.

Typically, service bureaus are processing users' data for standard business functions, such as payroll, accounts payable, and fixed assets. However, the data output of service bureaus often becomes input to the users' in-house equipment for further processing and for creating customized management reports. Therefore, the service bureaus will certainly be affected by the vendor approval process.

Manufacturers of such specialized computer supplies as ribbons, paper, and floppy disks also have to concern themselves with the results of the approval process. They, too, would suffer if they manufactured supplies for the equipment of an unapproved vendor.

Both users and vendors employ the services of systems consultants. It is common for a user to hire an outside consultant to study vendor offerings in relation to user needs and then to recommend vendor finalists in the selection process. Given many consulting firms' experience in this role, users are sure to take increasing advantage of this expertise as the approval process becomes more crucial to an overall office automation strategy.

Knowing that consultants have a wealth of information about the user environment, vendors are also more eager to use outside consultants. In fact, The Omni Group's multi-client TechTrends study was initiated by vendors. By analyzing vendor standings among users, the study reveals what prompts users to put particular vendors on their lists. The vendors that participated in that study now use those results to gain leverage with users in the approval process.

There are three basic reasons why clients call upon consultants for assistance: the client lacks expertise in a specialized area; staff trained to study the specialized area are unavailable; or the client is unable to decide between two or more internally generated solutions. Any of these three blocks can surface during the approval process, so that, rather than being called in on the basis of case-by-case acquisitions, consultants will participate throughout the full term of the vendor selection process in most cases.

9.3 SELECTION CRITERIA

William Allen, the vice-president of a California engineering firm, pinpoints four basic criteria for selection in the multi-vendor environment: performance, price, support, and compatibility. This list is surprisingly succinct. Any of the detailed criteria for hardware or software selection that industry experts have invented can be assigned to one of these four basic headings. Laying out the relationships among these four criteria is thus essential to understand why and how companies establish approved-vendor lists.

Performance versus price is the most familiar trade-off in equipment selection. Better performance is generally accompanied by a higher price. Given this relationship, price and performance are weighed against each other using a standard cost-benefit analysis. The cost elements in the analysis are easy to identify. Expenditures result from the purchase of hardware and software, personnel costs, and operation costs. On the other hand, the benefits of better systems performance are more difficult to identify. Generally, benefits can be classified under three separate categories: cost savings from reductions in processing or operating costs attributable to the new system, operational improvements such as faster processing and more timely access to data, and unquantifiable or intangible benefits such as improved customer relations. If cost-benefit analysis is used on a case-by-case basis, a different vendor might be selected every time. As a result, the price-performance trade-off for any specific application would be maximized by shopping from the most diverse buffet of vendor products.

Both support and compatibility, on the other hand, can be simultaneously maximized; they are complementary attributes rather than substitutes. The objective of the approval process is to narrow the field of possible vendors to those offering compatible products. This endeavor increases the relative importance of the user company as a client to the approved vendors. Thus, the vendor is likely to offer higher quality support to the user. Large companies select primary vendors because they offer a system of worldwide compatibility. To protect its stake as the company's primary vendor, the vendor of choice can be expected to provide a high level of product support in the frequently difficult conversion to the new system.

A recent research study indicates that the four basic selection criteria differ in relative importance to users. The study shows that, of the four, vendor support is cited as the most important selection criterion, regardless of company size. Compatibility, the study indicates, leads the other three vendor criteria in large and medium-sized companies, followed by price and then performance. Small companies, however, rank price immediately after vendor support in the hierarchy of criteria. It might be argued that for small firms, price is more important because capital constraints are tighter.

The two criteria most frequently cited as important, support and compatibility, are maximized when product purchases are mandated by the organization as a whole. Therefore, the use of an approved-vendor list is the best way to ensure support and compatibility. While the results of attention to compatibility and vendor support are obvious to the user in the trenches, the responsibility for them rests in the overall corporate relationship with vendors. The global reverberations of the vendor selection process highlight the importance and benefits of a centralized mandate of approved vendors.

Performance criteria, which are not always maximized through the use of approved vendors, are optimized by application-specific purchases. But performance seems to be less important to users. Users recognize that performance can often only be maximized at the risk of losing compatibility with other users in the organization. If taken to its logical conclusion, maximizing the performance criterion for every project might result in a different vendor for practically every user in the organization. There are almost enough vendors to make that possible. Obviously, with dozens of vendors supporting different products throughout the organization, vendor attention would be so scattered that vendors would not be able to provide adequate support for all the users.

Price, on the other hand, is a criterion which can often be maximized as a result of the list-forming process and the vendor response. As the company restricts its vendor representation to a few approved vendors, its eligibility for volume discounts grows, and vendors increase buying incentives. In the long run, the magnitude of these discounts could very well outstrip the aggregate, short-run discounts of application-specific price shopping.

9.4 CONDUCT OF THE APPROVAL PROCESS

The approval process is distinguished from case-by-case vendor selection in one important way: it takes an organizationwide, rather than an application specific, perspective. In most respects, the approval process is an aggregation of application specifications to the highest level possible, at which point vendors are evaluated according to their abilities to meet user demand both individually and in concert with other vendors.

A centralized systems staff should be responsible for aggregating application specifications. Regardless of whether central or departmental staff are used to collect the necessary specifications, a centralized staff should be responsible for evaluating the collected data and transforming the individual pieces into a cohesive group of specifications that defines the organization's global systems needs.

Only a centralized department can maintain the expert staff needed to conduct this in-house review and, in turn, to deal with the vendors. To exploit the benefits of centralization, this department's responsibilities should include both office automation and data-processing applications. This will ensure that the organization does not duplicate efforts in collecting specifications and in evaluating vendors.

9.5 WEIGHING THE SELECTION CRITERIA

Clearly, the importance of the four basic criteria used to evaluate vendors varies from department to department and from company to company. This suggests that a weighting scheme should be devised for the overall ranking of vendors, in addition to the individual evaluations of support, compatibility, price, and performance.

Rather than using a predetermined formula for this weighting process, it is best to solicit user input and devise an internal weighting scheme appropriate to the company and its overall goals. Weights can be derived from the results of an internal user survey. The information gathered in the following subsections is derived from a research study undertaken by The Omni Group.

9.5.1 Vendor Support

It is important in appraising vendor support that the user company be realistic in judging both its leverage with vendors and the tremendous variation in support levels among the vendors. Vendor support will be highest from an approved multi-vendor combination that synthesizes the advantages of user leverage and support-minded vendors.

This combination may involve some compromises, for the user may have the least leverage with vendors known for the best support. IBM, for example, is widely cited for providing excellent support, but small users could obviously increase their purchasing leverage by dealing with a smaller vendor. The user should take advantage of the approval process to build a vendor list that balances this critical trade-off between user leverage and vendor support.

The user's leverage with a vendor is an essential element to the evaluation of that vendor. The user has greater bargaining clout with a small vendor that wants to penetrate the user's industry. For this reason many users have leaned toward smaller vendors. The buyer should beware, however, that small vendors are vulnerable in a booming market, and some will not survive the industry shakeout. Of course, the large user ready to make a significant purchase is in the fortunate position of holding a good deal of bargaining clout with any vendor, large or small.

In addition to making this assessment of its leverage, the user should consider the different levels of support that are typical of vendors representing various distribution channels. Essentially, purchases can be made from any one of three types of dealers: the direct sales force of a vendor, a distributor that specializes in the product of a certain vendor, or a retail store. Obviously, the vendor's direct salesperson is in an ideal position to make a firm commitment for product support. The salesperson has a first-hand knowledge of your account, knows your operation, and is acquainted with your needs. As a direct representative of the vendor, the salesperson represents a large organization that must support the users of its product and provide maintenance. Distributors are one step removed from the vendor, but they generally offer only a limited range of products, and so they tend to be fairly well versed in the operation of these products. Therefore, one should expect a high level of support from distributors. The retail store is still further removed from the original vendor, but nevertheless it maintains a staff devoted to repair and maintenance. Because the retail store is likely to be chosen for its convenient location, users can take advantage of its storefront operation to get quick service and to purchase add-on features.

Within any particular distribution channel, there are additional variations in vendor support that the user can best evaluate only by consulting other users. The process of checking out user references can be done best in an on-site visit to other users of the same distributor. In addition, visiting some users other than those names offered by the vendors can yield some beneficial information. Exhibit 9.1 lists some questions that are helpful in evaluating vendor or distributor support of a typical software package.

Exhibit 9.1
Evaluating Vendor or Distributor Support

Typical questions to ask other users about a software package:

1. When was the package installed?
2. How long did it take to get the package up and producing?
3. What are your experiences with the vendor's service department?
4. How is the documentation?
5. What in-house modifications were required?
6. How much assistance did the vendor supply?
7. How could or should the package be improved?
8. What is the overall performance and throughput level?

9.5.2 Product Compatibility

There is no universal definition of compatibility, and the fact that not all vendors are even striving for compatibility underlines the challenge the user faces in the multi-vendor environment. There are few standards in the contemporary computer industry, and companies often rely on the telecommunications sector of the industry to provide hardware attachments that will allow incompatible products to operate within the same network.

However, the worst may be over. Most computer manufacturers admit that they are concerned about compatibility and claim a variety of methods that already allow for some interface.

Some general guidelines for compatibility can be put forward even while recognizing that specific definitions may vary from user to user based on broad differences in a company's office automation strategy and on specific departmental needs. First, it is not only important that the machines be compatible in the sense that they can be connected, but it is also beneficial to choose vendors that offer some sort of support compatibility. Some vendors manufacture high quality products but have rigid rules which restrict support for interfaces with other vendors' products. Some vendors have procedures to identify problems with their own product that work fine when the product stands alone but fall apart when the product is attached to others. Another problematic area in product support results from installing one vendor's software on another vendor's hardware. Most software vendors are very specific about which machines can support their product and which ones can't.

Problems with hardware and software compatibility can be classified into one of three general areas. First, the software operating mode may not operate under a given hardware architecture. For instance, a menu-driven program may require a touch-screen or a mouse which is not offered by the hardware manufacturer. Second, the software may require the use of special function keys which do not exist on the keyboard. Third, some software applications may not operate under the hardware manufacturer's operating system.

9.5.3 Price

Purchasing directly from the manufacturer usually brings the most favorable price for the user. The logic is simple: the direct sales force represents the manufacturer, and without the middleman the vendor should be able to offer the lowest price. Furthermore, because the large corporate accounts are critical to vendors, centralized large-volume purchases provide an important bargaining chip in negotiations with both hardware and software vendors.

When comparing prices for vendor approval, it is useful to obtain unbundled prices where available. Unbundled prices are per-component prices which, when aggregated, provide a configuration cost. Unbundled prices are critical in the vendor-approval process because the prices of main system components rather than of total configurations will be compared. Vendor approval does not evaluate specific configurations because the approval process is a periodic comparison of vendor prices for selected basic system components that the company has or needs. This point must be stressed because vendors, for competitive reasons, usually avoid providing component prices unless they are specifically asked. Some vendors, particularly in software, follow a policy of bundled pricing. If a vendor has a bundled pricing policy, the user can expect less flexibility from that vendor once the vendor becomes approved.

9.5.4 Performance

Hardware performance is typically compared in terms of rated speeds. These ratings are based on the average speed of the central processor in executing a typical mix of instructions. In evaluating processing speed, however, it is critical to remember that since many business data applications are input-output bound, the speed of input-output hardware may often determine the rate at which each application may be processed. This means that the performance abilities of the main processor of a super microcomputer, minicomputer, or mainframe computer configured with a separate input-output processor must be evaluated differently from those of a central processor that runs the same input-output hardware. Typically, separate processors for input-output hardware improve performance speeds and, as such, add points to a vendor's rating.

Two popular methods of comparing performance are the benchmark problem and the mathematical model. Both methods should reflect the organizational requirements laid out in the criteria for approving vendors. Application-specific comparison of approved vendors would later be made on a case-by-case basis.

Mathematical models are computer programs that simulate the performance of each proposed system relative to the complete processing requirements of the user. While mathematical models are commonly used in the evaluation of large-scale data-processing applications, a benchmark problem is probably a more useful tool in assessing office applications performance. A benchmark problem is a typical task that a new office system will be required to perform, such as remote editing capabilities on a document generated in a word-processing center. The vendor should be asked to provide a test site where the user can fully evaluate the benchmark problem.

To get to the point of testing performance, the company must develop a checklist of performance needs. Exhibit 9.2 provides an example of a grid used to evaluate the technical attributes of a hardware vendor's product. Exhibit 9.3 offers a checklist of considerations valuable for assessing software packages.

Exhibit 9.2
Technical Factors to Assess Hardware Performance

• *System Structure*

1. Bus: type, word size, bus clock, bus width, addressing range, transfer rate.

2. Processor: type, clock rate, instruction rate.

3. Memory: capacity, word size, access time.

• *Peripherals*

1. Disk Subsystem

   a. Disk controllers: type, number.

   b. Disk drives: type, number, storage capacity, average access time, transfer rate.

2. Tape Subsystem

   a. Tape Drives: type, number, storage capacity, read-write speed, rewind speed.

3. Printers: type, speed.

4. Workstations: type, functional capabilities, processing ability.

- *Communications*

1. Serial line multiplexors, I/O processor, line controllers, ports (type and number), lines supported, bits per character, framing, parity, speed, maximum number devices supported.

- *Local Area Network Support*

1. Bus or ring: data transfer rate.

2. Tree or star: Network interface processor, number of networks supported, stations per network.

- *Software*

1. Operating system: type, resource sharing system, print spooling system.

2. Languages supported.

Source: Richard Haines, Arch Associates.

Exhibit 9.3
Software Evaluation Checklist

1. Specify what the package needs to do to solve the problem and what specific features the package needs to have. List hardware and operating system capabilities, file sizes, and run times.

2. List required reports, file contents, inquiry capabilities, report generators, database file structures (if applicable), and any other desirable features.

3. Specify required arithmetic capabilities. If you are looking at a payroll package, for example, make sure it meets with federal, state, and local tax regulations. If the package must run both on the mainframe and smaller computers or multiple-mainframe, state that requirement.

4. Describe hardware needs, including possible conversions.

5. Note any desired high-level programming language interfaces, program design and construction standards, documentation needs, service code availability, recovery/backup capabilities, transaction logging and auditing facilities, and security provisions.

6. Write down file architecture, processing or turnaround constraints (response time).

Source: Dan Kamoji, Systems Standards Analyst.

9.6 INFORMATION SOURCES

In the user's quest for information on vendor support, price, compatibility, and performance, the numerous publications that specialize in rating information systems products and software are the best places to start. Auerbach and Datapro offer possibly the widest variety of systems evaluation services. These two subscription services have long been known for comprehensive reporting on new data-processing products and have more recently applied their expertise to office systems products.

The Auerbach and Datapro publications offer product-to-product comparisons and some vendor background information. The services are provided in the form of a basic starter volume such as Auerbach's *Microworld* or Datapro's *Automated Office Solutions*. These volumes are periodically updated with new product information sent to the subscriber for an annual fee. While these publications do not provide all of the information needed to complete the technical grid for performance comparison described above, they do offer enough data to get rough comparisons—particularly on price and performance.

Other good sources of technical evaluations are the trade journal buyer's guides. An example is *The Office* magazine's annual "Buyer's Guide to Word Processors." The *Computerworld* magazine has taken this concept a step further by offering a series of product-specific reference guides which are published on a regular basis throughout the year—for example, the *Computerworld* "Buyer's Guide to Computer Systems" and the *Computerworld* "Buyer's Guide to Terminals and Peripherals."

9.7 TAKING THE NEXT STEPS

After making preliminary comparisons from the published product evaluations, direct contact with the vendors should be established. The first step is a request for technical brochures to supply the detailed technical grid information unavailable from published sources. This is the best method of getting the details without arousing the vendor's interest. Until the field is narrowed, it is best to avoid contact by phone or in person. Personal contact usually prompts the vendor to push for a sales call, a time-consuming activity at such an early stage in the selection process. When the vendor brochures have been thoroughly digested, the user has enough knowledge to create a list of vendor finalists. These finalists will compete for positions on the approved-vendor list. The process of filing user requests and the submission and evaluation of vendor proposals will be the subject of the next section.

9.8 DEALING WITH THE VENDORS: RFPs, PROPOSALS, AND CONTRACTS

Critical vendor distinctions emerge after the list of vendor finalists has been compiled and the user initiates vendor contact. Because vendors are competing seriously to survive the predicted industry shakeout, users will find it absolutely essential to work from a list of vendor finalists. If the vendor search is not limited, users will suffer paralysis by analysis.

Vendors are promoting their product aggressively but not always informatively. There was a time when vendors would speak only to the data-processing director in a large firm. These days vendors have undertaken mass marketing campaigns on an unprecedented scale. They have even taken to advertising on TV and radio. Despite all the coverage, the vendors do not seem to be differentiating themselves through their advertising. Even an office automation consultant can have a difficult time telling the products apart solely from their advertising. Every vendor promises the same thing to the user and claims that none of the other products has the features that his does.

Vendor contact gives the user a chance to sort out the different products and to catch the distinctions among the products. The user's opportunity to scrutinize the vendors of choice comes in three stages of vendor contact: making the request for proposal (RFP), critiquing the vendor proposal and presentation, and cutting the contract.

9.8.1 Making the RFP: Form, Content, and Submission

The RFP is critical because it essentially sets the limits for information gained in further vendor contact. The vendor's proposal and presentation should address the user's needs as set out in the RFP, and any eventual contract will build from requirements stipulated in the original request. The content, form, and submission of the RFP are therefore crucial.

The content of the RFP should be developed according to the four selection criteria: support, compatibility, price and performance. In the RFP the user should request background information about the vendor to formulate an impression of the vendor's support potential, including the vendor's familiarity with the user's industry. Questions concerning the size and solvency of the vendor may also be asked. This financial history can be requested in the form of quarterly sales results and annual reports. In addition, getting data on the location and capacity of the vendor's maintenance facilities as well as the vendor's current position in any litigation can be valuable. Specifically, the RFP can ask directly whether the vendor is a defendant in any lawsuit where the damages sought by the plaintiff exceed a half million dollars.

Compatibility issues can also be explored as part of the company background information. In addition to probing a vendor's compatibility within its own product line, it is important that the RFP address compatibility with products from other vendors. The user will then have the opportunity to discover whether the vendor is trying to sell only one product or offering different products and options that are compatible within a larger framework.

One surefire clue to product compatibility can be gained by looking at the spate of mergers, acquisitions, and joint ventures that have recently occurred in the vendor industry. Vendors are discovering that users want complete systems to solve specific problems. IBM is a leader in the trend toward using ownership in other vendors to gain compatibility; for example, IBM now owns 19.1 percent of Rolm Corporation, the chipmaker. Control Data, NCR, Sperry, and Western Union have joined IBM in the ranks of vendors buying into other vendors.

If price is a consideration, it should be noted as a high priority in the RFP, but the user's specific budget constraints should not be mentioned. If the user discloses specific budgetary constraints, the vendor will be prone to fit the system to the budget rather than to the needs.

The RFP can, however, target the desirability of leasing versus buying. The outcome of a lease-versus-purchase decision will depend on the best deal the vendor can arrange, and this deal should be based on the priority of the user's particular cash and tax benefit needs. A product leasing arrangement can provide the user with an opportunity to get the job done with a minimum of cash expenditure, to meet a need until the next budget cycle, or to take advantage of tax deductions.

Performance specifications have traditionally formed the heart of the RFP and are probably the requests with which the vendor feels most comfortable. For the purposes of the RFP it may be better to keep questions about performance specifications phrased in a more general manner (see Exhibit 9.4).

Exhibit 9.4
Example Inquiries on Performance

1. Does the vendor have any or all of the products (hardware or software) or services which can perform the user's critical information functions?

2. Can the vendor specify a quantified level of performance (maximum production turnaround time) for such products or services?

3. What does the vendor know about the performance experience of other users

of the product or service, the average expected up-time during normal usage, for instance?

Most experts agree that the RFP should be a written document, but no one has devised a standard format. A written RFP does have a clear advantage over oral interviews with vendors. The written request gives the user the chance to submit identical requests to all vendors—a process which will be helpful in later comparisons of proposals.

While the RFPs submitted to vendors should be identical, they may not necessarily be formal documents. An RFP could take the form of an informal letter. If a formal RFP looks too technical, a vendor may simply ignore it, particularly if it comes from a smaller operation. Finally, a user should not submit an RFP if it seems the project might not be undertaken. If a vendor is leery of your intentions, you might not get another bid when you become serious. The issue of credibility is not, however, as likely to arise in RFPs for the vendor-approval process, as it is in later case-by-case RFPs issued to approved vendors.

9.8.2 Critiquing the Vendor Proposal and Presentation

In accepting proposals for evaluation the user should adhere to the deadline set out in the RFP. Vendors should take no longer than two weeks to respond to the initial RFP. For this reason, the RFP should not demand more than the vendor can respond to within a reasonable amount of time. The user can send a follow-up letter of greater detail to those vendors that respond. The lack of a vendor's timely response to an RFP tells the user a lot about the vendor, and, normally, the vendor's failure to respond should prompt the user to remove the vendor from further consideration.

Once all the final proposals are in, the user should evaluate them according to the firm's priorities. At this stage the vendor's response should be evaluated in the context of the priorities expressed in the RFP. Budget and time are almost always important, but it is up to the user to decide the priorities given his or her company's particular situation.

The user should form a vendor evaluation team composed of several specialists to critique the vendors' proposals and presentations. The team should have the participation of a technician, an accountant, and an attorney. The technician, who could be an outside consultant, can provide input on the best available products to resolve users' technical needs. The accountant is equipped to evaluate the relative merits of various acquisition methods. For instance, the accountant can help decide whether leasing or buying is more advantageous or whether used equipment, with the combination of a lower break-even point and a generally higher price-performance ratio, is preferable to new equipment. The attorney should be on the team to provide legal opinions and to draft documents.

After the proposals are examined, the entire team should attend each presentation. In this way the salesperson's claims can be compared with those made in the vendor's proposal and with information provided by proposals received from other vendors. The team can then ask questions that compare and contrast the vendor's product or service with those of its competitors.

The vendor's responses to questions during the presentations are prime clues in the evaluation process. The amount of information vendors are willing to provide may indicate how well they will support the product. This guideline holds for technical information as well. The vendor should be forthcoming in response to the user's technical questions. After all, once a vendor becomes approved, a close cooperative relationship between user and vendor will be necessary. The user should beware of such dodges as "that feature is coming out next month," "we can't worry about that right now," or "everything is explained in the manual."

9.8.3 Cutting the Contract

The final step in the selection process is the securing of a contract, which represents the opportunity to get the vendor's promises in writing. Without a contract the value of the approval process is negligible, since the user cannot force the vendor to perform. The computer contract as a performance agreement should define the expectations of both parties, how the expectations are to be implemented, and the consequences for failure to perform.

Three tricky issues in negotiating the contract call for special attention: legally coordinating multiple vendors, attaining corporate licenses for software, and finalizing the lease-versus-buy decision. Each of the vendors in a multiple-vendor project can be contractually required to warrant the compatibility of its products and to provide general maintenance for those products. In its warranty, special responsibility rests with the key vendor, which usually establishes a tie-in with the junior vendor. This makes it fair to place the burden of "failure of performance" on the key vendor.

Corporate licenses for software are usually well worth the trouble of negotiating them. Although corporate software licenses are rare, a one-time $20,000 fee is a clear savings when contrasted with 100 copies of a $300 program.

With the last special negotiating issue, the lease-versus-purchase decision, there are three major considerations: the time value of money, taxes and depreciation (whether the user needs the investment tax credit and the write-offs that come with ownership), and product flexibility (leasing typically allows a user to escape from an agreement more quickly than the user can sell the equipment).

The signing of the contract marks the end of one phase of the implementation process and the beginning of the ongoing challenge to keep the system in step with the operational needs of the company. The next chapter discusses the mechanisms which can be used to ensure management control over the new environment.

QUESTIONS AND ANSWERS

Q. At what point in the office automation process does vendor selection enter?

A. At the very earliest stages, consideration should be given to narrowing the field to vendors you desire to work with and who wish to work with your organization. The goal is to increase the level of service for the buyer, the future role of the vendor, and the satisfaction of both parties.

Q. Who makes the selection?

A. The final decision rests with the user. What department or functional position makes the choice varies from organization to organization. A preferred vendor or vendor of choice list is often the means used in larger organizations.

Recent surveys performed by the Omni Group show that the decision process is often a tripartite one, with user, consultant, and vendor all participating.

Q. Are there different types of vendors?

A. Yes, four types may be characterized. These are hardware manufacturers, software houses, service bureaus, and computer supply companies.

Q. What role do consultants play?

A. Consultants can be utilized by either the vendor or the potential user during the selection process. With their specialized expertise and experience, consultants can and do play a crucial role.

Consultants note three basic reasons for their participation: The client lacks expertise in a specialized area; staff trained to study the specialized area are unavailable; or the client is unable to decide between two internally generated solutions.

Q. What are the criteria for vendor selection?

A. There are four basic and succinct criteria for selection: performance, price, support, and compatibility.

Others weigh price over performance in a cost-benefit analysis. This can, however, ignore the longer view and intangible factors of vendor support and vendor-user compatibility. In fact, an Omni Group study shows that support is the number one factor in the selection process, with the other three varying by company size and individual user.

Q. Is there a typical selection process?

A. There is no standardized formula which can be applied in a majority of cases. The process, to be successful, needs to be customized. However, one can state that companywide user input should be obtained and that the decision should be made with weighted consideration given to company needs.

Q. How does a user deal with a vendor?

A. Once again, there is no hard and fast methodology. One can isolate three distinct stages in the vendor contact process: making the request for proposal (RFP), critiquing the vendor proposal, and cutting the contract.

10

Operating in the Multi-Vendor Environment: Concepts and Case Studies

Once equipped with the hardware and software products of more than one vendor, a company is operating in the multi-vendor environment. Obviously, some companies manage this environment more successfully than others, and the single most important contribution to a company's success in this venture is the maintenance of a secure control management function. This chapter first describes the concepts of multi-vendor control and then takes a look at two companies in different stages of the climb toward control over the multi-vendor environment.

10.1 CONCEPTS OF MULTI-VENDOR CONTROL

The lack of control in the multi-vendor environment is attested to by the bad reputation attached to the term. Because a computer can often fit into a department manager's unsupervised discretionary budget, top managers need to devise a sensible means of making sure the company's computers start—or continue—talking to each other. There are five basic concepts surrounding the necessary control: the relationship between the technology of very-large-scale integration (VLSI) and computer proliferation, the benefits of distributed processing versus decentralized processing, the technical and organizational difficulties in achieving distributed processing, the multi-vendor solutions to technical problems, and the centralized solutions to the organizational problems.

10.2 VLSI AND PROLIFERATION

As a result of the mind-boggling performance of the integrated circuit industry, just about anyone can afford a computer. Every year since the integrated circuit industry began in 1960, the number of components per silicon chip has roughly doubled. In the last twenty years the cost of mainframe computers has decreased by a factor of 1,000. Minicomputers often reduce processing costs by an additional factor of five, and microcomputers can cut the cost of a job by another factor of 100. Thus the computer increasingly is being brought to the job rather than jobs being collected and run by an autonomous computer center. Significantly, computers are now economical to own even if they are not in use.

10.3 DISTRIBUTED PROCESSING VERSUS DECENTRALIZATION

The new proliferation of computers raises the issue of the optimum level of decentralization of each company's information processing. If a firm strives for complete decentralization, then every department manager can outfit his or her own department with computers according to the department's specific needs. The process is similar, for instance, to allowing each crew foreman in a large shop to purchase hand drills with special drill bits that can be interchanged depending on the job at hand. If every work crew on the shop floor has a different kind of hand drill, all tasks will get done, but each work crew will be dedicated to a single task.

If, on the other hand, a company wants to achieve distributed processing, equipment must be purchased according to some balance between the department's specific needs and the need to interface with central equipment and that of other departments. The company that wants distributed processing is not unlike the shop steward who saw the benefits of making sure his crews all possessed the same hand drills so that they could share the bits and perform a wide variety of specific tasks as needed.

10.4 TECHNICAL AND ORGANIZATIONAL PROBLEMS

The benefits of distributed processing are not easily achieved. As evidenced by the previous discussion of integrated software, distributed processing faces both technical and organizational barriers. Without a doubt the most significant contribution of VLSI has been to make distributed data processing feasible in a business setting. Nevertheless, distributed processing still faces technical challenges, particularly in systems design and programming, since hardware development has always preceded software development. In addition, the organizational problem of what information is held and processed locally and what gets sent to the home office still plagues many companies.

10.4.1 Multi-Vendor Solutions to Technical Problems

Because many vendors are now designing products that are compatible with other products on the market, vendor competition is becoming more intense. Still, increased vendor compatibility and vendor competition are creating solutions to the technical obstacles to distributed processing. VLSI and heavy vendor competition have led to the introduction of distributed processing systems composed of plug-compatible products. Obviously, the wider choice of compatible products means that the user can now package a multi-vendor system that meets its business needs.

Companies can take advantage of vendor compatibility to consolidate control over the acquisition process. The corporate strategy to accomplish this has been described in detail in the previous chapter. In the past, when most products were standalones, users were more limited by vendors than by products actually on the market. Firms tended to vacate the responsibility of decision-making and to rely on the supposedly expert vendor. But today, as has been pointed out, the user can create clout by dealing with several vendors.

10.4.2 Centralized Solutions to the Organizational Problems

The organizational problem in distributed processing can only be solved through some measure of centralized planning and control. Competitive strategy theory supports the argument that users can increase their leverage over vendors by dealing with more than one. Competitiveness does not ensure compatibility, however. Global systems compatibility can only be achieved through the use of an approved-vendor list. The key to the operational success of such a list is that it is maintained by some centralized office and not by individual departments.

Given the current trend toward decentralized processing, centralization is practically anathema. Distributed processing is a more acceptable term because it connotes a movement away from centralization. The term is not to be confused with decentralized processing, however. If a company wants the benefits of distributed processing, it has to allow the shop steward—and not the crew foremen—to oversee the shop.

Neither the existing technical nor organizational solutions have made management in the multi-vendor environment problem-free. Vendor competition and innovations in VLSI technology often bring technical headaches before technical relief. While some centralization of the management information services (MIS) function has been retained during most companies' decentralization moves, the office management function has almost always been dispersed. The organizational solution, by reining in the freedom of department managers to choose equipment, will therefore bring tension before relief. Nevertheless, the results are usually well worth the pain, as the two case studies that follow will illustrate.

10.5 A PHARMACEUTICAL COMPANY ON ITS WAY TO CONTROLLING THE MULTI-VENDOR ENVIRONMENT

The U.S. headquarters of a major Swiss pharmaceutical company is learning how to operate in the multi-vendor environment. The scope of this user's information processing requirements is broad and formidable, and the obstacles to its controlled distribution are intimidating. Located on a New Jersey campus, the massive headquarters complex of new office buildings and old facilities houses about seven divisions organized into over 100 departments. Although physically bounded and centralized, the departments operate autonomously with management functions decentralized.

Departmental information processing needs are as varied as the departmental functions. There are the numerous research departments which design experimental applications to test newly synthesized drugs for safety and effectiveness. Operating departments require automated control over drug mixtures and the blending process. Finally, specialized law departments use word-processing applications to speed and improve their communications with patent offices and regulatory bureaus.

Despite their decentralized structure, these departments need to communicate. The mixture requirements and experimental results formulated in the research labs have to be passed along to the operating and legal departments for calculation of the actual drug blends and for filing various reports on the new drugs. Similarly, new laboratory regulations and procedures must be passed from the legal department back to research and development. Preferably, all information traveling among departments in the pharmaceutical complex should be electronic, passed through a communications network, and managed by computer. The network would access a complete, up-to-date data base at the hub of the network. The cumbersome process of sharing hard-copy information would be eliminated. This scenario captures the ultimate goal of the company's office automation strategy.

The initial call for change came from the top. Top management was motivated by the high cost of the existing decentralized approach to managing information equipment. Department managers were competent in managing specialized staff and operations but did not possess the expertise to buy and manage information equipment.

Although managers chose to automate their departments in order to reap the expected benefits, lack of equipment expertise prevented the full benefit from being realized. They had often purchased equipment on the basis of gut feelings rather than systems analysis. As a result, departments accumulated a wide variety of equipment, most of which was incompatible with similar equipment in other departments. Because of this, when one department suffered an equipment outage or failure, there was no backup procedure available. With so many different vendors involved, the company had to rely on the various three-day standard training programs offered by the vendors. The company could not identify any primary vendors to justify the development of internal training programs.

The company began its information realignment with an executive order to create a department to control and manage business equipment throughout the company. This department's staff was responsible for developing standards and guidelines for compatibility and communications in the company's business equipment. The staff studied individual departments to assess needs and equipment inventory and to make recommendations to achieve the overall goals. To improve user training, this department also became responsible for developing an internal training program.

Progress has been made. The business equipment and services (BE&S) department established an approved-vendor list. From their departmental studies the BE&S staff identified a dozen vendors that were represented in the company. Based on the results of a needs analysis in the department under study, BE&S selected four primary vendors that would best provide specific application needs and ensure general compatibility.

The BE&S manager says his objective in selecting vendors was to "keep my customers satisfied, so I picked the vendors that had been most willing to hold the user's hand." One indication of this support was the vendor's record for customizing products to the company's specific needs. One of the vendors approved, the BE&S manager recalls, was "not considered an industry leader but had customized for us a chemical scientific text editor." Using these four vendors, BE&S set up compatibility guidelines for all the components in the vendor's product lines.

Based on the approved-vendor list, BE&S established programs for in-house training and a staff to provide internal equipment maintenance. Consistent with the company's customized vendor products, the in-house training programs were tailored to meet each department's specific needs. Such programs were a substantial improvement over the standard vendor offerings. Outside maintenance contracts were reduced as the internal service staff gained specialized expertise.

Even though the company has cleared the initial hurdles, further improvement opportunities exist. For one thing, BE&S should establish one department to control and manage all information equipment—BE&S has been given authority to oversee word-processing and typing equipment while the MIS department manages data-processing equipment.

The BE&S manager admits that there is little coordination between MIS and BE&S. A user in the diagnostics administration department says that as a result, "We're caught between MIS and BE&S, who don't talk to each other, and we don't know which department is responsible for helping us." If industry experts are no longer able to draw the line between word-processing (WP) and data-processing (DP) equipment, how, then, can these departments make the delineation?

The company should develop strategy and tactics for achieving compatibility and communications goals. In other words, this company knows it wants compatibility and networks but has not decided how to go about it. Some saw centralized optical character recognition (OCR) equipment as a mechanism for compatibility. Typing from department A was sent to the OCR center, department B, where it was converted for further processing in department C. While OCR can serve as an interim compatibility solution, direct communications between departments A and C would certainly be more efficient and a better fit with the company's organizational strategy which emphasizes a certain degree of departmental autonomy.

The company should use the approved-vendor list as a control mechanism (BE&S had not aggressively controlled acquisitions). Departments were not always notified of the approved-vendor list and unknowingly submitted requests for nonapproved vendors. Other department managers simply ignored the approval process and used discretionary budgets to build isolated equipment empires. A user in the general law department concluded that the approval procedures made it "too easy to buy low-end equipment," when higher-priced equipment could have been justified "from a productivity standpoint."

Given the product leeway provided by the company's list of four vendors, department managers should be restricted to acquisitions from approved vendors. Of course, there will be unusual circumstances where a study of additional vendors is warranted. In these cases, the acquiring department should justify the purchase of any incompatible equipment and be "fined" for any traceable incompatibility costs. The benefits of training and maintenance should also be promoted to encourage compliance with the approved-vendor list.

10.6 AN OIL COMPANY IN CONTROL OF THE MULTI-VENDOR EQUIPMENT

In connection with the relocation of its home office, an international oil company prepared to achieve worldwide compatibility among all of its facilities. The plan involved more than 70 subsidiaries operating in over 60 countries. With locations as diverse as Bahrain and South Africa, the company wanted worldwide headquarters and each office tied into the same 24-hour network linked to the petroleum market.

The key to reaching this goal was, again, the centralization of fairly decentralized information systems. Centralized switching was essential to provide a 24-hour communications cable that could run a batch packeting system complete with video security and voice messaging.

But the company had a long way to go before these changes could be implemented. There were 22 different filing systems in operation simultaneously, and each new departmental manager designed a new filing system with no attention to those already in existence. Simply by setting up a consistent filing system for use throughout the organization, the company, with the aid of outside consultants, cut the number of paper files by about 60 percent.

Although there were major obstacles, the company did possess one decided advantage: it was primarily a one-vendor organization. In addition, an acquisition policy was carefully conceived and carried out. Even though their primary vendor offered one of the few well-integrated network systems, the company considered other vendors as well. For example, the vendor of choice was not represented in South Africa. So, rather than attempt to operate without a local vendor, the company opted to use another vendor, trading some loss in compatibility to optimize vendor support. Using selected subsidiary offices, the company tested the primary vendor's system. To further evaluate the integration of these products as well as those of other vendors' systems, the company's implementation team visited at least a dozen test sites where the various systems operated in other corporate environments.

Following a vendor selection process, which analyzed their past relationship with their primary vendor and the costs and benefits of switching, the company elected to stay with the original vendor. The systems used to make the evaluation were only test systems with no guarantees, but the knowledge that the primary vendor already had a lot invested in the company was tantamount to a warranty.

Because there were no guarantees, the vendor of choice concentrated the use of management's funds on backup systems to make the conversion virtually fail-safe. Two identical central batch packeting systems were installed in the new headquarters. Although it cost the oil company more to run the two systems simultaneously during the conversion, management considered it a worthwhile investment to minimize the risk of losing data or contact with any of the worldwide locations.

Another important element considered in the relocation was attention to staff needs. In this case, management was prepared to provide the support and funds needed to make the conversion work. First, it appointed a team of high-level functional managers to oversee the move and conversion. Then it gave the human resources manager great leeway to ease the transition. He was so successful in designing relocation incentive plans that over 85 percent of the existing staff pulled up their stakes and accompanied the corporation to its new headquarters 1,500 miles away.

Today, the company is established in its new home office that houses the central processing units for the worldwide communications network. Matching its success in solving the technical and organizational problems of relocation, the company has achieved impressive results in the realm of office design as well. A visitor to the new headquarters is immediately impressed with the way ergonomics and efficient work-flow designs have been incorporated into the elegance of reception rooms that display art from all over the world.

In fact, the company has a lot to be proud of. All of its worldwide systems are integrated and working. They have achieved the 24-hour coverage that they strived for and, as their reward, the competitive edge in their industry.

QUESTIONS AND ANSWERS

Q. What are problems encountered in the multi-vendor environment?

A. Lack of control is the biggest problem encountered by companies that operate with more than one vendor. The largest factor contributing to the success of a firm operating in this environment is a secure control management function.

Q. What approaches or concepts can be brought to bear?

A. Five concepts can be utilized when examining a company's status and proposed course of action. These basic concepts surrounding the necessary control are the relationship between the technology of very-large-scale integration (VLSI) and computer proliferation, the benefits of distributed processing versus decentralized processing, the technical and organizational difficulties in achieving distributed processing, the

multi-vendor solutions to technical problems, and the centralized solutions to the organizational problems.

Case studies are an additional means to arrive at an optimum course
of action.

11

Staffing and Training the Office of the 1980s

11.1 THE OFFICE REVOLUTION AND THE STAFF OF THE FUTURE

The technological revolution that is creating the office of the 1980s leaves no aspect of the modern business untouched. From the machines themselves, to the space they occupy, to the staff who run the office, no stone has been left unturned. The staff that has been adequate since the 1870s, when the typewriter was first introduced, are now seeing their skills become outdated. Managers and executives, who in the past simply delegated computer responsibility to "techies," are now facing automation on their very desktops. The implications of this penetration for staffing and training procedures are phenomenal. During the next decade 80 percent of the white-collar work force will have to be retrained. How each business can deal with this situation is the subject of this chapter.

11.1.1 Computer Use in the 1980s

If there is any doubt left as to what the trends are, the facts should convince even the most stubborn entrepreneurs. In the first place, the proportion of staff members, both in secretarial and managerial positions, who are using electronic machines is expanding by leaps and bounds. On the average, about half the support staff use office computers today. Significantly, the same firms have between two-thirds and three-fourths of their staff operating personal computers (PCs). For managers and professionals the figures are not so startling, but the trend is still clear. While only about a third of those in this category now operate computers, over half are expected to do so within a year. In addition, the number of companies in which only a select group (less than 20 percent) has computer access is dropping rapidly.

11.1.2 Changing Job Descriptions

When translated, these figures paint a picture of substantial penetration and, as a result, a probable overhaul of existing job categories. For instance, once a word-processing center is established, other secretaries are free to take on responsibilities other than document production. Nearly two-thirds of the firms that have secretaries using PCs indicate that their secretaries are now spending more time on higher level tasks. Some of these tasks involve traditional administrative functions, but, more and more, managers are delegating professional tasks to support personnel who are trained to run various software programs on PCs. Over two-thirds of the companies surveyed reported that, collectively, many accounting, database management, spreadsheet analysis, and graphics tasks are being entrusted to nonmanagement personnel.

"What we're trying to get our support staff to realize," says Marilyn Calvert, manager of administrative services at Sencorp in Cincinnati, "is that office machines open doors for them. Here we have all these secretaries worrying about being replaced and dehumanized by the machine, but really it allows them to do more things."

As shifting tasks become permanent, more companies are finding old job titles and descriptions inadequate. A majority of firms indicate that their job qualifications are undergoing substantial changes. Soon, over one-third of these firms expect computer skills to be required in virtually all positions. Already, firms that have begun the office automation process are noting shortages in personnel who have the requisite computer skills, and many firms are now relying more heavily on temporary employees.

11.1.3 Staffing New Jobs

To this problem and to the general upheaval in the office, there are various ways to react. A firm can try to hire people who are well versed in the new skills, but there are no assurances on the open market. Well-qualified people are rare and expensive, and they enter a new firm knowing nothing about the business. To compound the difficulty of the hiring process, the structure of the labor market has changed dramatically over the last few years. More than half of the American women are now working, most of them in white-collar jobs. But expanded managerial options for today's women mean that skilled support staff are harder to find. These facts and figures point to the importance of training within a company's overall strategy.

Any training program will have plenty of obstacles to overcome. For one thing, convincing nonusers that computers will enhance and simplify their job is not always an easy task. Managers in particular continue to express fears and doubts about the usefulness of computers to their jobs. Many seem to be confused by computer command structures and baffled by software programs. Negative attitudes toward computer use also focus on work quality considerations, such as boredom, loss of creativity, or lack of human interaction.

On the other side of the coin, however, most managers seem to feel that learning is worth the effort and that the time saved using a computer will outweigh the time spent mastering it. More present computer users express enthusiasm about the benefits of automation than do nonusers. One clue to be derived from this information is that the more exposure people have to computers, the more favorable their outlook toward them becomes. As Jim Cunningham, vice-president of corporate human resources at GAF Corp., notes, "My feeling is that most of the general alienation stems from a simple resistance to change. Sometimes you have to switch the usual process and get people to learn before they'll finally accept." Since the concept of the automated office has already been generally accepted, at least on the company level, it only makes sense to spend some time and energy on the micro level in educating and training workers to actually participate in the new program.

"As far as I'm concerned, the hot topic for this decade is not networking or parallel processing or artificial intelligence, but training," asserts Charles Mitchell, publisher of *Office Systems '85*. "If you can't get people to actually use the stuff, who cares how sophisticated the applications get?"

11.2 CREATING TRAINING PROGRAMS

Training objectives have both general and specific facets to them. For this reason, it is usually advisable to break employees into distinct training groups. Thus, while it may be a general goal to achieve companywide computer literacy, professionals need to use different software applications than do secretaries. Similarly, a training agenda should include a segment on business goals and the industry, but managers and support staff will view these goals from different perspectives. In this book, training has been subdivided into three categories: for secretaries, for professionals, and for the office automation (OA) management team which is overseeing the automation process.

Before the OA team can set up a training agenda, it must be clear what the purpose and implications of such a notion entail. The point of these programs is not to provide piecemeal instruction, but to create a holistic curriculum capable of building an integrated office unit. As the upheaval in the office has upset traditional relationships and procedures, employees need to be made comfortable in their new environment in order to work effectively.

Walter Kleinschrod, former editor-in-chief of *Administrative Management*, explains, "It's not just that staff members can't run spreadsheets or send electronic messages. Fundamentally, people are confused about what they're doing or even about what the company is doing. As long as office workers have to be trained in specific applications, there's a perfect opportunity to start the education process from scratch."

To this end, a training program should cover four distinct sets of activities or goals. First, it should take advantage of the overhaul of the office environment to offer remedial training in those traditional office skills which are still useful. Second, it should take care to reinforce existing office procedures and to educate workers about newly created ones. Third, it should deal with more abstract notions of business goals, departmental goals, and game plans. Finally, training must address the new technology, with both general computer education and specific operating instructions.

11.3 TRAINING SECRETARIES

Secretaries and secretarial tasks have been most directly affected by trends in the labor market as well as by office automation. These jobs are still filled predominantly by women, but the pool of available talent is shrinking as skilled women move to fill management and professional positions. At the same time, secretaries are usually the first office workers to be confronted by electronic machines and the first to have to adapt their jobs to them. With the need for new skills and with even the old skills in short supply, businesses have no choice but to invest in a substantial retraining venture.

"The importance of secretarial effectiveness cannot be overemphasized," says Edith Chance, word-processing manager at Ciba-Geigy in Greensboro, N.C., "You're not just talking about numbers of documents or phone calls. Without productive secretaries you're not going to have productive managers, so the running of the whole business is at stake."

11.3.1 Remedial Training

Although companies don't like to admit they may have hired support staff who can't spell or type, the problem exists. More and more managers are reporting dissatisfaction with skill levels of both applicants and employees, so that remedial programs are likely to be required for at least some staff members. Such programs should be designed to rapidly review language skills but not to provide in-depth elementary education. They should work on improving basic spelling, grammar and punctuation usage, as well as typing proficiency and telephone technique. In addition, secretaries should be coached in writing business letters, including format and style.

The key to devising a successful yet cost-effective program is to make it as nonthreatening and uninterruptive as possible. Edith Chance explains, "Even though this part of the retraining is the least complicated, you're likely to run up against a lot of resistance if you're too blunt. Signing workers up for Remedial Training 1A is not going to be good for morale." Although classroom instruction is an option, some innovative managers have put together worksheets which can be completed during lull periods. These exercises utilize otherwise wasted time while stimulating improved performance.

11.3.2 Office Procedures

Other than possessing the basic skills addressed above, clerical workers need to be proficient in coordinating all sorts of office-related activities. As secretaries have more professional tasks delegated to them and individual workstations become more self-sufficient, it is crucial to decentralize such paraprofessional skills as time management, task prioritization, and planning techniques. As with the basic tasks, none of these more sophisticated skills is new to the business world or unfamiliar to any good personnel department. First and foremost, the OA team is responsible for improving each employee's level of proficiency in the general area of work organization. "What's interesting about the revolution in office procedures is what has to be done to restore order," observes Sharon Canter of Manpower, Inc., "It's not just rewriting the manuals—it's reevaluating what basics are needed to make any procedures work."

Procedures which cover work organization contain elements of the old office and the new. Facilitating teamwork and developing interpersonal communication skills are traditional personnel objectives. Likewise, setting task priorities and allotting time to complete them have always been facets of administrative planning. Other advanced administrative procedures such as business report writing and spreadsheet formatting have enhanced secretarial duties to fill in gaps left by more efficient document production.

The rewriting of procedural manuals must accompany the redistribution of skills. Indeed, part of the training challenge is to get employees to apply the old skills to novel applications. For example, procedures regulating document production and retention must be adapted to conform to the company's distributed or centralized processing system. Likewise, some office tasks will have disappeared completely, others will take less time, and yet others will be newly created.

All of this transitional shifting must be eventually settled and standardized before the running of the office returns to normal. To achieve this end, each secretary should create a procedures book which outlines his or her daily, weekly, and monthly activities. An OA team's review of these books can lead to more formalized guidelines and written procedures, which can help to expedite and standardize instruction for temporary or new help. Such a book could act both as a training manual and as a monitor of performance.

As part of the general effort to improve coordination in the support staff, training in secretarial teamwork can counteract some of the dangers of isolated specialization. As many clerical jobs are broken down into separate components, more effective production can be derived from a team approach to handling departmental activities. The communication links opened between team members can ease the sharing of shortcuts and ensure the even distribution of workloads. "I've had incredibly positive feedback from secretaries assigned to teams," notes Marilyn Calvert. "At first they're afraid they'll lose their independence, but the satisfaction of working in a bigger picture seems to compensate."

11.3.3 Corporate Computer Literacy Program (CCL)

The skills described in the previous two sections are, in a sense, prerequisites to establishing a successful computer literacy program. Such a program should represent the culmination of the office automation process and the integration of all its human and technological components. As such, it involves much more than training on specific machines. Simply, CCL would seek to instruct workers at all levels and in all fields of information processing on how the automated office affects both their own positions and the objectives of the company as a whole. Phil Jones, editorial director of *Training* magazine, adds, "The concept of CCL represents, I think, the merging of various business trends—in attitudes as well as technology. On the one hand you have the simple problem of machines out there mystifying people. On the other, you have these new ideas of decentralization and worker participation."

11.3.4 Business and Departmental Training

To initiate workers into the big picture of company goals and auto-mation strategies, departmental workshops or focus groups can be given the task of defining their own functions. Caught in "forest for the trees" myopia, many workers have no sense of operations beyond their indi-vidual information needs. Employees should know something about the industry and their company's position in it. Without being informed about their product or service, it is impossible to evaluate what is im-portant and why. In addition, they should have a clear notion of who's who in the firm's hierarchy. Telephone secretaries, for instance, need this information to set call priorities and dispatch messages.

A better understanding of broad company strategies, however, may have little impact on an individual's personal flexibility in adapting to change. Before the first machine is installed, employees need to be con-vinced that OA is a positive step and assured that they have something to gain. The phenomenon of cyberphobia, or fear of computer technol-ogy, is rooted in anxieties about status loss and possible replacement or simply in a fear of technology itself. An effective way to overcome such resistance has been to publicize in your company case studies of how similar workers in other companies benefit from learning about com-puters. Additional motivation can be provided by tying bonuses and pay scaled to savings generated by streamlined processing.

11.3.5 Technical Instruction

Once the attitudinal ground has been prepared, users should be ready for a technical overview. Before specific programs can be learned, both managers and support staff must gain a general appreciation of how computer systems operate. Even the very basic concept that information, whether letters or numbers or lines, can be electronically encoded in a binary system, may be novel to many workers. More generally, users should have a sense of what components make up an office system—from input, output, storage, and central processing, to the important communications network. In addition, they should have a rudimentary understanding of the different potential of mainframe, minicomputers, and microcomputers. Needless to say, this introduction should avoid excessively complicated or technical information. The purpose is not to further mystify but to make the new machines less threatening.

The process of training support staff to use computers becomes more involved as normal office applications multiply. Word-processing and accounting programs are most commonly associated with secretarial du-ties, and both uses are projected to grow steadily over the next few years. Electronic spreadsheets and graphics programs, traditionally operated by technical experts and managers, are being rapidly introduced into the support staff repertoire as clerical roles continue to expand. The most dramatic growth potential, however, seems to be in electronic mail and scheduling software. Although scant use of these programs is reported today, department managers have targeted this application for substantial expansion.

What all these figures mean is that the clerical workers of the 1980s will not be able to survive without being familiar with one or more of these widely used software packages. In addition, it is crucial to emphasize that programs take some time to understand. While many employees report that simply operating a computer or following commands is relatively easy, only a minority said the same thing about understanding programs. But as Joyce Lippman of Merrill Lynch points out, "It is the most short-sighted of strategies to balk in the face of a little extra effort up front. The alternative is to keep paying expensive experts and let your secretaries do nothing."

While learning to operate PCs is the most complex aspect of technological training, there are other office machines which clerical workers use daily. Staff should be made familiar with handling microfilm, with operating facsimile devices and photocopiers, and with managing complex phone systems.

11.4 TRAINING PROFESSIONALS

Because professionals have not been confronted as immediately as support staff by the office automation process, it is crucial to integrate them into the new system with a training program designed especially for them. If the support staff has been well prepared to perform in the computer environment while the principals remain ignorant as to how to tap the new resources, little progress has been made. Managers need to be convinced of the value of computer use both by their secretaries and by themselves. While decision-makers can more objectively analyze the needs of their staff and organizations, when it comes to ordering a computer for their own desk, reason sometimes turns to rationalization.

"Training professionals to benefit from automation is, to put it bluntly, a chore," states Jim Cunningham of GAF Corp. "Most of them have been in their business a long time, and accepting the need for such fundamental changes comes hard. The key is to be short, sweet, and very persuasive."

11.4.1 Remedial Training

Although managers should not need spelling refresher courses, some basic managerial skills do deserve attention. Lack of supervisory competence can be especially common among low-level word-processing and administrative supervisors who have been promoted through the ranks. Often these people find it hard to make the transition to directing their former peers and should be exposed to some type of assertiveness training. In addition, supervisors should be able to construct work-flow charts and schedules and to compose training and procedural manuals. Managers with more responsibility should be familiar with allocating budget items and cost-justifying their department's projects. To be complete, a basic skills seminar or manual for managers would review writing and dictation techniques and go over procedures for delegating work and utilizing available workers.

11.4.2 Office Procedures

One of the problems professionals often come up against is the gap between business school theory and office practice. Although it is imperative that managers understand the resources that are available to them, university curricula rarely address the ins and outs of working with other people in an office. Thus, before the system can be made to serve them, they must learn how it works.

In the realm of document production, for example, managers must be provided with guidelines on the kinds of documents which should be channeled to the word-processing center, such as repetitive letters, statistical charts, and reports and texts requiring extensive revision. In addition, standard procedures linking departmental typing to the document production center should be written up and distributed. Managers also need guidance in setting reasonable deadlines for work completion and in communicating special format requirements.

As document production becomes more efficient, managers' time-management skills need to be directed toward reallocating the tasks just described. Decision-makers have to be aware of the implications of changing clerical roles and of the new possibilities for delegating professional tasks. Managers can even operate under new productivity goals to ensure that such a redistribution takes place.

As professionals, like their support staffs, learn to adapt to the new environment, revised operating procedures for managers can be compiled as well. Although desk books are naturally more difficult for managers to keep, an effort should be made to reduce even the most complicated projects to a series of tasks within a timeframe. "Unless professionals get over the notion that what they do is too lofty to be quantified," observes Charles Mitchell, "they're never going to get to the point of accepting that machines can help them do more than type their reports." In other words, establishing new office procedures can be a first step in drawing reluctant professionals into the automated environment.

11.4.3 Corporate Computer Literacy Program

Many of the concepts underlying professional, as opposed to clerical, computer literacy training are similar. The various components of the program are identical, from the overcoming of fears and clarification of business goals to instruction in specific applications. Even though professionals tend to have a broader perspective on their company's role in the industry at large, and even on the industry's place in the local or national economy, they can still be blinded by departmental competitiveness and by ignorance as to how employees further down the corporate ladder contribute to the overall project. A seminar for professionals on business and departmental goals should focus not only on long-term objectives, but on the mechanics of how they are implemented.

11.4.4 Technical Instruction

As indicated previously, managers and executives are considerably more reluctant to recognize the value of computers in their jobs than are the clerical workers below them. Negative attitudes among top managers focus on several perceived problems, and it is the responsibility of any training program to deal with these obstacles.

First and foremost, many managers don't accept that any potential usefulness could outweigh the tremendous output of time they would need to invest. Second, some managers fear that computers are incapable of protecting confidential data or of maintaining the integrity of the data as it is stored. And third, some simply express doubts as to their ability to master technical operations. Interestingly enough, studies seem to show that these fears and doubts become stronger the further one climbs up the corporate ladder. One explanation for this discrepancy is the age distribution across professional categories. "There's nothing surprising in that statistic," explains Phil Jones. "The longer you've had to get used to one way of doing things, the less likely you're going to even see the need for change, let alone be ready to jump into the fray."

Despite some hesitance, many executives and managers agree that having their own PC could improve their decision-making efficiency without harming their interpersonal functions. Professionals can learn to use PCs to monitor support staff as well as to raise their personal productivity level. Because managers have always been collectors and disseminators of information, the computer's potential to store, sift, and transfer data at will could cut out the intermediary verbal network that they have always relied on. Once the professional comes to appreciate the nature and potential of distributed processing, he or she can reap the full benefits of direct terminal access. In the larger sense, the training in managerial applications and the overview of staff computer use will give professionals the necessary tools to make the automated office work for them.

11.5 TRAINING THE OA MANAGEMENT TEAM

The OA team will be at once the most difficult and the most important to train, as its competence will determine the success of the ongoing education process. "The problem we were faced with at the outset," agrees Joyce Lippman, "is who is going to teach the teachers? You've got personnel people, trained in interpersonal skills, and MIS techies who know how the machines work, but bringing everything together is a feat."

As the next chapter will elaborate, the OA team has responsibility for overseeing the entire automation process, from evaluating needs to choosing equipment to preparing employees for the change. The skills it will need to plan and implement such a project are multiple. Its members must possess all of the communications skills of the human resources department along with the planning perspective of top management and the technical knowledge of data-processing experts. Given the scope of these requirements and its heterogeneous representation, the OA team must be given clear directives and channels of authority. More than likely, an outside coordinator or consultant should be brought in for the initial stages of the process to help the team set priorities and goals.

Although the team will consist of representatives from all the operating divisions, as well as MIS, personnel, facilities management, and administration, MIS should shoulder the major burden of implementation. Obviously, MIS has the greatest experience in acquiring and using automation equipment, and, as stressed elsewhere, one of the explicit objectives of the OA team is to mold MIS into a department more oriented toward service.

To this end of promoting communication and feedback from the user community, MIS members of the OA team should be instructed to coordinate the computer literacy and other training programs. Whether they actually perform the training or not, MIS people will gain the expertise that will allow their department to continue to update staff training procedures even after the OA team has completed its mission. In addition, MIS must be trained to apply its technical knowledge to standardizing and supporting new office procedures regarding document production and storage, security systems, and equipment purchase.

"There's no doubt that to make an automation overhaul work, MIS has to be the lynchpin of the operation," agrees Walter Kleinschrod. "They're the ones who will be modernizing and working out bugs long after the implementation team has gone back to its departments."

11.6 CHOOSING THE TRAINING MEDIA

The vast majority of companies today offer their employees some type of computer training, however cursory. The methods and teaching tools are as varied as the applications they claim to explain. If they are well chosen, computer training products can yield a substantial return on investment. Consideration should also be given to developing custom in-house training, especially for more sophisticated software. Reliance on off-the-shelf packages can often result in underutilized systems.

The key to a successful training program is its flexibility in adapting to each user's individual learning requirements. For example, enthusiastic users could benefit from audiotapes and self-paced workbooks. More hesitant learners might need group or even one-on-one instruction. Also, the appropriateness of methods will vary depending on the content of the instruction material. Thus, departmental seminars provide a good forum for discussions about company objectives, while various video formats can be helpful in visualizing operational procedures.

Of all the training methods available, most people still prefer the traditional classroom environment. Over 40 percent of the firms with OA plans train their personnel in a classroom setting. Second in popularity were self-training manuals, cited by one-fourth of the companies. Interestingly, newer methods like computer-assisted instruction, videotapes, and videodisks were listed as major training methods by fewer than one-fifth of those interviewed. When ranking different training methods by level of desirability, companies with OA plans lean even more heavily toward the nontechnological face-to-face option. Over 50 percent ranked classroom training highest, while less than 20 percent preferred either computer instruction or self-study. One reason why videodisks may be judged so negatively is that, although they are highly interactive, they are also extremely expensive and therefore difficult to justify the cost.

Whatever training methods are used, it is a good strategy to begin educating users with fairly simple applications. Once they become confident and proficient, more advanced operations can be added to their repertoire. For example, VisiCalc's electronic spreadsheet gives managers a glimpse into the computer's problem-solving capacities without requiring excessively complex data conversion or communication. Word-processing skills provide similar ease of passage for support staff who may go on to use database management, electronic filing, or graphics packages.

11.7 APPOINTING TRAINERS

Assigning responsibility for implementing training programs is not always a clear-cut task. Although in-house training in on-site facilities seems to be the most popular choice, it can have its drawbacks, especially in the short run. While in-house personnel have the advantage of being familiar with the company's objectives, philosophy, and products, it is often difficult to find a group capable of supervising the overall program. Again, MIS is the most common candidate, but the department's computer experts often have no training skills. On the other hand, trainers from the personnel department frequently have only a rudimentary knowledge of computers. Another option could be to decentralize the process by assigning training responsibilities to department managers. This option derives strength from the manager's intimate knowledge of his or her own section's needs, but suffers from a possible lack of co-ordination and standardization. On the other extreme, the OA team itself could supervise instruction, but its impermanence would detract from the sense of continuity which an ongoing training program should cultivate.

The ideal situation is to train the trainers, but since that takes time, it may be advisable to bring in an outside consultant to design and implement a training program. While this option is the most costly, consultants are specialists in these areas and should be able to construct a functional training program in a short period of time. In addition, once permanent qualified staff are found, these programs can be taken over and maintained in-house.

Nevertheless, assigning permanent staff is still fairly costly, and smaller companies may have to rely on vendor-provided training. As in most cases, however, costs and benefits tend to even out, and vendors offer the most uneven and the least useful training. Reliability of course varies with the vendor, but generally these programs suffer from being too generic and not focused enough on the company's specific problems. They are most valuable when used in conjunction with more customized programs or when employed to train operators to run basic software packages.

Whoever is chosen to train the staff of the 1980s, it is clear that the deep penetration of office computers into today's corporate world has made training a top planning priority. After all, computers themselves do not increase productivity; it's the people who operate them that really matter.

QUESTIONS AND ANSWERS

Q. On the human side, what are the effects of office automation?

A. As it affects personnel, office automation is truly sweeping through all levels of the organization and widening its already large sphere of influence. Surveys and polls show that more and more staff are operating computers and that existing job categories and duties are being overhauled.

Few people realize that many tasks and functions which used to be strictly management duties are now entrusted to nonmanagement personnel.

Q. How can an organization cope with this revolution?

A. Wholesale outside hiring of skilled personnel is not normally a viable solution. It can demoralize present staff, and newly hired employees have no previous knowledge of your business. In-house training and development is much more strongly recommended.

Q. How does a company go about training its employees?

A. In-house programs must be developed. Although a general goal of companywide computer literacy may be in effect, differing user groups will have specific learning goals and outlooks.

To address specific user needs, training has been subdivided into three categories: for secretaries, for professionals, and for the office automation management team which oversees the automation process.

Q. What are the elements of a training program?

A. A comprehensive program would address four sets of activities: remedial training, office procedure formalization or reinforcement, business and departmental goal orientation, and finally general computer education and specific technical operating instructions. Programs must be customized for the levels of the organization they address.

Q. What role can outsiders play in this process?

A. The office automation team, which has responsibility for overseeing the entire automation process, needs multiple skills and a diversity of perspectives. Often an experienced outside coordinator or consultant should be brought in for the initial stages of the process to help the team set priorities, goals, and methodologies.

Vendors too may be able to offer assistance, although vendor training may be too general. Often vendor training offers real benefits only at the low and high ends of the software spectrum.

12

Establishing an Integrated Office Automation Strategy

Although the central focus of this entire book has been to equip the reader with the tools to create and implement an office automation (OA) strategy, it is helpful to gather the pertinent information in a "how to" chapter for easy reference. By this point the reader should be convinced of the importance of strategic thinking. As has been repeatedly stressed, the directing of a company through the OA conversion cycle involves more than just the installation of new machines. If carefully planned and executed, a strategy creates a management forum as well as a planning process by which corporate groups can better integrate business goals and information management. Specifically, the effective dissemination and control of information has become an indispensable component of a competitive business strategy. With this fact in mind, this chapter makes a final effort to clearly outline the procedures which should be followed. The rest is up to the reader.

12.1 PREPARING THE GROUND

Because the office automation strategy must incorporate the firm's overall business objectives into the problem of technology selection, the office automation process must begin with a mandate from top management. Departmental management support is helpful, of course. Nevertheless, the parochial views often espoused by individual departments are bound to provide only partial solutions because the departments alone lack the general perspective and sufficient resources to support a major OA planning effort. The only way to secure adequate financing and personnel is to send a clear message of priority from the top.

To do this, a compelling business case must be made that focuses on top management issues. Technology for technology's sake is not the way to top management's heart and pocketbook. Any presentation should focus on two major issues—namely, the current state of OA at your firm including any existing expenditures and efficiencies, and the benefits of assessing OA needs and developing a comprehensive plan. More specifically, the case for automation must consider the financial implications (current costs, proposed equipment costs, potential savings, potential cost avoidance), the business implications (competitive advantage, cash management, information management impacts of OA), and the next steps (your proposal for the number of staff and the amount of funding needed for the action plan you will follow).

Clearly, companies with an OA strategy have a stronger profile of top management support than those companies that do not. One could use chicken-or-egg logic here and say that only more strongly committed top management would have a strategy, but the very act of formulating a strategy helps to build the business case and win top management support.

12.2 BUILDING AN ORGANIZATIONAL STRUCTURE

Once OA is funded and staffed by top management, the next step is to institutionalize the OA planning process, and the practitioner must first create an organizational framework for supervising the OA conversion. The most common procedure is to establish an interdepartmental committee to coordinate the OA effort. Representatives to this body should be drawn from all the major functional participants and the user community. As pointed out earlier, such a committee should include representatives from MIS, personnel, administration, facilities management, and each operating division. Management should take care to balance individual responsibility and authority with globally agreed upon guidelines and policies.

Within the OA planning group, which may be either a committee, a task force, a new department, or subgroup within a department, major operational responsibilities are most often delegated to MIS. If methodological, managerial, or technical expertise is unavailable or absent, outside consultants can be brought in, but they should still work closely with the functional group described above. One of the important upshots of the prominent role delegated to MIS should be the grooming of MIS as a service department with a strong commitment to the end users. Thus, MIS may have the primary responsibility for successfully introducing the OA system to the users. It will coordinate training and supervise computer literacy programs. In addition, it will be saddled with more technical tasks, such as defining the systems architecture and communication links as well as developing approved-vendor lists for workstations and software and equipment standards.

The essence of the department's role, however, should be to facilitate the end user's adjustment to the new technology. To this end, its conduct of needs assessment studies and audits should contain some widely accepted mechanism for user input and participation. One such vehicle is an information center, where equipment and software can be brought in for evaluation, testing, and training. Another method is to bring MIS and user task forces together to deal with specific departmental requirements, project by project.

12.3 ADAPTING CORPORATE POLICIES

Once the OA planning and implementation structure is in place and responsibility is assigned, yet another ingredient is necessary to make the action channels effective. Key corporate policies in five basic areas must be changed or created to reflect new office automation priorities. These policies include business planning, information management, equipment purchase and management, financial management, and human resource management.

12.3.1 Linking the OA Process with Business Planning

As a reaffirmation of management's commitment to improved information systems, this step will allow the incorporation of divisional OA objectives into the business planning cycle. Through its participation in corporate decision-making, the OA team can better set project priorities and determine their funding levels. Moreover, it will have the perspective with which to evaluate progress toward both divisional OA objectives and overall business goals. In fact, an insular, isolated OA group is an ineffective group, and the more closely linked to the business planning process it is, the more opportunity for success the project has.

12.3.2 Establishing Information Management Policies

The capacity to generate what even ten years ago would be unthinkable amounts of information through increasingly accessible channels has created new problems in the realms of information security and retention. Yet, few companies have created information management policies that cover security, storage, type of media, access to data, database management, and other issues. Responsibility for setting standard procedures in these areas should reside either in the OA group or with a single person or subcommittee, but additionally the participation of the legal department and facilities management is advisable. Once recommendations are formulated, they should be submitted to the central OA committee for approval or alteration. Policies should seek to define the various levels of information security, as well as to consider alternative security methods and techniques, such as passwords, lock-and-key systems, or encryption schemes.

A second set of policies, developed and approved by the procedures described above, should govern record retention. With the explosion in storage capacity and classification techniques, attention must be devoted to purging procedures, long-term records storage, retention schedules, and file classification. No less attention must be paid, of course, to ensuring that these new policies are actually carried out. Again, enforcement depends on sufficient authority, but management can aid the delegated committee by setting time lines for development, implementation, and enforcement.

12.3.3 Regulating Equipment Purchase and Management

The selection and ongoing management of OA systems is a time-consuming task which requires an optimal mix of technical expertise and a sophisticated knowledge of business needs. While most MIS departments have certain policies that deal with the evaluation and procurement of hardware and software, these should be aligned with OA objectives and streamlined to avoid frustrating development delays and overlaps. They must also integrate with the purchasing group and adapt or use the guidelines and techniques for mass purchasing developed already. As was made clear in Chapter 9, an important component of effective technology management is the preferred-vendor list. The list should be geared to establishing compatibility with existing mainframe systems and communication between divisions and workstations. To briefly reiterate the considerations that should be taken into any vendor evaluation, they are the vendor's support and service record, the availability of appropriate software, the price-performance ratio, and the degree of compatibility.

Software evaluation procedures should be more flexible than those for hardware (see Chapter 5). Because of the rapidly changing market and the relatively low cost of most PC software, experimentation with different programs is not only possible but beneficial. Nevertheless, tentative standards for performance and compatibility of various types of packages should be recommended, by MIS or an outside consultant.

The ideal is to achieve a balance between reasonable budgetary constraints and individual experimentation. The OA policy group can bring these objectives together by monitoring and evaluating end user's experiments which, if successful, can be used to adapt existing standards.

12.3.4 Setting Financial Policies

While it is true that office automation components are declining in price, systems costs as a percentage of the corporate budget are rising. Consequently, the control of financial policies, of cost justification and allocation, is more crucial than ever. Cost justification, while not always possible to quantify (see Chapter 2), must nonetheless be systematically projected, even when a portion of the savings will be "soft." Whether OA tools are meant to increase document production or to achieve intangible improvements in customer service or competitive positioning, some means to establish realistic budgets and to measure progress are a must. The eventual costs of the development of new systems should be borne equitably by the divisions, the user groups, and the corporation itself. Using a chargeback system, the costs of centralized information services can be assessed, and distributed processing can be regulated. By offering premiums for desktop computing, the demand for work can be regulated. In addition, chargeback schemes can allocate the costs of supporting local systems from the design phase to the training of personnel.

Another prime financial concern is whether to lease or purchase equipment. The decision often depends on where the company is situated in the automation process. For instance, leasing equipment for short-term needs makes sense if no long-term strategy has yet been formulated. Once primary vendors are chosen, equipment purchase may prove to be the more attractive option, although different classes of equipment may require different policies. Appropriate solutions can be derived from a careful analysis of cash flow and upgradability versus investment credits, depreciation, and projected obsolescence.

12.3.5 Managing Human Resources

Redistributing access to computer power can precipitate major changes in the structure of an organization. Given the expectation of redefined job categories and shifting positions, hiring, training, and staffing policies need to adapt to the new technology (see Chapter 11). Job descriptions for employees who will use advanced office systems, word processors, and PCs must be amended to include such responsibilities. As Chapter 11 points out, automation is altering traditional career paths, and attention needs to be focused on designing alternative options. As part of this shift, pay scales and compensation analyses will probably be altered to suit the new environment.

To integrate the new categories, the corporation is faced with the major challenge of training and retraining and managing human adaptation to technological change. The development of a corporate computer literacy program can be crucial to smoothing the transition. The details of such an enterprise will be discussed later in the chapter.

12.4 ADDRESSING SHORT-TERM NEEDS

While the groundwork is being laid for the creation of a long-term strategy, a corporation may have immediate information needs which cannot be postponed. Thus, the structure set up to evaluate larger goals may also be called on to propose interim maintenance measures.

For example, the information center may be backlogged with user requests for PCs, and, as such, it would be a target for OA overhaul. While a systematic study is being performed, several things could be done to temporarily improve the situation. One option would be to hire an automation specialist to deal with the emergency. The consultant, while handling the specific problem, could also become a major force in the OA planning scheme. This alternative is attractive for companies that have no available in-house advisor who has a good working knowledge of both hardware and software requirements.

Regardless of the solutions chosen to plug crucial information gaps, they should be tied, whenever possible, to the parallel process of strategy development. Even short-term measures can give clues for long-term decision-making by providing equipment information and testing, training opportunities, and needs analysis. By the time a company is meeting short-term needs while being fitted out with an organizational structure poised to direct major changes, it is clearly ready to develop a concrete strategy for office automation.

12.5 DEVELOPING A STRATEGY

12.5.1 Assessing Needs against Business Objectives

The core of a successful automation plan is its capacity to overlay technologies against business objectives, which were defined earlier in this process. This, in turn, depends on the nature of the organization's business and its competition, its information requirements, its size, and the character of the marketplace in which it deals. As an illustration, compare the different benefits that a typical publishing company and an investment banking firm might derive from an automation program. For the publishing company, the enormous potential of electronic communication as a marketing tool could alter the very nature of the business itself. On the other hand, the bank will probably change the way it does its business, with the transformation of certain tasks and job categories, but the essence of the business itself will not be altered by automation alone. Each firm must understand the expected impact of new technologies before it can set priorities for change. Likewise, the company must clarify its mission before any impact can be projected.

12.5.2 Evaluating Existing Performance and Productivity Levels

With the company's general objectives in mind, existing modes of operation and personnel performance can be more profitably evaluated. Various techniques for targeting departments for OA projects have been suggested—all of them based on the measurement of white-collar productivity as outlined in Chapter 2. To produce an array of indicators for OA needs, profiles can be used to chart and quantify several areas of managerial and support staff activity. Information transfer profiles are indexed according to format, speed, and frequency. A personal processing profile is based on each manager's document production needs. Indexes include time spent in calculating, in preparing graphic displays, and in forecasting. An information retrieval profile summarizes the volume, frequency of use, and location of filed information. An activity management profile addresses the value and complexity of a manager's contribution to business objectives. Activities are indexed by the number of subordinates involved, by the complexity of each project, and through its priority ranking. Finally, a conferencing profile provides an indicator of telephone and face-to-face communication requirements.

More specific indicators of support staff productivity can be calculated using surveys geared to measure clerical activities. A general support staff/management profile looks at secretary-professional ratios and attempts to gauge the overall balance between the departmental work load and the number and skills of the resident and backup support staff. Document production profiles measure output and the suitability of existing equipment to handle it. Finally, intangible indicators of management satisfaction with clerical and administrative performance should be taken into account.

12.5.3 Utilizing the Screening Study

As has been repeatedly stressed, information in and of itself has no value. The results of the compiled profiles should be employed to set concrete goals and priorities within a time frame and to select a pilot project in a targeted department or division. Several considerations, stemming both from the magnitude of the need and from the potential benefits, should be taken into the decision of which group to pilot. Projected benefits include an increase in the quality or quantity of the output, a decrease in labor input, or an enhancement of the quality of the staff's work life. For pilot projects, it is also important to avoid areas which require massive data conversion, user training, or the revamping of standard work procedures. Nevertheless, some changes will be necessary, and it is obviously important to the future success of the company's automation effort that the pilot project be attentive to questions of upgradability and compatibility.

12.5.4 Matching Business Goals with Appropriate Technology

When the time has come to choose the technological components which are expected to achieve the company's automation goals, care should be exercised to strike a balance among user satisfaction, financial constraints, and technological imperatives. While a completely user-directed approach might result in a spate of incompatible machines with specific applications, an approach centered on systems compatibility might result in an inflexible but tightly integrated automation system. Underlying either extreme are each company's financial directives and constraints. Whatever needs have been ascertained, unless a strategy can be developed which realistically addresses these limitations, success is unlikely. Not only implementation but maintenance costs must be considered and justified when technological alternatives are examined. Not even the largest firm can support an unlimited array of database systems, programming languages, or mainframe systems. It is the responsibility of the OA planning committee to strive for optimized equipment performance within the context of specific constraints.

The methods for selecting hardware and software components have been discussed in detail in previous chapters, but a quick summary of the general steps is useful at this point. As always, one begins by gathering as much information as possible from a variety of sources. As has been shown, the task of educating oneself is not easy, as the computer marketplace often behaves like a moving target. Before vendors are actually queried, researchers should consult published vendor brochures, computer magazine supplements, and, most important, user groups.

When types of systems and components are identified, the more specific vendor selection process can be undertaken. As detailed earlier, requests for proposals (RFPs) will be submitted to vendor finalists, and representatives should be invited to present each vendor's sales pitch to the OA committee. The resulting approved-vendor list, which identifies one or more acceptable primary vendors, will be incorporated into the firm's long-term equipment purchase policies. If successful, the vendor list should provide the flexibility for individual departments to design their own technological solutions and the standardization which will insure companywide compatibility. With the general framework established, specific approval can be leveled according to a project-by-project cost-justification analysis.

12.6 IMPLEMENTING AN OFFICE AUTOMATION STRATEGY

To have reached the implementation phase of the automation strategy, a firm has already invested considerable time and energy. Nonetheless, it is arguable that the biggest challenge has yet to be faced. A well-defined mechanism for smoothing out the human and technical traumas of substantial or rapid change can make the difference between a system's optimal or marginal functioning, no matter what its theoretical potential.

12.6.1 Procuring, Installing, and Testing Equipment

Once equipment selection has actually been made, the process of installing it should provide only minor inconveniences. In regard to this technical phase of implementation, MIS should already possess the necessary expertise to orchestrate the move. If not, common sense recommends simple guidelines focused on minimizing work disruption. It is best, for instance, to carry out major physical changes during nonwork hours. And whatever schedule is agreed upon, MIS people should be sure to keep user managers informed and participating. Department participation in testing the new systems is also advisable, as it will begin the process of integrating the new technology as well as illuminating potential operator problems.

12.6.2 The Human Factors Surrounding Implementation

Although installing equipment is the simplest aspect of the implementation process, it frequently receives the most attention. What planners seem to neglect is the design and human element (see Chapter 11) of the transition—getting staff to understand, accept, and finally use the new equipment. Too often OA is introduced to employees who are given no conceptual framework and little training beyond basic button-pushing. Today we can point to enough instances of underused or misused systems to assert confidently that an OA system is only as effective as the people who use it. Still, it is easier to acknowledge this fact than it is to provide concrete mechanisms for "putting people first." In broad terms, this entails facilitating communication between MIS and DP departments and the company's end users. On the one hand, MIS should be encouraged to incorporate a service mentality into its framework of technical expertise. As noted previously, MIS's responsibility in the automation process is meant to equip the unit for such human services functions. On the other hand, user feedback should be regularly channeled back into the ongoing planning process.

12.6.3 Designing a Corporate Computer Literacy Program

This communication network then becomes the foundation for a more ambitious and systematic program for establishing corporate computer literacy (CCL). A successful program would strive to inform workers at all levels and in all information functions as to how electronic processing affects both their own jobs and the company's mission. In addition, the staff would receive all the skills necessary to fully utilize the system's processing capacity. This training should include empowering managers to employ computers as business tools. If the program is effective, the firm should find itself with a knowledgeable user community that is able to pay back its training costs with on-the-job innovations and planning suggestions.

12.6.4 Maintaining Equipment: What to Do If It Doesn't Work

The most likely functional problems will probably be associated with software use. Sources of difficulties can be numerous—from inadequate power sources and dirty disk drives to malfunctioning hardware or bugs in the software program. An additional hazard is that software packages are not returnable once opened, except in the case of a manufacturing defect. Although such defects are more common than in other industries, it is often difficult to prove that it is not the user's skills which are deficient.

The first recourse should be the software dealer, who may solve your problems by exchanging the disk. Otherwise, call the software vendor and present their technical support people with the problem. More than likely, they've heard your complaint before, unless it's a new program or the application is unusual. If this route leads to a dead end, you can try the program's author or the company's president. If all else fails, consult a local user group. Chances are, someone will have worked with the package before or will be able to direct you to a programmer who has. Bugs can be worked around without dooming a program. Another alternative, of course, is to secure a service contract with the vendors or the consultants who supervised the OA process. Although service contracts can be costly, the difficulty of distinguishing hardware and software troubles often makes them worth having.

12.6.5 Performing Audits

Audits are often divorced from the implementation process, but it is essential to see office automation as an ongoing, adaptable process. Audits can point to needed adjustments and chart improvements in personal productivity brought about by the use of office systems. Surveys can illuminate the users' evolving attitudes and demonstrate ongoing support. On the other side of the coin, an audit can gauge how well users are living up to management expectations of improved performance and productivity.

The first weeks of operation are the most crucial in working out bugs, altering standard procedures, and creating a functional system. During this period of four to six weeks, MIS or OA team support must be available, and professional time should be allotted accordingly. Weekly meetings with end users may help smooth the transition and can be used as formats for conducting frequent informal audits over the first six months. After this, the frequency of the audits will decrease, but the criteria will be constant. Through either interviews or periodic output surveys, such as those discussed in Chapter 2, the auditors can gauge changes in the quantity and quality of work produced, in the time allocated to various tasks and in the perceptions of quality of work life. If expectations are not being met, the audit may propose new policies, software, or training programs.

With the establishment of periodic audits to keep the system efficient and up-to-date, a company has completed the OA conversion cycle and is ready to enter the business world of the 1980s and beyond with complete confidence. Although the road to the successful automation of today's office is far from direct, it is safe to say that there are no other roads to travel. The increasing expense of an expanding white-collar work force, the mind-boggling pace of business transactions, and the exponentially growing need for immediate information are trends that will not reverse themselves. The choice that today's entrepreneur makes is not whether to automate or to continue as is, but whether to prosper or to be left buried in the file cabinets and typewriters of a bygone era.

QUESTIONS AND ANSWERS

Q. What is the first step in formulating an integrated automation strategy?

A. Securing a mandate from top management, so that technology may be best integrated with business objectives, is a necessary first step. Since the automation process will have an impact throughout the organization, an overall approach and integrative strategy must be supported from the top.

Q. What company policy areas are affected by an integrated strategy?

A. Five basic areas of corporate policy will be affected or changed by the office automation process. These are business planning, information management, equipment purchase and management, finance, and human resources.

Q. Who should participate in the process?

A. As has been stressed, a companywide integrated approach is needed for success. Who is in charge of the office automation process will vary from company to company and business to business, but should include representatives from MIS, personnel, administration, facilities management, records management, and each major operating division. In larger companies MIS is often delegated the major operational responsibilities based on technical expertise.

Q. When is the process complete?

A. Although the major responsibility of the office automation task force may be viewed as completed after the successful installation, start-up, and early operation of the chosen system, the process should not be viewed as complete. It is essential that office automation be viewed as an ongoing evolutionary process, and audits and surveys (similar to those described in Chapter 2) must be undertaken periodically even after installation.

Appendix: Case Histories

It is one thing to follow and to understand the arguments in favor of the automated office, in favor of integrating front-office and back-office processing, but it is an entirely different matter to take managerial responsibility for an implementation yourself. While a general, "how-to" type of discussion is valuable to instruct the manager on the central issues involved, no guide to automating the office could be considered complete without a discussion of some concrete examples. For this reason an appendix containing nine case histories has been compiled.

The source material for these case histories has been gathered from interviews performed by the staff at Butler Cox & Partners and The Omni Group. The interviews were conducted from a standard questionnaire and focused on the implementation of one particular system within each firm in question.

The sequence of questions began with the determination of the nature of the organization, its business, the number of employees, and the level of use of information technology before the implementation. Next, the reasons for installing new office systems, the office systems strategy, and the applications for which the new office system was intended were examined. Specifically, the questions focused on the hardware and software chosen and on the staff that would use the new office system. For instance, was the system intended for managerial and professional use or for secretarial and clerical use?

The survey sought to determine what benefits were expected from the office system, whether the system was strictly cost-justified or qualitatively justified, what problems were encountered during the implementation, what efforts were made to train and educate new users, and what organizational or job changes had occurred or were expected to occur because of the installation of the new office system. Finally, the survey attempted to discover the firm's future office systems plans, any constraints placed on those plans by the current implementation, and any future plans for major organizational change within the firm in question.

The case histories concentrate on office systems that include managers and professionals among their users. Also noted are the important messages and signals to others that have emerged from each organization's attempts to implement new systems. Special attention has been paid to ways in which the system has changed the way a firm does business.

A.1 AT&T COMMUNICATIONS

The following study clarifies some of the problems that can be encountered as office systems become widespread and user demands for more facilities increase.

AT&T Communications is the AT&T company that handles the supply and sales of long distance international communications services. The company employs more than 100,000 people, some 40,000 of whom are office staff. As with any organization this size, AT&T has many computers at various locations, including seven major data centers with large IBM or Amdahl mainframes, 14 DEC VAX 780 machines, and over 2,000 microcomputers.

A.1.1 Electronic Messaging System (EMS)

Electronic messaging constitutes the largest part of the office systems network. More than 8,000 terminals are connected on a dial-up basis to an electronic messaging store-and-forward system based on the VAX 780s. Almost 90 percent of the EMS users are professionals and middle managers (excluding supervisors, technicians, and engineers). Of these, more than half are marketing managers and sales staff. This group also constitutes the majority of the 1,000-plus users of home or portable terminals.

The marketing and sales staff have many uses for electronic messaging, some that include improving communications across different time zones and widespread geographic locations. For example, monthly revenue statements, new price or product announcements, and variance reporting are often sent via electronic messaging. In the early days it was not easy to cost-justify the use of electronic messaging. The marketing department, by pressing hard for the introduction of EMS, by identifying qualitative benefits, and by preparing to pay for the service, was the driving force behind the electronic messaging system. By the end of 1984 the system served 22,000 users.

A.1.2 Benefits Identified

Installation of the electronic messaging system realizes many qualitative benefits. First, a less bureaucratic communications culture is developed. The electronic messaging system saves time when compared with the formal nature of memos and letters. A cryptic note is acceptable when sent via electronic messaging; whereas a letter is often sent back to the typist even if only one or two words are misspelled. Second, EMS reports back to the sender when messages are received. Because messages are received and contact is made with another person, the sales environment is sharpened. Third, EMS reduces telephone usage. Time management improves significantly because marketing and sales managers can handle mail at their convenience. Fourth, EMS eliminates the familiar situation called "telephone tag," where about three out of every four telephone calls fail to reach the intended recipient, who then calls back only to find that the original caller is unavailable. Fifth, managers gain early access to information, particularly when they can access the system from home. Managers now have better control because they can sometimes intervene before actions are carried out. This is particularly important in the sales area, where special deals are often negotiated with large customers.

Although the telephone is still the dominant form of communication within AT&T, electronic messaging is now the norm for sending short messages that do not require an immediate reply and for distributing the same message to several different people—for example, to sales staff who are at different locations.

A.1.3 Training and Support

To develop and administer the electronic messaging system, a central group of 25 staff members has been established. User-coordinators have also been designated in each of the major user departments (or regions) to provide an active liaison between users and the central group. So that specific requirements for electronic messaging, text editing, and other features can be tailored to individual requirements, formal training seminars are modular in nature. Hands-on experience along with videotaping is used extensively in the training session.

Early electronic messaging users required more training and encouragement than more recent users. The change is due in part to pressure now being exerted on individuals to use the system. Infrequent use of the system has now dropped to less than 10 percent as a result of the change and the implementation of time-sharing.

A.1.4 Problems Encountered

Once accepted as a common form of communication, the electronic messaging system soon became overworked. No central mechanism or authority had been established to deal with the excess demand for the system's resources. Potential users would obtain microcomputers and then demand immediate access to the electronic messaging system. Compatibility became a major strategic problem. The number of potential users proved a major hurdle to overcome in implementation. Maintaining timely and efficient service became difficult, as the number of users increased from 8,000 to 22,000 in less than one year. In many cases, the text-editing facilities on localized personal computers or word processors proved a more feasible solution than using a VAX-based mail system.

Although many current users did not have word processing facilities until regular terminals were upgraded to personal computers, AT&T recognized the need to tailor applications to meet individual user requirements, in addition to providing general-purpose facilities such as electronic messaging.

A.1.5 Future Developments

AT&T plans a number of enhancements to their office systems in the near future. The top priority is to improve the ability of users to communicate through the system. By using artificial intelligence techniques, they hope to make office systems proactive rather than reactive. Switching from regular terminals to microcomputers will provide local processing capability as well as access to the central EMS. Ideally, every professional and manager will have a microcomputer or personal computer. Local slide production and presentation facilities will be based on the PCs, and business graphics facilities will be developed further. All of these planned developments will evolve under the umbrella of a UNIX environment. It is interesting that AT&T anticipates no significant organizational change to result from the implementation of new office systems. Only the responsibilities of the secretarial and typing support staff will be transformed significantly.

A.2 STANDARD OIL

The following case study shows how a major oil company has installed general-purpose office systems, such as electronic messaging and information retrieval, both for first-time terminal users and for established terminal users.

Standard Oil (Amoco) is one of the largest international oil companies; it employs some 44,000 employees in the United States. The company uses a large and sophisticated range of IBM-compatible computers, including two Amdahl 5680 mainframes, two IBM 3083 machines, and two IBM 3033 computers. These machines, and many other smaller computers, which are located at different sites throughout the United States, are linked together with IBM's Systems Network Architecture (SNA) using IBM 3704 and 3705 controllers.

A.2.1 PROFS System Installed

Since 1977, Amoco has been using a forerunner of the IBM PROFS system in its Tulsa production research facility. Until 1981, members of the research staff worked with IBM on the development of the system, but now they use a slightly modified form of PROFS.

Throughout the United States, users are located at five main sites. Communication facilities have been installed at these sites for authorized users.

Two word-processing centers have Displaywriters connected to the PROFS system. Thus, users of the system have direct access to a large document production facility with the capability of transmitting the finished product electronically. There are now over 2,000 users on the system.

The installation of the PROFS system was achieved in two steps. First, PROFS facilities (keyword-based information retrieval, telephone directories, document creation, electronic mail, calendars, and short message capabilities) were provided to existing terminal users. Second, access of PROFS facilities was extended to users in specific areas who had not previously used computer terminals, so that they too could benefit from the general-purpose facilities.

Because the PROFS system was developed in the technologically advanced research department, the problem of penetrating the business areas was deemed critical. To do this, a fairly simple approach was used. Any business area that already used computers or had a relatively senior manager who was identified as a "technology champion" was targeted for penetration. Using a high-level management supporter, the installation process in most cases proceeded smoothly. A clear tendency for "downward migration" of technological enthusiasm was observed.

About 60 percent of PROFS users are professional staff, and the remainder are secretarial support personnel. The system is also used by senior and middle managers. On one or more of the mainframe computers, many professional users employ end-user computing facilities. The most common end-user computing facilities are spreadsheets, report generation, and financial modeling.

A.2.2 Training and Support

An in-house introductory training course lasting two and a half days is given before a new user is provided with PROFS facilities. Further training courses are available if necessary. Classroom training sessions and self-study manuals are now being supplemented by an experimental computer-based training facility. Three members of the training staff at the Chicago headquarters carry out PROFS training, and there is also one trainer available at each of the four largest sites where PROFS is used. Six technical staff members work on user support and technical enhancements for the system.

A.2.3 Benefits Identified

To evaluate the benefits of its PROFS system, Amoco used outside consultants. The consultants found that the identified cost savings were about equal to the costs of the PROFS system. In particular, AMOCO reduced its labor costs while maintaining an increasing work load. In many cases the existing 3720-type terminals had already been cost-justified for specific computing applications. Many users also recognized qualitative benefits, including an improvement in the quality of written output, a shorter response time, a decrease in the number of interruptions during the working day, and a reduction in the time required to complete specific projects.

In 1981 PROFS facilities were installed in the offices of the Public and Government Affairs Department in the Chicago headquarters and eight main field locations in the United States. The department has the responsibility to gather information, evaluate it, and give a corporate response to questions from legislative bodies and the media. Through the use of PROFS, the staff can record responses that in turn can be accessed by other company locations. The chances of different responses being given to the same question can now be reduced significantly. Conflicting answers can no longer cause errors that will distort the original quote.

A.2.4 Problems Encountered

The PROFS installation has a very high level of acceptance among its users. This may be due to the top-down commitment from senior management, or it may be due to the technically experienced user-base. Both factors have a positive impact on acceptance. Senior managers are a major obstacle, since they have a lack of interest in technological development that is not financially rewarding. Although IBM's long-term commitment to the PROFS system had been in doubt, IBM reduced that concern by incorporating PROFS into its architecture for document transfer (DIA/DCA).

A.2.5 Future Developments

About 85 percent of the electronic mail traffic travels among users in the same department, and in most cases sender and receiver are at the same site. Amoco, therefore, plans to install local area networks with gateways to the inter-site network. Then, the large volume of wide-area traffic that is associated with the PROFS electronic mail system will be reduced significantly. The number of people using the system is slated to increase by about 10 percent each year because of the increase in new users. The company is also attempting to link Wang office systems into the PROFS system.

As of mid–1984, Amoco had not experienced any major organizational change due to the PROFS installation, but as developments are consolidated over the next few years, the number of middle managers in Amoco will probably be reduced.

A.3 A MULTINATIONAL PHARMACEUTICAL COMPANY

The following case study illustrates the successful implementation of a voice-messaging system for a group of users defined by common requirements. The head office contains 400 data-processing terminals and about 30 word-processing stations.

A large multinational pharmaceutical company based in the United States employs some 2,500 office staff at its head office. Its most significant office system application is a VMX store-and-forward voice-messaging system which improves communications with the sales force out in the field.

A.3.1 VMX Voice-Messaging System Installed

The VMX voice-messaging system is currently used by over 1,000 staff people, about 80 percent of whom are in management or in the sales force. The VMX system allows uniform messages to be transferred quickly to a dispersed sales organization. When the sales force is spread out over several time zones, the person to whom a message is destined may not be at work to receive it. The VMX makes communication possible under these circumstances without being intrusive. Voice messaging has been found to work very well for sales and marketing functions.

A.3.2 Benefits Identified

As the use of the system has grown, several benefits have led to a favorable response from the sales force generally. The immediate nature of communications with the system has reduced the need for formal correspondence, and sales staff queries can be handled in a much shorter time. A study conducted in 1981 showed a reduction in the number of meetings and sales-related telephone costs because of the VMX system. When a message is received, it is recorded by the VMX so sales staff can no longer claim that they never received it. The major drawback is that voice is not a sufficient medium for communicating complex information. Nevertheless, the system has become accepted as an effective communications tool.

A.3.3 Training

The price of the VMX system (about $300 per user) was considered insignificant when compared with the total cost of the selling function. Training costs also were very low. The company used the vendor's standard training course. As the use of the system spread quickly through the sales force, there was a considerable incentive for everyone to learn how to use it, and no major user-acceptance problem was experienced. Acceptance among the sales force is now universal.

A.3.4 Future Developments

A new enhancement that would allow a salesperson to inspect customer and product information data bases at any time is now being explored. For example, if a doctor were to inquire about product safety during a sales call, the salesperson could access the appropriate information instantly. Because the system has been so successful in sales applications, the company plans to extend the voice-mail facility to all office staff within the next two years.

A.3.5 Organizational Impact

The VMX system now has remarkably few problems and has become one of the major tools for communication among the head office staff, sales management, and the sales force. The installation of the voice-messaging system has not led to an organizational change.

A.4 MANUFACTURERS HANOVER TRUST

This case study shows how a large bank built an electronic messaging and decision support facility for an established and growing base of terminal users.

Manufacturers Hanover Trust (MHT) has some 30,000 employees, 10,000 of whom are professional, front-office staff. At the company's headquarters there are a large number of IBM mainframe computers, including eight 308X machines and many 4300s. In addition, the retail banking operations make extensive use of NCR machines. About 6,000 members of the professional staff at corporate headquarters have access to the 4,000 terminals installed there.

Mainstream computer developments are provided through four independent data-processing divisions serving four groups: corporate departments, retail banking, wholesale banking, and securities. MHT's entire user population is served in turn by several centralized technologically oriented divisions: architecture and technical staff services, office automation, standards, systems development, and telecommunications.

A.4.1 Various Office Systems Installed

Word processing, electronic messaging, and time-sharing are the main office systems at MHT. There are approximately 1,000 word-processing workstations attached to Wang OIS or VS machines, used mainly by typists and secretaries. (Historically, a 20 percent productivity increase was achieved by the introduction of word processing.) Some 600 personal computers run word-processing and spreadsheet packages and provide access to an electronic messaging system which runs under the MHT wide-area network, called Geonet.

The Multi-Comet electronic messaging system has 5,000 managerial and professional users worldwide (the vast majority of whom are in the United States) and operates via dial-up telephone lines connected to three PDP–11/70 minicomputers, one of which acts as a standby machine. About 66 percent of the electronic messaging users also use their terminals for some other purpose (mainly decision support or word processing).

Three DEC System 20/60 machines provide the professional and managerial staff personnel with admission to the decision-support facilities. These facilities include database management, data access and report generation, financial analysis, and econometric modeling. Geonet links MHT operations in 16 countries, using packet-switching technology to support both voice and data communications.

The use of computing facilities as an alternative to traditional system development is also quite advanced at MHT, where more than 1,000 users have each developed at least one program using BASIC, APL, or Focus. Typically, credit officers, economists, and financial analysts make up the users.

A.4.2 Electronic Messaging

In 1979, electronic messaging was born in the office automation group with a small pilot system. The Comet electronic messaging service was used because it had low start-up costs and was easy to use. The system started with only six users and was quickly expanded to 30 at three management levels in different offices around New York City.

Because they were technically oriented, the original 30 users represented an important core group. The system was readily adopted. There was a low dropout rate even at this early stage because of peer pressure to use the system.

This implementation exercise was repeated using another group of amenable users. The office automation strategy aimed to establish person-to-person communication for a critical mass of users in a professional working group. By organizing critical mass groups in this way, the office automation team was able to expand the system in discrete stages before beginning to link the individual groups together to form a critical mass for the use of the whole organization. Groups who worked together but were separated geographically or by time zones, such as newly formed task forces, were selected first for inclusion in the new system.

Corporate use of the Comet EMS had spread to 650 users by 1981. The success of the two-staged implementation at corporate headquarters spawned a "me too" attitude toward the new system. More than 5,000 people were using the electronic messaging service in 1984, 1,000 of whom were using portable terminals. The system now has 4,000 regular users. On average, users log on twice a day for seven minutes, and each user sends about seven messages to an average of 2.7 people per day. Since the introduction of electronic messaging at MHT, messages are sent to associates within the same building as frequently as they are sent to distant locations.

The electronic messaging system was used by more than 500 support staff personnel in the end of 1984. The demand to use the system was so heavy that the cost of the service was charged back to the users, unlike other data-processing services, which are treated as corporate overheads. This charge-back scheme has not stopped people from sending even the most unimportant message via the messaging service. Staff users resent receiving telephone calls that are not urgent or that contain a message that could have been sent by electronic mail. Some users have started telling the callers so, thereby reinforcing the new electronic messaging culture.

A.4.3 Benefits of Electronic Messaging

Among the benefits realized by electronic messaging, a quantitative survey of its users revealed that on average the system saved users 37 minutes per day. The system was regarded as an invaluable form of communication. Several more benefits resulted from the system. EMS reduced the time wasted by telephone tag and the time required to type and check formal internal correspondence. Electronic messages are usually short and often grammatically incorrect. They are accepted, nevertheless, in a way that an incorrect memo or letter would not be. Secretarial typing has fallen by as much as 50 percent in some areas as a direct result of the introduction of electronic messaging. More effective work management resulted from a reduction in telephone interruptions.

A.4.4 Problems of Electronic Messaging

Several problems followed the introduction of electronic messaging. There were some dropouts from the system (about five percent of the total). This was particularly noticeable as the early expansion in numbers (200 to 500 users) began to take place. Small pockets of nonstandard electronic mail services have developed as new and different office products have been purchased locally. Some fears about the security of the Comet bureau service existed initially because the service was shared by many other companies, but a problem never arose. Surprisingly, about $500,000 was spent on the system before upper-level management approval was obtained, and the success of the implementation made approval a mere formality. In 1983 another PDP–11/70 minicomputer had to be installed to handle a demand that exceeded current capacity.

A.4.5 Support Team

Five staff members make up the electronic mail and decision-support team. Such a low number of dedicated system support personnel has been maintained by setting Multi-Comet as the corporate electronic mail standard and supporting only DEC, IBM, and Wang devices on the system. If other products are purchased, users have to arrange for an interface both to Multi-Comet and to the decision-support systems.

A.4.6 Future Developments

MHT plans to use in-house videotex to provide a bulletin board for in-house publishing, accessible through existing terminals and new terminals. The firm will promote the IBM PC as the first-choice terminal. The office automation group and users will be able to tailor applications to meet individual or group needs. Improvements in image storage, video conferencing, and business graphics will be offered by the decision-support service.

Nevertheless, the firm anticipates the need to overcome challenges to the automation process. Delays in resolving the arguments in favor of central control with those in favor of free innovation by users may hinder the further expansion of information technology at MHT. The signs are that the controls will be guidelines rather than detailed constraints and that MHT will continue to be a pioneer. Inability to assimilate new technological changes into existing services may also present technological integration problems.

A.4.7 Organizational Impact

The use of office systems at MHT has not led to significant organizational changes. Besides a change in secretarial and typing support, no organizational change with users has been ascribed to office systems.

A.5 ABBEY LIFE

This case study shows how an office system, based on portable computers, can be used to complement a mainstream business application based on a mainframe computer. Abbey Life was formed in 1962, as a division of ITT, and has since become one of the leading life insurance companies in Great Britain. It has remained a comparatively small company with 4,000 employees, specializing in life insurance and pension fund management. Combining life insurance funds with long-term investment funds has made a significant contribution to the company's success. This linkage has been employed in 25 insurance companies that have been formed in the past 20 years in Great Britain, and it has been adopted by all the established competitors.

More than 60 percent of the employees are field staff, and almost 2,000 of those sell insurance. The high proportion of direct sales staff reflects the importance of the sales activity to the company. The insurance products sold are highly complex and specialized. Organizationally, the sales staff are controlled through local branches. The sales staff's main task is generating new business since established clients constitute only 25 percent of the sales. Abbey Life also provides insurance through 1,500 independent brokers in Great Britain, who offer services from several other companies.

A.5.1 Sales Support Systems Developed

Sales information at Abbey Life was processed manually until 1980. The central computing facilities handled administrative routines, but the majority of procedures at the branches were based on forms and card indexes. The result was time delays of up to five weeks in handling new policies, which affected both the service to customers and management's control and information. Abbey Life recognized the problem and introduced a new system. Management initiated the development to alleviate the problems inherent in manual processing. Several functional attributes were deemed necessary in the new systems. Once-only input and easy access to data are essential. The system must have the capacity to change and grow without entailing an organizational expansion. Customer service must be improved by enhancing the quality of information available to the sales staff and by shortening the access time for information. More effective management control through improved information flow must be achieved. The ALADIN and LAMP systems were developed after 1980 for use in sales to handle these requirements.

A.5.2 The ALADIN System

ALADIN (Abbey Life Assurance Distribution Information Network) is a mainframe system based on an IBM 3083 supporting 200 terminals located in the head office in Bournemouth and at the 270 branch offices in Great Britain. The new system provides extensive facilities. Users may obtain details on new insurance policies, existing policies, and policy surrender. The system identifies opportunities to provide additional services such as providing the renewal date on expired policies. The system maintains details on investment funds and customer quotations on different policies. Users can make underwriting inquiries, and the system even includes a special branch inquiry facility for nonstandard underwriting risks. The system supports an interface with the billing system. And finally, it provides a processing capability to managers who wish to analyze sales information in such categories as product, salesman, branch, and type of customer.

The system is very large and quite complex with extensive on-line checks and editing facilities. It handles approximately 15,000 new business policies every 20 days, with inquiries for quotations amounting to several times this figure.

The system has proved to be very successful. Since its introduction, the company has handled 25 percent more business without any need to increase headquarters staff. A two-day service standard has been introduced, with 75 percent of business being turned over on the same day (and 90 percent within two days).

The quality of management information has also improved, thus assisting management control.

A.5.3 The LAMP System

The LAMP (Life Assurance Marketing Package) system is a self-sufficient, portable-microcomputer application based on Epson HX20 devices and specially developed software. The system's objectives are threefold. To assist the information facilities of ALADIN, LAMP produces information instantaneously for the customer. LAMP augments the internal cooperation of the sales staff and assists in the sales presentation to customers. LAMP was designed also to reduce the errors made by associates while making sales presentations.

Programs were developed to quote prices of various pension plans, insurance plans, and capital funds for insurance. The applications were designed so that they provide backup to the sales presentation as well as hard-copy output tailored for each customer's insurance requirements. The application was launched with a short video presentation. The results have generated new business.

The programs were designed to allow sales personnel to show potential customers the benefits derived from matching insurance to one's personal requirements. The company absorbed the development cost. The associates were expected to purchase the briefcase terminal, which was offered at a slight discount. Since its introduction two years ago, over 25 percent of the sales staff have purchased a microcomputer. New information is regularly provided on cassettes, which are fully compatible with the ALADIN system. The implementation of the LAMP system has not required any organizational changes.

A.5.4 Future Developments

The management of Abbey Life has acknowledged that portable computers have successfully aided their sales staff. The possibility of linking portable terminals to the mainframe and allowing two-way information flow of policy details is one way of expanding the systems at Abbey Life.

A.6 A SENIOR MANAGEMENT OFFICE SYSTEM PILOT TRIAL

This study outlines some of the dangers associated with installing office systems for use by senior managers. It is adapted from the experience of a medium-sized firm in Great Britain.

At the outset, management perceived the success of a step-by-step approach to the electronic office of the future as dependent on a top-down strategy. The data-processing department presented a proposal to its computer steering committee to try out an office automation pilot trial. After several months of discussing various alternatives, it was agreed that the facilities provided should be based on 12 multifunction terminals linked by a local area network with the potential to connect into the company's mainframe computer.

Six senior managers and their secretaries took part in the pilot trial. The six managers were selected for two reasons. First, it was believed that a successful pilot trial at a senior level would make subsequent installations more acceptable to all managers who would then understand the issues more clearly. Second, the six managers were eager to take part; whereas some other senior managers were skeptical.

No formal justification exercise was carried out and no organizational changes were made, but the data-processing manager expected a savings in managers' time of at least 10 percent. This saving would result in the managers' having more time to make important decisions, thereby improving the overall quality of managerial performance. Every three months during the year, the views of the participants in the pilot were to be obtained through interviews. In addition, the six secretaries were sent to the supplier's standard two-day training course.

Two systems analysts organized a one-day training course. The original aim of the course was to educate the users on six general applications: an electronic spreadsheet, electronic diary and appointments scheduling, access to the mainframe computer using an inquiry language, access to the telex system, word processing, and electronic mail. Although some managers and secretaries found parts of the system difficult to grasp, the initial training was considered a success. There were follow-up training sessions over the next few weeks, but lingering difficulties were not completely resolved.

Besides the problems of the training course, difficulties surfaced in the first month of the pilot trial. Management chose one of the leading products on the market. Nevertheless, there was a delay in providing access to information on the mainframe computer. Attempts by managers to use the spreadsheet facility were short-tempered and short-lived. Secretaries were the only ones using the telex, thereby leading to a lack of enthusiasm for diary scheduling and electronic mail. Despite pressure on the data-processing manager to increase the support level and to generate ad hoc reports on demand, use of the system slowly died out.

Excluding two managers who (together with their secretaries) had established diary routines and text editing, the system was not used to any great extent. After a short-lived period of experimentation, disillusion set in. A feeling of disappointment and anticlimax was present among the users. When the information was finally transferred to the new system, managers still complained of unsuitable formats or incomprehensible listings.

After six months, four of the managers' terminals were removed. The remaining terminals were being used (mainly by secretaries) for word processing and simple selective text retrieval. Alternative pilot areas and equipment are being considered, but progress is expected to be slow.

A.7 STEWART WRIGHTON

This case study provides an example of an organization with traditional mainframe systems and comparatively few word processors. In the last few years this organization has moved toward a decentralized approach with very clear ideas on the development of office systems.

Stewart Wrighton is a large insurance brokerage based in Great Britain in Kingston-upon-Thames and London. Annual turnover is $77.3 million and the company employs some 1,600 office staff and spends $3.2 million annually on computer systems. The computer department consists of an 80-member staff, centrally organized, and reports to a group systems director. Staff and equipment are split between the Kingston and London offices. The current computers include 30 Wang PCs, five Wang VS 100 computers supporting about 200 terminals, and an IBM-compatible NAS Hitachi mainframe running under the VMS operating system.

A.7.1 Office Systems Installed

The insurance brokerage business requires data-processing applications mixed with word processing, and the company's approach to office systems reflects this underlying requirement. Stewart Wrighton's financial system has been run on a mainframe computer which is being phased out. In recent years the Wang VS computers have increasingly been used to run all the front-end administration systems such as claims analyses and correspondence. The Wangnet system, which is a local area network, handles local communications. Installation of office systems is judged on the basis of two factors: the unit cost of a business transaction and the service provided to customers. Two out of three people on the office staff will have terminals by 1987, if the present pace of system installation continues. As a result of the move toward distributed processing, the firm expects its computer department staff to fall from 80 to 30 people by 1990.

The Wang-based systems are used primarily by clerical staff, although secretaries also use the systems for word processing. Professional staff in the systems and finance departments use the Wang PCs for spreadsheet applications, for word processing, and, to a lesser extent, for diary management. A trial system using Wang's wide-area system network has been implemented between the offices in Kingston and London.

A.7.2 Office Systems Strategy

Two key elements of the company's office systems strategy are to gain the support of senior management and other end users generally. These elements are considered to be of prime importance, as indicated by the significant education and training program which includes in-house word-processing training, personal computers for any manager or senior professional who requests the use of one, job rotation between junior brokers and the computer department, and three-day executive familiarization courses—regardless of the justification. In addition, the strategy mandated a team of up to five people who currently answer some 200 inquiries and requests for assistance per month.

Clerical activities are transferred away from clerks to the professional staff in three stages. In the first stage, clerks who serve different business areas such as shipping, aviation, or construction are centralized and provided with Wang terminals. The staff savings due to the change are substantial. In the second stage, the staff reverts to serving their individual business areas. In the third stage, brokers are encouraged to carry out administrative activities on the system and to discontinue the use of manual pro forma procedures. The unwillingness of brokers to do this is seen as a major potential problem.

Office systems should encourage end users to develop many of their own systems using application generators and prototyping where appropriate. In addition, business-related systems, many of which are integrated data-text systems using the Wang VS 100 machines, have been developed. General-purpose office systems such as diary systems, spreadsheets, word processing, and electronic messaging will be added on to support these business-related systems.

A.7.3 Future Developments

Stewart Wrighton's plans also include development of an integrated spreadsheet system to handle the budgets of all managers with a significant budgeting responsibility. Electronic mail systems will carry both intra-office messages and inter-office communications. Local data bases will be used for "what-if" applications, information gathering, and data manipulation.

A.8 NATIONALE-NEDERLANDEN

This case study illustrates how a leading insurance company is adopting a staged approach to the introduction of office systems. It shows how office systems are being used to integrate text and data in clerical activities. Nationale-Nederlanden, a large Dutch insurance company, whose main business deals with general insurance and life insurance, employs about 6,000 office personnel in three locations in Rotterdam and The Hague. Most of the company's routine business transactions are handled by large computers in The Hague (one Siemens 7890 machine, one IBM 3083, and one IBM 3033). A centralized systems group has the responsibility for office systems development.

A.8.1 Office Systems Installed

The office systems at the head office locations have been developed around 100 terminals on mainframe computers, 50 IBM PCs, five IBM 5520 shared-resource systems running 65 terminals, 70 IBM Displaywriters, and one IBM 8100 DOSF system running 20 terminals. During the last few years, IBM 5520 systems and Displaywriters have been acquired to assist secretaries and typists in word processing. At this point there is general satisfaction with the improved typing service provided. Many authors believe that some time has been saved by the new facilities.

The IBM 8100 DOSF system has been installed recently for use by about 60 clerical staff to assist in normal transaction processing in the mortgage department. These applications give users access to mainframe computers via CICS and also permit text processing to be carried out on the IBM 8100 machine. Secretaries who had previously typed a great bulk of customer correspondence have their typing load reduced. Typed transactions now contain fewer errors, particularly in the data, since two stages of transcription have been avoided. The turnaround time for correspondence has also been reduced by about one day.

The improved performance of the typing service has coincided with a disintegration of traditional typing pools in favor of departmental and personal secretaries. As a result, some personal problems have arisen in the typing pools.

Many typists have feared moving from the social environment of the typing pool to isolated departments.

The rejection of an early version of the IBM 8100 DOSF office system by secretaries has been another interesting aspect of the introduction of text processing in Nationale-Nederlanden. The combination of a fear of screen-based text processing systems and insufficient user training has been attributed to the reason for rejection. Once introduced, electronic typewriters were widely accepted, thereby increasing morale and putting the process back on track. Ironically, as screen-based word-processing equipment has become accepted by some secretaries, those using only electronic typewriters have demanded the screen-based system as well.

During the past year, 50 IBM PCs have been installed with spreadsheet, text editing, and other packages for use by professional staff. End-user computing is supported by an information center staffed by six full-time systems professionals. Nationale-Nederlanden has also been using APL to provide computing facilities to professional staff including accountants and actuaries.

A.8.2 Training

Throughout the office automation process, local staff and equipment suppliers have organized and carried out the training program. Those responsible for the introduction of office systems have, in recent years, devoted much effort to encouraging the exchange of knowledge and experience at all levels about the advantages and limitations of office systems.

A.8.3 Future Developments

The use of optical storage systems such as Phillips Megadoc and image archives is expected to be the next stage in the automation of the company's mainstream transaction processing routines. IBM's image capture, storage, and viewing facilities are actively being considered. The company, however, is waiting for the cost of disk storage to fall; therefore, a large installation may be about two years away. The turnaround time for archive-related correspondence is expected to fall by as much as three or four days, once this system is installed, compared with the use of the existing centralized paper-based archives and a microform facility.

Achieving a successful installation of office systems at the managerial level is the most difficult and sensitive task in the automation process. Since managers are often reluctant to devote time to learning how to use the system, and their requirements are often diverse, the benefits of introducing new systems are difficult to quantify. Managerial office systems, therefore, have not yet been installed. The middle-level managers will use storage and processing facilities on computers dedicated to the individual departments. At the highest level, centralized mainframe computers will handle corporate processing and storage.

The use of multifunction workstations by the secretaries of senior managers, however, is under investigation. These facilities might include electronic mail, calendar management, links to mainframe systems, text editing, document archiving and retrieval, and some personal computer facilities.

All of the company's future plans for office systems are built on a strategy of compatibility with an IBM communications infrastructure. Three levels of storage and processing have been identified within this strategy. Standalone applications will run initially on a network of communicating personal computers. Later, some PCs will be replaced by terminals that are patched directly into mainframes within a local area network.

A.8.4 Organizational Impact

As office automation systems are implemented, three main trends are expected to become apparent. As more typing is done by professional staff and clerks on their own terminals, the number of typists and secretaries will decline. Administrative services such as facsimile transmission, microform, photocopying, and telex will be progressively decentralized and eventually will be carried out by the users themselves via electronic media. As the decentralized office system strategy and end-user computing are implemented, the centralized computer department itself will slowly become partially decentralized and begin to act as a free-lance consultancy on office systems throughout the organization.

A.9 MASSEY-FERGUSON

This case study illustrates how a multinational company installed an advanced office system during a period of stringent financial restriction. Massey-Ferguson is a Canadian multinational corporation that manufactures diesel engines and farm machines. It has 37 wholly owned factories in nine countries, and, together with its associates and licensees, it makes products in 31 countries and sells them in countries around the globe. The company employs some 30,000 people worldwide, about 20,000 of whom work in offices.

A.9.1 Office Systems Installed

It was necessary, given this type of international corporate structure, that information flow efficiently and quickly between the Toronto head office and the various operating units. In 1981, development began on an advanced in-house office system that would provide text editing, integration of text and data files, electronic information storage and retrieval, and a store-and-forward electronic mail system that would make use of the existing telecommunications network for worldwide access. As part of the development process, system demonstrations were developed to gather management interest and support.

The system was installed in 1982 for use by some 2,200 office staff throughout the world, using about 2,000 IBM 3270-type terminals. The MIS staff at various international locations were the first users to test the facilities provided by the new office systems. This arrangement had the advantage that local MIS staff became familiar with the system, so that they could later install terminals in other local departments.

Those staff members who had access to an existing data-processing terminal and who had a need to carry out large amounts of international correspondence were then introduced to the system. Where terminals were not available, electronic messages were printed and distributed manually to the intended recipient through internal mail services. This approach, Massey-Ferguson found, was widely used and accepted. Professional staff and especially managers who were not provided with the new facilities had an increasing demand for the system.

With some 2,200 people, including senior managers, middle managers, professionals, clerks, and secretaries using the system, the level of acceptance was very high; only 15 people stopped using the system. Strong control was exerted to ensure that electronic storage was used only for important documents that would need to be retrieved later.

Specially designed systems that used the general-purpose system as a base were developed after the general-purpose systems were installed. For example, the purchasing department can now file orders into a "bring forward" file which sends them automatically through the telex system to suppliers at the appropriate time. Farm machinery distributors in North America are automatically informed when new products are launched, when special promotions are offered, and when stock is available through the electronic mail system. This system also enables distributors to place orders electronically with Massey-Ferguson.

A.9.2 Training

Five members of the head office staff invited each division using the facilities to conduct the training sessions for the general-purpose office system. The head office staff train the divisional staff, who in turn train other staff at each location.

A.9.3 Problems Experienced

The high transaction rate provided one of the few problems experienced during the installation process of the office systems. To avoid response-time problems, the computer staff had to ensure that computer applications with high processing requirements and low transaction rates were timed so as not to interfere with the office system, which had low processing requirements but high transaction rates. Inefficient disk-packing routines installed in the system caused the initial storage calculations to be inaccurate. As a result, the information storage data base had to be reorganized once a month during the first year of installation.

A.9.4 Cost Justification

While the new office systems were being installed, Massey-Ferguson was experiencing a period of financial stringency. A detailed cost justification was therefore necessary for the new system, which had a total cost of less than $200,000. The type of cost justification that was carried out is illustrated by considering a typical document that is typed, duplicated, and physically distributed from Canada by mail to 100 recipients in Switzerland, Canada, and England. The traditional method cost nearly four times more than using the new electronic mail system.

A.9.5 Future Developments

Massey-Ferguson's future plans for office systems include an increase in the penetration of terminals, facilities to handle business graphics and business forms, and links to a publishing and phototypesetting system that will incorporate graphics information from the company's computer-aided design systems.

Glossary of Terms

Access time. (1) The time in which a machine is operating and available for use. (2) The time required to receive information once the computer has been signaled.

Acoustics. An ergonomic consideration relating to the level of noise within an office and workstation. Noise can be controlled through the engineering and/or the architecture of the space.

Active files. Files that contain records that are used frequently.

Active records. Those records consulted in the performance of current administrative work, or records in working files.

Actuating. (1) Implementing or starting a process. (2) Putting a process into action.

Administrative support. The job function of assisting management in performing tasks of a nontyping nature.

Alterable information. Information in digital form that can regularly undergo deletions, additions, and revisions and is ever changing.

Analog. Operating by directly measurable quantities from a continuum as opposed to operating in a digital manner.

Analytical staff. Personnel who collect information and data and analyze and define what is revealed by both statistical data and subjective collection of feelings and thoughts.

Anthropometry. The study of human body measurements for the scaling of sizes, heights, and shapes of furniture and equipment to the dimensions of workers.

Applications software. Sets of instructions used to tell the computer how to do a specific job.

Archival record.   Records once considered current files that are now semiactive or inactive and are retained for legal, fiscal, administrative, or historical reasons.

Archive.   To store information.

Archives repository.   An area established to preserve records for the benefit of posterity.

ASCII (American Standard Code for Information Interchange).   A character coding system used for data storage and transmission.

Asynchronous transmission.   The mode of transmission between equipment with different protocols, in which a "start" signal precedes and a "stop" signal follows each character to check synchronization, and characters move one at a time along the line.

Back-office processing.   Functions associated traditionally with the data-processing group in a firm that concerns the internal functions of a firm. Payroll and large number-crunching applications are typical back-office activities.

Bar graph.   A chart that presents information through the use of horizontal or vertical bars.

Baseband.   A digital pathway ranging from around 1 million bits per second to 50 million bits per second.

BASIC.   This language (Beginner's All Purpose Symbolic Instruction Code) was developed in the mid–1960s at Dartmouth College as a simple, basic interactive language.

Batch stream.   A method by which a computer deals with doing a number of tasks. A batch stream is a queue of tasks. The computer takes on one task, finishes it, and moves on to the next.

Batched.   Sent in a group; usually refers to the grouping of information and its transmission to an information system.

Baud rate.   In telecommunications, the rate of signaling speed. The rate of speed expressed in bauds is equal to the number of signaling elements per second.

Benchmark.   A point of reference used in determining a plus or minus accomplishment.

Benchmark position.   A job which has been measured; performance criteria have been established that provide a determination as to the worth and value of the position.

Best-guesstimate study.   A study in which estimates of work loads and time expended are based on input from the support staff being studied.

Beta site.   A site, usually a department within a company, that is used as a test case for an office automation feasibility study.

Black box.   An intermediate interpretation device or program used with equipment having different protocols; often called a translator.

Boilerplate.   Presorted documents, such as letters or contracts, to which variable fill-in information can be added via the keyboard.

Broadband.   Common-cable TV cable that employs modems and allows multiple streams of data to be transmitted simultaneously.

Bubble memory.   A magnetic memory that must be accessed serially but has a higher storage density than many other storage media.

Bus network.   A network that consists of a length of co-axial cable (called a bus) along which individual devices tap into the communications cable. There is no centralized hub. Signals from one station move along the bus in both directions to all stations tapped into the cable.

CAD (computer-aided design).   The use of the computer's processing capability to generate representations of aesthetic or functional ideas. This capability is often employed by engineers, architects, or artists.

CAI (computer-assisted instruction).   The use of electronic equipment as a training tool.

CAR (computer-assisted retrieval).   The retrieval of historical information from a company's records through the use of a VDT. Information can be read from the screen or produced in hard copy.

Carbon copy collection.   The collection of the copies of all typing accomplished during a set time period.

Cassettes.   Magnetic tape for recording information.

CAT (computer-aided transcription).   The capture of keystrokes onto a magnetic media that is then processed through a computer and printed out.

CBMS (computer-based message system).   A system that allows the transmission of text messages to and from the users who are connected to the computer on which the system is based. It can be a service offered inside a particular firm only or a service to which a number of subscribers outside the system supplier can subscribe.

CBX (computerized branch exchange).   A digitally controlled communication switching device.

Centralization.   The location of one or more functions at a single site with a central support staff organization.

Checkpointing.   The process of shuffling discrete quantities of data in and out of main memory as they are needed by the processor.

CIM (computer input microfilm).   A microform based information storage and retrieval system.

COBOL.   This acronym stands for Common Business Oriented Language which was developed in the late 1950s, and it is intended for use in the solutions of problems in business data processing.

Cold type.   Typesetting on typewriterlike machines or by photocomposition.

COM (computer output microfilm).   A micrographics form of output whereby microfilm and microfiche are produced directly as computer output, without the intermediate hard-copy and microfilming steps.

Communication processing.   The manipulation and distribution of information through video display terminals.

Compaction.   A reduction in the number of characters per page achieved by reducing the length of the lines and size of the characters.

Computer graphics.   Graph representations produced on the computer.

Computer output mailing system.   A mailing system that allows computer-printed continuous forms to be fed into equipment that automatically bursts the forms, inserts them into envelopes, designates zip code breaks, and meter-stamps them for mailing.

Computer teleconferencing.   A telecommunications process in which words, data, facsimile images, and voice are transmitted from one geographical location to another.

Conference method. A training session in which trainees are encouraged to express themselves orally and to exchange and compare ideas.

Conventional planning. The designing of office space with many enclosed areas divided by permanent walls.

Cost avoidance. The elimination or reduction of costs in a budget through elimination of the necessity for temporary help, overtime, or additional budgeted personnel.

Cost-benefit. The hard- and soft-dollar savings achieved by implementation of an automated system.

Counting-documents method. A method used to determine the amount of typing produced whereby any completed task (letter, report) is counted as one document and documents are then totaled over a set time period (a day, a week, and so forth).

Counting-lines method. A method of determining the amount of typing by counting the lines produced within a given period of time.

CPU (central processing unit). The information storage area shared by multiple data- or word-processing terminals.

CRM (certified records manager). A professional classification granted to records managers who have completed prerequisite training and met the accreditation requirements for certification.

CRT (cathode ray tube). An electronic vacuum tube, similar to a television picture tube, that displays text as it is entered from the keyboard.

Data base. The compilation and storage of information consisting of data and text for the purposes of access, retrieval, and printout.

Data-base management. The management of data via machine storage rather than paper files.

Data processing. The manipulation of numbers through various computations to deliver meaningful totals and create useful statistical information.

Data retrieval. The recall of prestored material from a system.

DBMS (data-base management system). A computer software that handles the storage and retrieval of records stored in direct-access computer data bases.

Decentralization. The locating of minicomputers and terminals, as well as word processors with standalone intelligence, in the various departments of an organization.

Decision package. A document that identifies and describes a specific activity in such a manner that management can (1) evaluate it and rank it against other activities competing for limited resources and (2) decide whether to approve or disapprove it.

Decision support system. Special software that provides significant aids for financial planning, portfolio analysis, tax planning, and market analysis, and for projecting business situations that require mathematical formula calculations.

Desk manual. A guidebook to particular duties and tasks that remains with the job and the workstation for which it was written.

Determinants of effective leadership. The situational elements that dictate which type of style will be successful in a given situation (for example, the size of the organization, the amount of interaction, the personalities of leader and group members, the level on which decision-making is encouraged, the organization's health).

Digital. Data transmission in the form of discrete units; a process that transmits data by translating sound waves into on/off digital pulses.

Disk drive. The device into which a disk is inserted that reads information, writes information, and physically spins the disk to find information.

Disk pack. A stack of hard disks that share a spindle, have a standard specification, and a large storage capacity.

Distributed system. A system that provides decentralized memory and storage capacity yet allows network connections and communication over dissimilar peripherals.

Documentary information. Information that is recorded in some kind of permanent form, such as in written or printed materials.

Documentation. (1) A memo that describes an incident clearly and fairly and thus permits a problem to be confronted supportively and with just cause. (2) Observation of a machine in operation, to determine its usefulness to an office.

Downtime. Time when equipment cannot be used because of malfunction.

DSK (Dvorak simplified keyboard). Developed in 1932, this typewriter keyboard makes it possible for 70 percent of the work to be done on the home row and a majority of the stroking to be done by the right hand.

EBCDIC (extended binary coded decimal information code). An eight-bit alphanumeric code used on all IBM computers.

Editing. The correction, refinement, or revision of written material.

Electronic blackboard. A blackboard developed by Bell Laboratories, division of AT&T, that transmits graphics and handwritten communications over telephone lines for viewing on video monitors in distant locations.

Electronic data processing. The manipulation of data through the use of electronic computers.

Electronic file. A logical grouping of information, data, or text that is stored and accessed on a computer as a discrete whole.

Electronic mail. A system of communicating messages electronically to a recipient who receives either a hard copy or a visually displayed message on a CRT screen. The message may be transmitted electronically by facsimile, communicating word processors, computer-based message systems, public-carrier-based systems, public postal services, or private and public teletypes.

Electronic mailbox. A computer-based message system on which messages can be left until the user makes an inquiry.

Electronic proof. Database storage from which information can be recalled and reconstructed by electronic means. Proofing is accomplished by viewing the copy and editing it right at the video display terminal.

Enclosure and access needs. These space design needs may be determined by type of work performed. Space design must also recognize the need to access areas such as restrooms and lunchrooms so as not to contribute to a congested traffic pattern.

Engineering approach. An approach to the analysis of office functions based upon the detailed study of individual jobs, which are broken down into their vital components, to see whether they can be eliminated altogether or combined with other jobs.

Ergonomic concerns. Workstation features designed to promote optimum employee performance.

Ergonomics.   Facilities planning focused on the aesthetics of the workstation and its surrounding space, for example, the needs for privacy, a smooth flow of paperwork and communication, balanced territorial and social concerns, adequate access to electrical and communications circuits, and proper lighting, climate, acoustics, and color/decor.

Event schedule.   A written timetable of steps to be taken to accomplish a goal (for example, a step-by-step plan to implement office automation).

Evidential-value records.   Records that show how an organization came into being, how it developed, how it was organized, what its function has been, and the results of its activities.

External information.   Data that originate outside an organization, such as information concerning the products and services of competitors.

Facsimile (also called *fax*).   A process that involves the transmission of an exact copy over communications lines; facsimile combines replication and distribution functions, since it duplicates exact copies of graphs, pictures, and other materials and transmits them to other locations.

Feasibility concepts.   Aspects of the traditional office that must be examined by the feasibility study and what changes are likely to occur.

Fiber optics.   The technique of converting communication signals to light pulses that are sent over strands of hair-thin glass fibers.

File server.   An extension of local disks in a personal computer environment that allows many workstations to share a common data library. A file server might be a large disk or disk pack to hold files accessible by all users with access to that library.

Financial lease.   A lease arrangement whereby the lessor recovers the full cost of the equipment plus expenses and a profit. The lessee may receive title to the equipment at the end of the lease period.

First-line supervision.   Management of ongoing operations at the department level.

Fixed information.   Hard copy, microfilm, and other image storage that is unalterable in time and format.

Fixed-frame video.   A video process in which a new picture is transmitted several times per minute; the monitor displays an image for a number of seconds, until the next frame is received.

Floppy disks.   A small flexible disk that has become the primary storage medium for personal computers. Floppy disks typically come in two formats—5 1/4 or 3 1/2 inches in diameter.

Flowchart.   A diagram that uses symbols to illustrate the flow of work and paper through the office, from origin to completion.

Formatting.   The process of composing the basic form or style of text.

FORTRAN.   The first widely used procedure-oriented language (a way of expressing commands to a computer in a form somewhat similar to language) originating in the mid–1950s was labeled FORTRAN, an acronym from the words "formula translation."

Front-office processing.   Processing functions that are performed by end users who deal with the firm's clientele directly or with the firm's nontechnical personnel. Word processing, database management, and spreadsheet analysis are typical front-office activities.

Full-motion video. A closed-circuit television setup in which all activity is captured and transmitted to another location.

Gantt chart. A graphic illustration (developed by Henry L. Gantt) of scheduled work on a vertical scale (function) and horizontal scale (estimated time).

Guideline method. A technique for interpreting and reflecting the value of jobs in the market place.

Half-duplex. A type of transmission in which signals travel in both directions, but only in one direction at a time. Half-duplex is satisfactory for most transmissions between computers and terminals.

Hard disks. A disk resembling a phonograph record that is used to store large quantities of information that can be updated. Hard disks are used in personal microcomputers but are known primarily as the storage medium for minicomputers and larger mainframes.

Hard dollars. Expenditures of money that can be measured and controlled (such as the salaries of employees or cost of equipment).

Hard-dollar savings. Those salary and fringe benefit costs that can be saved through reduction of staff.

Hardware. A basic piece of equipment.

Hierarchy of needs. Abraham Maslow identified a hierarchy or ladder of needs and theorized that people can attempt to satisfy a higher-level need only after satisfying at least some of the lower-level needs.

Historical data approach. An approach to studying an office that involves gathering information from past records about the time and amount of work associated with a certain job.

Horizontal software. Generic software designed to perform a general application in any business.

Icon. A picture or symbol on a video display that depicts or symbolizes a computer function. When a user points to the icon with a "mouse" (a pointer displayed on the screen), the computer performs the function depicted.

Image copying. The process of replicating images through the use of OCR, laser copiers, or facsimile duplication.

Image network. See *electronic blackboard.*

Image printing. A printing process in which the entire image is produced in hard-copy form from a stored picture of that image in a cathode ray or an internal source.

Inactive files. Files that must be retained only because of legal guidelines or that are awaiting destruction at a time specified by the company's retention schedule.

Inactive records. Records infrequently referred to. Inactive records often are transferred to a records center or other storage area.

Incident process. The presentation of an incident or a problem situation in only a few sentences, designed to force trainees to ask careful questions in order to obtain additional pertinent facts.

Incremental budget. A budget in which expenses for the coming year are based on the preceding year or on some average of preceding years.

Information management. Supervision and control over a system that creates, gathers, processes, replicates, distributes, stores, and destroys the information utilized by an organization.

Information processing. An integrated system created by the merger of data processing and word processing. In an information processing system, all forms of business information (data, text, image, and voice) are freely accessible to workers at all levels, within necessary security restrictions.

Informational-value records. Records that provide information that should be preserved for future generations.

Input. The entering of source data or text into a system for processing.

Instruction. A coded sequence of binary numbers that is interpreted by the processor and causes the computer to perform a primary function.

Integrated circuit. An electronic circuit made up of a large number of components, semiconductors, or transistors fabricated onto a computer chip. ICs are the building blocks of computer processors.

Integrated software. A type of software which is becoming increasingly dominant and which features programs that combine the functions of word processing, spreadsheets, graphics, communications, and sometimes accounting, often by using "windows" to promote ease of use and entry from one function to another.

Integrated systems. Systems that permit multiple functions to occur simultaneously and permit the user to combine text and data in a single application with little or no difficulty.

Intelligent copiers. Copiers that can electronically store materials such as often-used forms and thereby eliminate the need for hard-copy storage facilities.

Interconnection. That part of the integrated electronic phase in which various electronic or technological components are tied together.

Interface. This term applies to an information exchange capability either between two machines, two people, or a machine and a person.

Internal information. Information generated within the organization (examples are production schedules, payrolls, policy manuals, and organizational directives).

Job classification. The analysis and rating of jobs according to predetermined classes (the same or similar task groupings).

Job description. A written, organized presentation of the duties involved in a specific job.

Job enrichment. The process of heightening both task efficiency and human satisfaction by providing greater scope for personal achievement and recognition in jobs, more challenging and responsible work, and more opportunity for individual advancement and growth.

Job evaluation. Any formal procedure for appraising, classifying, and weighing a set of functions.

Job redesign. The rethinking of a job and what it contains, with a view toward expanding the job by including in it more horizontal and vertical activities.

Job specifications. The minimum requirements of a job.

Keyboarding. The process of logging data into a system and assigning to the data an index designation for future distribution and retrieval.

Keystroke counters. Electronic counting devices that count the number of keystrokes produced on input devices.

Knowledge worker. Any management, professional, or clerical worker who processes information for use in decision-making.

LAN (local area network). A network that is designed for a particular installation to connect various elements of its office systems. A LAN could connect large computers, personal computers, remote terminals, or telephone lines.

LAN (local area network) duplex. An interlinked arrangement of computers (usually microprocessors) that permits a single computer in the network both to operate independently and to access directly other computers in a network over a limited area (1,500 feet to three miles).

Laser (light amplification by stimulated emission of radiation). A device that uses the natural oscillations of atoms to generate coherent, focused electromagnetic radiation. Lasers are used to cut optical disks and to read them.

Laser printing. A printing process similar to image printing, except that it operates by laser control rather than direct impact.

Lateral file. A drawer file turned sideways, with the side opening to the front.

Leader-member-relations task structure. The extent to which leaders and subordinates get along with each other.

Learning curve. A measure of the rate of learning in relation to the length of training.

Life cycle. A system that meets the objectives of the organization. When the office becomes too crowded, equipment is out of date, and procedures are no longer relevant, a new system cycle should be implemented.

Life span or cycle of a record. The successive stages undergone by a record (creation, processing, storage, retrieval, and retention or destruction).

Line counting. The electronic or manual process of counting typed lines.

Line graph. A chart that uses various types of lines to show fluctuations in a value or quantity over a period of time.

Logging. The act of putting information onto a log sheet or into a system.

LSI (large-scale integration) circuits. The process of mass-producing electronic circuits by etching up to 10,000 transistors onto silicon chips.

Machine dictation. The act of speaking into a microphone and recording ideas on magnetic tape for later transcription onto paper by a secretary or word-processing operator.

Magnetic media. Any type of magnetically charged belt, card, disk, or tape used to store, make corrections, erase, or rewrite documents.

Mailgram. Correspondence sent via the E-COM system, an electronic mail facility.

Main memory. The storage capacity built into the computer itself.

Mainframe. The central processing unit (CPU) that houses the hardware, software, and operating controls of a computer.

Make-ready and put-away time. The time spent dealing with roughly drafted reports that can be eliminated through the use of proper equipment.

Management by objective (MBO). A management strategy that focuses on goals.

Managerial workstation. A work area designed for the professional knowledge worker. It usually contains a computer terminal with time management controls, text editing features, electronic mail capabilities, files processing capability, and other features.

Manipulation. The process of rearranging the format of text and data (for example, changing the order of the paragraphs) to come up with the most workable form in which to present the information.

Matrix management. An organizational setup that combines centralized and decentralized characteristics.

Memory. The capacity of a computer to store information electronically. Information in main memory may be accessed at any time to allow the computer processor to complete its functions.

Menu. A list on a display screen that gives the extent of available choices in response to a prompt.

Message networks. See *electronic mail.*

Microcomputer. A small standalone computer that is operated from only one console and can perform only one task at a time. Personal computers are microcomputers.

Micrographics. The process of recording and reducing paper documents or computer-generated information on film and providing a system to store and retrieve that information.

Microprocessor. A minuscule logic circuit on a microchip of silicon that can perform over 1 million calculations per second.

Minicomputer. A minicomputer comprises a central processor, a console, and also a number of peripheral devices such as disk drives and operating terminals. More than one user can perform tasks at the same time in either a real-time or time-sharing operating environment. The minicomputer is distinguished from larger mainframes by not being suitable for massive number-crunching tasks.

MIS. An acronym for management information systems.

Mobile storage system. A storage system in which files are put on tracks in order to eliminate the need for aisles for each set of files.

Mouse. The electronic pointer on a video display screen with which a user designates the function he or she wants the computer to perform.

MS-DOS. A microcomputer operating system developed by Microsoft for IBM and compatible microcomputers.

MTM (measure time and motion). The measurement of time by applying time measurement units (tmu) to each singular function or task to determine time and motion standards.

Multifunction terminals. Systems based on mainframe computers or minicomputers equipped with special software that provide specific services on computer terminals; such terminals generally are used for many functions.

Multi-tasking software. This software gives a computer the capacity to simultaneously perform two functions.

Needs assessment study. A study aimed at providing an overall perspective on an organization's needs as a basis for future planning.

Network. A system that interconnects a wide assortment of information processing devices through a communications line or data base.

Networking. The linking of various information processing devices, such as word processors and data entry units, storage devices, printers, processors, and other peripherals, to send, receive, exchange, store, or reproduce information.

Node. A terminus in any sort of network. In a computer it could be a terminal, a disk drive, or a communications interface. In a PBX it would be any telephone.

Nonaction information. Information on which no action is required.

Nondocumentary information. Information that is not recorded. Usually obtained through word of mouth or personal observation.

Nonimpact printers.   Photocomposition printers.

Nonoriginal input.   That information already existing in a system.

Nonrecord.   A convenience copy that normally is discarded when no longer needed.

Nonrecurring information.   Information that is reported and used once in its lifetime.

Objective data.   Data that deal with things rather than with thoughts or feelings.

OCR (optical character reader).   A machine that can read printed or typed characters and then digitally convert them into input to a data or word processor.

OCR (optical character recognition).   The process by which a system scans typewritten pages and stores the scanned characters in digital form.

Off-the-shelf applications package.   Software packages sold by computer vendors or by separate software outlets. Such packages provide freedom and flexibility to experiment, as they can be obtained and used or discarded quickly and easily.

Office automation (OA).   The introduction to the office systems that offer word processing as part of a bundle of office functions that include electronic mail and message distribution, electronic filing, data access, data processing, and administrative functions such as calendaring, scheduling, and tickler systems.

Offset printing.   A printing process in which copies are made from an original copy produced on either a paper or a metal plate.

Open-office planning.   Designing office space with minimal enclosed areas, using movable wall panels.

Operating lease.   A lease arrangement whereby equipment is leased for a fixed sum each month. The lessor does not normally recover the full cost of the equipment over the period of the lease.

Operating-systems software.   Sets of instructions used to tell the microprocessor how to act.

Optical character reader (OCR).   A device that scans hard copy printout, reads the characters, and writes them digitally onto a disk.

Optical disk.   A disk that uses laser technology to provide high-density storage of either data or image information.

Organization chart.   A graphic presentation of the organizational structure that points out responsibility relationships.

Organizational culture.   A company's values, attitudes, and degree of competitiveness and commitment, which reflect top management's approach to decision-making.

Organizational objectives.   Company goals.

Organizational structure.   The hierarchy of authority, span of control, and areas of responsibility within an organization.

Orientation or induction training.   Training that acquaints new employees with the company's history, philosophy, policy, practices, and procedures (such as office rules and regulations or employee benefits).

Original input.   Information put into a system for the first time.

Originators.   Individuals who create information or text.

Overhead transparency.   A clear plastic sheet that, when placed on a lighted glass surface, projects the image on the sheet in magnified form onto a screen.

Overlay.   A memory management process whereby certain segments of data share the same physical location in a computer's memory while being processed. When not being processed, the segments of data are stored on disk.

PBX (private branch exchange).   An electromechanical communications device— usually a staffed switchboard.

Peripheral device.   A device not central to the operation of a computer but which is connected to it and supports it functionally.

Personal computer.   A computer designed for use by managers and professionals rather than by computer specialists.

Phase-in process.   An area-by-area approach to office automation.

Phototypesetter.   A device that converts text in digital form to printed material.

Phototypesetting.   A method by which information can be reproduced efficiently through a printing process that prints characters optically by taking pictures of them at high speeds.

Pie chart.   A circular diagram divided into sections ("slices") that normally is used to present information in percentages.

Pilot.   A prototype installation.

Point method.   A method of evaluation in which a range of points is assigned to a set of common factors (for example, education or skill).

Presorted mail.   Mail that is sorted according to zip codes, carrier routes, and so on before mailing.

Primary group.   A close-knit group whose members know the norms that govern the conduct of each member.

Problem-oriented solution.   The process of identifying and isolating a problem and providing a solution to that one problem.

Processing.   The manipulation of information that has been input into a system for replication and for distribution in the form of communication.

Processor.   The central device within a computer that executes the instructions provided by the user.

Productivity.   Measurement of the ratio of work done to time spent doing it.

Productivity gains.   Improvements in employee work output.

Programmed instruction.   A self-instruction method in which information is systematically presented to the trainee.

Protocol.   The language in which a message sent from one machine to another is packaged and handled.

Prototype.   A test situation involving installations or equipment being considered for wider use in the company.

Qualitative data.   Employee perceptions of how and why things are done within the system.

Quality circles (QC).   A group or circle of employees that meets to discuss how to improve the quantity and quality of work.

Quality of work life (QWL).   A factor of work life that can be enriched when employees are involved in decisions affecting their work environment.

Quantitative data.   Measurable work being accomplished, the type of information required by management, and the time it takes to produce such information.

RAM (random access memory).   A memory device from which information may be accessed by pointing directly to its location.

Random access.   A method of finding a piece of stored data by pointing to its location and picking it out.

Real labor costs. All labor costs, including payroll costs.

Record. Official document that furnishes information that is stored for future reference.

Recording density. A measure of how tightly data bits may be stored; a measure of the storage capacity of a medium for a given space occupied.

Records center. Areas established for the storage and servicing of inactive or semiactive records.

Records format. Formats designed to meet requirements of paper systems, micrographics, and computerized systems.

Records management. The systematic handling of documents from creation to destruction, including filing and micrographics, archiving, and destruction.

Records series. Identical or related records that are normally used and filed as a unit and that can be evaluated as a unit for purposes of retention or destruction.

Recurring information. Information that an organization regularly and frequently uses, such as sales, inventory, and production reports.

Reduction ratio. The size ratio between a film image and the original document.

Reference documents. Documents that contain or communicate information needed to carry on the business.

Replication. The duplication of information in another form.

Reprographics. The various techniques of replicating information with the ultimate objective of distributing it in some form. Replication techniques include printing, phototypesetting, duplicating, and COM (computer output microfilm).

Resource sharing. The facility that enables a number of users to operate the same piece of hardware or software.

Results-centered leadership. Leadership that is concerned with the "work itself" approach to motivation.

Retrieval. The recalling of stored information for reuse.

RFP. An acronym for a request for proposal—a document prepared by a potential user addressed to a vendor which delineates the user's needs and requirements.

Ring network. A network in which individual devices are connected in a loop or ring via a string of signal repeaters. If one device in the ring breaks down or is added to, the entire network is put out of operation.

ROM (read-only memory). A memory device from which information may be read but to which it may not be written.

Satellite communications. Electronic telecommunications via worldwide satellite transmission.

Self-paced instruction. Instruction through individual learning packets that consists of a planned program through which an individual moves at his or her own pace.

Semiconductor. A material that is neither a good conductor of electricity or a good insulator of the flow of electricity. It is used in transistors to permit the flow of electricity in one direction, but not in the other direction. Semiconductors allow the bifurcation of electrical current and are therefore essential to computer processors.

Sequential access. See *serial access.*

Serial access. A method of finding a piece of stored data by reading through the medium from the beginning until the desired piece is found.

Shared-logic system.   A system in which multiple video display screens and output devices simultaneously use the memory and processing powers of one computer.

Short-range strategy.   A short-term plan for implementing office automation.

Silicon chip.   See *microprocessor.*

Single-element typewriter.   A typewriter that uses a typing ball containing characters (Selectric typewriters are one example).

SNA (Systems Network Architecture).   A data network product offered by IBM that allows data transfer among different office machines.

Soft dollars.   Expenditures of money that can be estimated but not controlled (for example, improved productivity through conversion from longhand to machine dictation).

Soft-dollar savings.   Reductions in expenditures that come about when management delegates work and uses time-management techniques.

Software.   A program that instructs a computer to perform operations it ordinarily cannot perform.

Standalone display system.   A self-contained word processing unit that uses its own memory and processing powers for keyboarding, storage, text editing, and printing.

Star network.   A network in which all communications pass through some form of switcher at the hub of the configuration.

Statistical approach.   An approach to studying an office that uses one or all of the following methods: historical data, work sampling, and time studies.

Storage.   The systematic preservation of information within the system in some form.

Study team.   A group of people responsible for conducting a study. The team is usually made up of representatives from key office areas, such as data processing, records management, and reprographics.

Support-systems feasibility study.   A study conducted to determine the volume and kind of work done in an office by both management and support employees.

Synchronous transmission.   The mode of transmission between equipment with different protocols, in which each character must arrive at a predetermined time—which requires synchronization between sender and receiver.

System.   A collection of office machines unified in their function and connected in some way to enable designated tasks to be accomplished and applications to be performed.

Task-oriented responsibility.   Responsibility without much opportunity for creativity or personal initiative.

Telecommunications.   (1) The electronic transfer of data or information from one point in an information system to another through a unit that performs the necessary format conversion and controls the rate of transmissions, including transmission from one computer system or station to remotely located devices. (2) The ability to relay messages from one place to another without paper.

Telecommunications manager.   A person who has total responsibility for the management of the personnel who plan, install, maintain, and create networks of communication and monitor the transmission lines for the communication functions of an organization.

Teleconferencing.   Simultaneous processing of data messages and visual connections for the purpose of sending pictures and voices through telephone wires to screens and speakers in other locations.

Territoriality.   The need for personal work space.

Text input.   The keyboarding of text into an information system.

Theory X and Theory Y.   Two theories of management. Theory X assumes that successful management of people requires total control. Theory Y assumes that employee self-control and self-direction, with minimal managerial involvement, will result in successful management. A combination of both theories usually is required to perform daily supervisory functions.

Theory Z.   William Ouchi's theory based on the belief that a management or company philosophy should be less rigidly structured than theories X or Y (for example, formal reporting relationships, job assignments, and divisions between departments are imprecise and unclear).

Third-party service.   Service obtained from a company other than the equipment manufacturer.

Throughput.   The volume of typing, including dictation, transcription, and revision.

Time ladder.   A list of functions performed together with colored-in time periods indicating when employees performed each task.

Time sheet.   A sheet that lists the functions performed each day and the length of time it took to perform them.

Time standards.   The amount of work that should be done under specified conditions and methods.

Time studies approach.   An approach to studying an office in which an individual job is analyzed or reduced to individual tasks, which are then timed to determine the average time per task.

Topology.   The physical and logical configuration of networks; the way in which devices are connected to one another and to a traffic processing system.

Total support system.   A planned structure for integrating all services formerly considered separate functions into a support staff under centralized supervision and control.

Total system solution.   A comprehensive, integrated support system in which priority consideration is given to compatibility with a mainframe.

Transaction documents.   Documents that record the individual day-to-day transactions of an organization.

Transaction processing.   The processing of a specific business action such as a sale, a paycheck, or a change in inventory.

Transcribing.   The keyboarding of information into a system for future access.

Transitional office.   The conversion of a traditional office into an electronic office through a series of logical steps and strategic plans.

Turnkey.   The total preparation of a facility by a contractor which includes the acquisition and setup of all necessary premises, equipment, supplies, software, and personnel so that a customer only needs to "turn the key" to begin full operation.

Typesetting.   Methods of printing, such as handset, casting, typewriter composition, and photocomposition.

Typing production.   Typing volume measured in lines, pages, documents, or other criteria for a specific period of time.

Unbundled services.   Services not included in the original purchase of equipment and provided by vendors for a separate charge.

Understaffing.   The hiring of too few people to meet the demands of the work load.

UNIX.   An operating system for computers developed by Bell Laboratories.

Upgrades.   Additions to or replacement of software or hardware that updates existing software or hardware.

User friendly.   The attribute of a system that is easy to use.

User manual.   A guidebook for principals describing the services that the support system provides.

Value added.   Additional benefits that accrue to the user of a particular product or service that are not paid for directly.

VDT.   An acronym for video display terminal.

Vendor.   A company that sells technology, furniture, supplies, and services to meet the needs of the automated office.

Verbal input.   The dictation of information into an electronic dictation system or the voice input of information into a voice recognition system.

Vertical files.   Conventional file cabinets, whose drawers open at the front.

Vertical software.   Software programs created for a specific industry or industry segment, and also those designed for a specific application, such as for attorneys, purchasing or sales agents, or research and development staffs.

Videodisk.   A television recording on magnetic disk.

Videotape.   A television recording on magnetic tape.

Virtual memory.   The storage capacity that the user of the computer can employ to accomplish a task. Virtual memory is larger than main memory when the architecture of the computer permits mapping onto storage media other than main memory.

Visual display.   The process of displaying information on a cathode ray tube (CRT) or video display terminal (VDT).

Vital records.   Information needed to establish or continue an organization in the event of a disaster.

VLSI (very-large-scale integration).   Circuits that incorporate vast quantities of logic; the compression of more than 10,000 transistors on a single chip.

Voice activation.   A feature on dictation equipment that activates the tape when a person speaks and deactivates it when there is a pause.

Voice mail.   The storing of messages in digital form for transmission to a receiving point at a later time.

Voice recognition.   The process by which systems "recognize" spoken words and convert them to digital signals sent to an attached system or display device.

Voice response.   The process by which systems "respond" to an inquiry by converting the answer stored digitally in computer memory.

Voice synthesis devices.   Machines that enable visually impaired workers to interact with computers or word processors.

Word processing.   The transcribing of an idea into a document by means of automatic equipment.

Work-count unit.   A standardized, predefined specific quantity, such as a character, a line, a page, or a document.

Work measurement.   A method for determining work load volumes and improvements in work or in work groups by comparing what has been accomplished against a standard.

Work sample.   A collection of sample materials for quantitative measurement by size, nature of the materials, and required format.

Work-sampling approach.   An approach to studying an office in which a manager observes work at random periods or gathers copies of work to determine the amount of work accomplished in sample periods.

Work standards.   Work measurement approaches—subjective, statistical, or engineering.

Workstation.   An office space equipped with automated technology that is designed either for a particular individual or a particular task. Typically, the central component is a personal computer.

Index

About the Author

RANDY J. GOLDFIELD, President, The Omni Group, Ltd., has contri-
buted to numerous studies of management and automation systems.

DATE DUE